THE knot BIBLE

2ND EDITION

THE knot BIBLE
THE COMPLETE GUIDE TO KNOTS AND THEIR USES
2ND EDITION

NIC COMPTON

ADLARD COLES

LONDON · OXFORD · NEW YORK · NEW DELHI · SYDNEY

ADLARD COLES
Bloomsbury Publishing Plc
50 Bedford Square, London, WC1B 3DP, UK
29 Earlsfort Terrace, Dublin 2, Ireland

BLOOMSBURY, ADLARD COLES and the Adlard Coles logo are trademarks of
Bloomsbury Publishing Plc

First published in Great Britain 2013
This edition published 2025

Copyright © Nic Compton 2025

Nic Compton has asserted his right under the Copyright, Designs and Patents Act, 1988, to be
identified as Author of this work

For legal purposes the Acknowledgements on page 320
constitute an extension of this copyright page

All rights reserved. No part of this publication may be reproduced or transmitted in any form or by
any means, electronic or mechanical, including photocopying, recording, or any information storage
or retrieval system, without prior permission in writing from the publishers

A catalogue record for this book is available from the British Library

ISBN: HB: 978-1-3994-0436-5; eBook: 978-1-3994-0435-8; ePDF: 978-1-3994-0434-1

2 4 6 8 10 9 7 5 3 1

Designed by Lisa McCormick & Richard Carr

Printed and bound in China by C&C Offset Printing Co., Ltd.

To find out more about our authors and books visit www.bloomsbury.com
and sign up for our newsletters

Contents

Welcome to knots	**8**
The basics	**10**
History of knots	12
Learning the ropes	16
Tools of the trade	18
Types of rope	20
Terminology	22
Top 10 most useful knots	24
Hitches	**26**
Round turn & two half hitches	28
Seized round turn & two half hitches	29
Round turn & buntline hitch	30
Innomiknot	31
Clove hitch	32
Slipped clove hitch	33
Clove hitch tied in the bight	34
Exploding clove hitch	35
BEST FOR tying a bucket	**36**
Camel hitch	38
Rolling hitch	39
Constrictor knot	40
Constrictor knot with loop	41
Double constrictor knot	42
Constrictor knot tied in the bight	43
Strangle knot	44
Ground-line hitch	45
Ossel hitch	46
Ossel knot	47
BEST FOR tying a fender	**48**
Fisherman's bend	50
Fisherman's bend & bowline	51
Marlinspike hitch	52
Cow hitch	53
Transom hitch	54
Knute hitch	55
Studding sail halyard bend	56
Gaff topsail halyard bend	57
Topsail halyard bend	58
Horse dealer's hitch	59
Timber hitch	60
Stopped half hitch	61
BEST FOR lashing things down	**62**
Killick hitch	64
Lifting hitch	65
Queen Clara hitch	66
Great Queen Clara hitch	67
Lighterman's hitch	68
Pile hitch	70
Crossing knot	71
Cleat hitch	72
Slipped cleat hitch	73
Cleat hitch on a bollard cleat	74
Cleat hitch on a pin	75
BEST FOR tying a mooring line to a ring	**76**
Blackwall hitch	78
Double blackwall hitch	79
Double cat's paw	80
Bubble knot	81
Trucker's hitch	82
Double trucker's hitch	83
BEST FOR tying an anchor snubber	**84**
Bends	**86**
Overhand bend	88
Figure-eight bend	89
Sheet bend	90
Double sheet bend	91
Triple sheet bend	91
Alpine butterfly bend	92
Lapp knot	93
Rigger's bend	94
Barrel knot	95

BEST FOR tying an ensign	**96**
Zeppelin bend	98
Broach bend	99
Carrick bend	100
Open carrick bend	101
Spanish hawser bend	102
Surgeon's knot	103
Simple Simon	104
Double simple Simon	105
Slackline bend	106
Jamming bend	107
Adjustable bend	108
Twin bowline	109
Reeving line bend	110
Double reeving line bend	111
BEST FOR joining two mooring lines	**112**
Fisherman's knot	114
Double fisherman's knot	115
Triple fisherman's knot	115
Racking bend	116
Heaving line bend	117
Single stopper	118
Sansome bend	119
Braided splice	120

Loops 122

Overhand loop	124
Figure-eight loop	125
Bowline	126
Fast bowline	128
Tucked bowline	129
Water bowline	130
Bowline in the bight	131
Midshipman's loop	132
Angler's loop	133
BEST FOR tying a rope harness	**134**
Honda knot	136
Carrick loop	137
Harness loop	138
Double harness loop	139
Broach loop	140
Peace knot	141
Butterfly loop	142
Eskimo bowline	143

BEST FOR tying a jib sheet	**144**
Braided loop	146
Braided interlocking loop	148
Running bowline	150
Ichabod knot	151
BEST FOR tying a mooring line to a bollard	**152**
Gibbet knot	154
Locking loop	155
Slip & nip loop	156
Adjustable loop	157
Hangman's knot	158
Scaffold knot	160
Spanish bowline	161
BEST FOR making a rope ladder	**162**
Triple loop bowline	164
Double angler's loop	165
Tom fool's knot	166
Handcuff knot	167
BEST FOR tying a halyard	**168**

Knots 170

Overhand knot	172
Double overhand knot	173
Slipped overhand knot	173
Figure-eight knot	174
Slipped figure-eight knot	174
Stevedore knot	175
Ashley's stopper	176
Quatrefoil	178
Cinquefoil	179
Reef knot	180
Heaving line knot	182
Martha's vineyard heaving line knot	183
BEST FOR tying a stopper knot	**184**
Monkey's fist	186
Monkey's paw	187
Sheepshank in the bight	188
Sheepshank tied with ends	189
Sheepshank with clove hitch	189
Yardarm knot	190
Poldo tackle	191
Versatackle	192
Prusik bottle sling	194
Indian jug handle	195

Lashings	**196**
Pole hitch	198
Square lashing	200
Diagonal lashing	201
Shear lashing	202
Figure-eight lashing	203
Filipino lashing	204
Japanese lashing	205
Jury mast knot	206
Marline hitches	208
Chain stitch lashing	209
Coils	**210**
Simple coil	212
Halyard coil	213
Clove hitch coil	214
Bell ringer's knot	215
BEST FOR coiling a rope	**216**
Alpine coil	218
Butterfly coil	219
Figure-eight flake	220
Wrapped coil	221
Cheesing	222
Decorative knots	**224**
Crown knot	226
Wall knot	228
Double wall knot	229
Diamond knot	230
Double diamond knot	232
Footrope knot	234
Star knot	236
Matthew Walker knot	238
Double Matthew Walker	240
Matthew Walker loop	241
Lanyard knot	242
Chinese lanyard knot	244
Japanese loop	246
Chinese crown loop	247
Good luck knot	248
Mystic knot	250
Three-strand plait sinnet	252
Two-strand plait sinnet	254
Crown sinnet	256

BEST FOR making a bellrope key ring	**258**
Turk's head 3L × 4B in the round	260
Turk's head 4L × 3B in the round	262
Turk's head 3L × 5B in the flat	264
Turk's head 5L × 4B in the flat	266
Oval mat	268
Ocean braid mat	270
Doughnut	272
Whippings & seizings	**274**
Plain whipping	276
Sailor's whipping	278
Palm & needle whipping	279
French whipping	280
Butane whipping	281
Crown whipping	282
West Country whipping	283
Flat seizing	284
Racking seizing	285
BEST FOR making a chafe guard	**286**
Splices	**288**
Short splice	290
Long splice	292
Back splice	294
Hard eye splice	296
Soft eye splice	297
Traditional chain splice	298
Grommet splice	300
Multiplait eyesplice	302
Multiplait chain splice	304
Dyneema reduction splice	306
Spectra splice	308
Dyneema loop	310
Dyneema soft shackle	312
Glossary	314
Index	316
Acknowledgements	320

Welcome to knots

What is it about knots? How can such an apparently simple occupation as twisting bits of string into preconceived patterns be so endlessly satisfying and have such wide-ranging appeal? Knots have intrigued writers and artists since ancient times, and even Leonardo da Vinci was not adverse to doodling the occasional turk's head when the fancy took him. So, if you like to tie knots, you're in good company! The knots in this book range from the practical to the decorative, the curious and the downright brilliant.

Hitches
It's the biggest section in the book, with 47 knots for tying a line to an object, ranging from old timers developed during the Age of Sail to ingenious new knots devised in recent years.

Bends
More than 30 ways of tying two lines together, including a neat option for slippery high-modulus ropes such as Dyneema® and Spectra® (page 111). Needless to say, you won't find a reef knot here (because it's not a bend!).

Loops
There's something for everyone in this section: Spanish, Eskimo, double, triple, sliding and locking, not to mention handcuffs and a couple of crazy braided loops. Are the days of the bowline's rule numbered? Find out on page 127.

Knots
Featured knots include everything from stoppers to heaving line weights (including the monkey's fist and paw), a rope tackle and a couple of bottle slings. Plus that much-misinterpreted reef knot.

Lashings
Need to set up a jury rig or build a shelter? These are the oft-neglected but essential building knots for creating all sorts of interesting structures.

Coils
They say cleanliness is next to godliness, so best keep your ropes tidy! We also discuss the pros and cons of cheesing rope.

Decorative knots
There are mats, turk's heads and lanyards, plus some of the most complicated knots in the book. Take a deep breath, and follow our specially extended step-by-step sequences.

Whippings and seizings
There is more essential rope care information here, plus a couple of decorative whippings which rarely see the light of day.

Splices
These include a few old standards, a couple of obscure ones from yesteryear, plus some bang up-to-date splices from the high-modulus camp. And just wait until you see our soft shackle. It's the next must-have item for every sailor!

WELCOME TO KNOTS • 9

IMPORTANT NOTE

Each knot is accompanied by a Knot Score box which gives a score, ranging from 1–5, for Strength, Security, Difficulty Tying, Difficulty Untying and Usefulness. The scores are solely based on observation and experience, and not on scientific testing. They should not be taken as definitive, nor should they be used as the basis for tying the knots for any critical purpose. In any case, results will vary depending on the type and condition of the cordage being used, as well as the particular circumstances in which the knots are tied (eg size of load, whether the line is wet or dry, etc). Readers are advised to test the knots for themselves and reach their own conclusion before using them for any critical activity.

For more information about the knot score boxes, see page 23.

“ To me the simple act of tying a knot is an adventure in unlimited space. A bit of string affords a dimensional latitude that is unique among the entities. For an uncomplicated strand is a palpable object that, for all practical purposes, possesses one dimension only. If we move a single strand in a plane, interlacing it at will, actual objects of beauty and of utility can result in what is practically two dimensions; and if we choose to direct our strand out of this one plane, another dimension is added which provides opportunity for an excursion that is limited only by the scope of our own imagery and the length of the ropemaker's coil. What could be more wonderful than that? ”

Clifford Ashley, The Ashley Book of Knots

THE BASICS 1

History of knots

Knots have existed for as long as there has been rope to tie them with, for a piece of rope is pretty useless without a knot to fasten it onto something. And rope was used for all sorts of things, from carrying loads, snaring and tethering animals, to building houses. It was also useful in wartime to trap, tie and even execute enemies. And a piece of stretchy animal's intestine tied to a stick made a wonderful slingshot. But all of them needed knots.

Above: The Tall Ships races have helped keep alive the art of sailing square-riggers – and tying complicated knots.

In the beginning

Not surprisingly, there's evidence of knot-tying all over the world. The earliest objects thought to require cordage – and therefore knots – are two pendants found at the Repolusthöhle in Austria, which are 300,000 years old. We know the Ancient Egyptians were familiar with knots, as a length of twisted twine was found in Tutankhamun's tomb (c.1620 BC). The Nootka and Clayoquot tribes of the west coast of America used cedar to make whaling lines 100–125mm (4–5in) thick and up to 360m (1,200ft) long. They also made lanyards for their harpoons out of whale sinews, twisted into three-strand rope, and tied with knots.

Both the Ancient Greeks and the Romans used knots extensively. In fact, so far ahead of their time were the Ancient Greeks that, back in the 4th century BC, Oribasius published a range of 18 knots and slings intended specifically for surgical use – surely the first such specialist knot list.

But perhaps the most imaginative use of knots were the 'number records' developed by the Incas before colonisation. Using a decimal system, numbers were recorded in lengths of cord, called *quipus*, using knots instead of numerals. Thus three knots (or a triple knot) in the 'unit' position represented three; three knots in the 'ten' position represented 30; three knots in the 'hundred' position represented 300, and so forth. A single *quipu* might hold up to 2,000 cords, each one colour-coded to indicate what was being counted, eg green for cattle, white for sheep, etc. *Quipus* were used in place of written records and were regarded as legal documents by the local government.

Heydays of knotting

Knot-tying really developed into an art form in the 18th century, starting

Above: The Incas used knots for counting several hundred years before the Chinese invented the abacus.

with the Age of Discovery and the explosion in world trade that followed. As ships ventured increasingly further afield to deliver cargo, lengthy passages at sea, often lasting several months, meant that sailors had time on their hands. Most were illiterate and could not seek refuge in books, even when those were available.

Instead, they turned to 'the arts': model-making, scrimshaw (carving whalebones), tattooing, sewing, knitting, crochet, basket-weaving and even hat-making were all practised by sailors desperate to alleviate the monotony of a long passage. But the pastime of choice for most was knot-tying.

Indeed, according to Clifford Ashley, in his definitive *Book of Knots*, the type of knots tied by a sailor indicated the service in which he was employed. The Navy was the most thrifty, and its sailors had to content themselves with 'small stuff' (ie thin cordage), such as log lines and fishing lines, leading them to specialise in decorative knotting and macramé. The merchant navy apparently had plenty of hefty old rope (known as 'junk') to give away, which had to be teased out and reconstituted before it could be made into mats and suchlike. But it was the whaling ships that provided the best habitat for the 'marlinspike sailor'. Not only did they spend the longest time at sea, thereby giving ample time for extra-curricular activities, but there was always some tired old harpoon line for their crews to practise on.

The development of knots was an international phenomenon that spread from ship to ship regardless of nationality or religion. For, while it is true that sailors guarded some of their more obscure knots like a secret family recipe, any knot that fulfilled a useful function was soon shared to benefit the whole ship – and indeed the whole seaborne community.

It was also uncontrolled and unregulated, which meant that the best knots emerged in time through trial and error and recommendation.

They also acquired different names, not only from country to country but virtually from ship to ship. The common reef knot is variously known as the square knot (US), the reef knot (UK), the Heracles knot (Greece), the Hercules knot (Rome), and the love knot (romantic literature).

Symbolic knots

Apart from their practical function, knots have long been used as a metaphor in art and literature. The Ancient Greeks and Romans were particularly fond of the reef knot and used it as a motif in clothing and jewellery. The knot's neat symmetry, showing two ropes in equal and opposite union, made it a natural choice for anyone wanting to represent romantic union, and it was used in marriage rituals in both great civilisations.

Above: The knot of Heracles (otherwise known as the reef knot) has captivated artists since ancient times. This gold chain dates from 300 BC.

Below: The Age of Sail, when great square riggers such as these sailed the world, was the peak time for knot-tying.

Knots could also be problematic and difficult to untie including, most famously, the mythic Gordian knot. According to legend, after Gordias became King of Phrygia, the ox cart he had been riding was tied down with a complicated knot, whose ends were hidden from view. The story went that whoever managed to untie the knot would go on to conquer the East, including the much-desired Persia. Many people tried without success, until Alexander (later Alexander the Great) came along and sliced it open with one stroke of his sword. The story has been taken as a metaphor for solving apparently intractable problems with simple (albeit brutal) methods.

Knots have long been thought by mariners to have magical properties, including the power to control the wind. So-called wind-knots were tied into a piece of rope or a rag and sold to superstitious sailors, who would then untie the three knots they contained at an appropriate moment to release the wind. The 17th-century Norwegian poet Petter Dass explained what was supposed to happen next:

> Untie but the one for a gentle, good breeze,
>
> The sails will be filled, you make progress with ease;
>
> But if you the second will loosen,
>
> You pull in the canvas to barely half mast.
>
> The third will send wind that will race you so fast
>
> That pumps you will have to resort to.

Even religion hasn't remained impervious to the potent symbolism of knots, which feature in both the Jewish Bible and the Koran. Indeed, Deuteronomy 22:12 states: 'You shall make yourself twisted threads, on the four corners of your garment with which you cover yourself.' This has been taken as an instruction by devout Jews, who attach precisely crafted lanyards, called *tzitzit*, to the four corners of their prayer shawls.

Into the modern era

The passing of the Age of Sail, and the advent of steam, is usually quoted as the reason for the lapse in interest in knot-tying at the end of the 19th and beginning of the 20th centuries. Steam ships needed fewer crew and passages were shorter, the logic went, meaning that sailors had less time on their hands to devote to the pursuit of knots. Clifford Ashley, interestingly, disagrees. He blames the passing of knots on improved education. As sailors became more educated and able to read, they found other ways to entertain themselves, mainly by reading books. Writing in 1944, he welcomed the emerging popularity of radio, which he said freed people's hands to play with bits of rope, and warned of the distracting effects of television and cinema.

Ashley may have been right about the dangers of TV, but what he didn't anticipate was the effects of post-war

Above: A prayer shawl decorated with knotted tassels, as prescribed by the Jewish Bible.

Left: Faced with an intractable problem such as the Gordian knot, Alexander had a typically direct solution: cut it off!

prosperity in the West. With more free time to indulge in their personal interests, hobbies of all kinds flourished in the 1950s and 60s. Later, came the reaction to mass-produced goods and a renewed interest in traditional crafts of every description – including knot-tying. Whereas Ashley believed he was witnessing the end of a craft, he was in fact anticipating its revival.

In recent years, knot-tying has seen an explosion of interest, with many new books and countless websites devoted to the subject. The International Guild of Knot Tyers (IGKT), formed in 1982, now boasts over 1,000 members, with branches in North America, the Netherlands, France, Germany and New Zealand.

How many knots?

If you thought that every knot that could be tied in a piece of string must have been invented by now, think again. *The Ashley Book of Knots* claims to include 3,800 knots – although this includes many repeats of the same knots in different situations, so the true figure is probably less than 3,000. That was nearly 70 years ago. New knots are being invented all the time, as witnessed by the IGKT's quarterly publication *Knotting Matters*. Of course, not all of them are all that useful, and there is always the temptation to add an extra turn to an existing knot to create a new one that performs rather less well than the original. But, while many inadequate knots will pass by the wayside, others will be taken up and may eventually challenge or even supplant the old favourites.

Even now, there is no definitive list of knots. In fact, finding exactly the right knot for the job is the main challenge. Few authors will agree even

Above: A group of ratings learn to tie knots. Knowing your hitches could be a question of life and death in the Navy.

on the top ten knots, let alone a bigger selection, and the aspiring knot-tyer will have to read widely to investigate all the possibilities. The selection published by *The Admiralty Manual of Seamanship* isn't a bad starting point. A recent edition includes the following:

Reef knot, figure-of-eight knot, marlinspike hitch, marling hitch, timber hitch, clove hitch, constrictor knot, double blackwall knot, midshipman's hitch, bowline, running bowline, bowline in the bight, French bowline, monkey's fist, heaving line knot, fisherman's knot, crown knot, wall knot, manrope knot, Turk's head, square lashing, diagonal lashing, and various splices and whippings.

But there is no better indication of the everyday nature of knots than the fact that so few are named after people. Of the 200 in this book, only the Ashley stopper and the Matthew Walker knot take their name from real or fictional people. Even there, Ashley played no part in naming 'his' knot, which he referred to as the oysterman's stopper, while Matthew Walker is quite possibly a mythical figure. The point being that now, as ever, knots are made to serve people, not vice versa.

Learning the ropes

Anyone can tie any of the knots in this book. All it takes is a bit of patience and a calm head. For the simpler knots, all you need are two 1.8m (6ft) lengths of rope about 9mm (¾in) in diameter, and only the most basic tools (page 18). There are a few basic techniques, however, that will ensure the experience is a pleasure rather than a chore.

Learning the ropes

The first rule of knotting is: start simple. There's a language of knot-tying which you must learn before embarking on the more complicated formations, and, like all languages, it can only be learned through practice. Familiarise yourself with simple knots, and after a while your hands will feel their way around and almost anticipate your brain. That's when you're ready to move on to the next level. Tackling a difficult knot before you're ready can be intensely discouraging and put you off the whole business – unnecessarily.

A simple rule to follow is never leave a knot until you can tie it without looking at the instructions (words or pictures) – not just minutes later but the next day and the day after that. Keep coming back and challenging yourself to tie the knot from memory. It's amazing how quickly it implants itself in your brain.

If you're struggling with a knot, or a particular step, try turning the page around and tying it from a different angle.

Rope care

The second rule of knotting is keep your ropes tidy. Badly coiled ropes, or ropes with frayed ends, create a distraction you just don't need when you are tackling a new knot. Use the coiling techniques described on pages 210–222 to keep the rope tidy. If it's old rope that's full of twists, shake

Below: Trainees aboard the yacht *Brilliant* are taught some basic knots, before heading out off the coast of Nova Scotia.

them out and start afresh. This is best done with the rope on the floor, shaking the whole coil to clear the twists – like a garden hose.

In the old days, new rope made from hemp was stiff and unworkable. One technique for softening it was to uncoil it and tow it behind the ship for a few hours. Once one end was done, you would turn it around and tow it from the other end – making sure both ends were properly whipped beforehand. Modern ropes are much softer and easier to work with and unlikely to need such treatment, but if you do try this, make sure you're well away from other boats and fishing pots – and beware of catching the line in the prop.

Keeping the ends of the ropes well sealed or 'whipped' pays dividends. An unsealed rope soon becomes frayed and, even when twisted back into shape, never quite regains its true shape. Use the whipping techniques described on pages 274–286 to keep your ends tight. Modern ropes usually come 'ready-sealed' and can easily be resealed using a small blow-torch or lighter – although there's something about an old-fashioned whipping that looks the part like nothing else.

The traditional way of cutting rope was with a hatchet on a block of wood. Nowadays, hot knives are available quite cheaply and seal the ends of the rope at the same time as cutting it. For most of us, however, a simple sailor's knife will suffice. Make sure it's sharp and make sure you cut onto a firm surface – such as a chopping board or a block of wood. Wrapping insulating tape or putting a stopping (eg a constrictor knot, page 40) on either side of the cut *before* applying the knife will prevent the rope unravelling.

If you're cutting to length, always cut a bit more than you think you need. It's generally easy to get rid of any extra length, but awfully hard to add it on. And remember the old carpenter's saying: measure twice, cut once.

Washing rope
Working with salty or dirty rope isn't much fun. It also creates abrasion, which shortens the life of the fibre. Soak it and wash it in a bucket or bath of warm water, using a mild detergent. Alternatively, most synthetic ropes can be put in a washing machine. Use the setting for wool (ie delicates) and don't tumble dry. The best way to dry rope is to lay it out in a well-ventilated place, preferably away from direct sunlight, which degrades the material.

Tightening the knot
Just because you've got the rope in the right position, doesn't mean you've tied the knot. Tightening is an integral part of the process and can make or break a knot – particularly the more complicated varieties described in Chapters 4 and 7. Work your way around the knot methodically, never losing sight of the intended shape. This can take as long or, in the case of the ocean plait mat, longer than tying the knot itself. If the knot is very tight, use a pair of pliers to work it, applying just enough grip to pull the rope through without damaging it.

Above: It can be worth investing in a hot knife, which automatically seals the end of synthetic ropes while it cuts them.

Tools of the trade

In the days of sail, there were only three items a rigger carried aloft: a knife, a marlinspike, and a 'horn' containing a dollop of tallow for greasing the rope. Anything else was a bonus. Nowadays, the advent of wire rigging means the modern rigger has to carry a much bigger range of tools (cutters, swagers, etc), but for most knot-tyers, only the basics are necessary.

Essential tools

The first and only truly essential tool is a knife. A traditional rigger's knife is made of mild steel, with a wooden handle and a squared-off blade – you don't want to stab yourself in the arm while you're swinging in the rigging. In truth, almost any knife will do the trick, as long as it's sharp and preferably has a sheath to protect it and you from any nasty accidents.

The other classic rigger's tool is the marlinspike. Traditionally, this was a steel spike about 225–300mm (9–12in) long, with a rounded head and a hole at the top for attaching a lanyard. This was used for opening strands of rope while splicing, as well as easing apart tight knots. The rounded head allowed it to be pounded with a mallet when working with stiff rope or wire. Nowadays, a diminutive marlinspike is included in most pocket knives designed for yachtsmen (such as the ubiquitous Captain Currey Lockspike Knife) or else combined with a shackle key in a holster kit. Either is adequate for the small and medium stuff, but will be completely inadequate for the larger stuff (25mm [1in] diameter and over).

A useful addition to the marlinspike toolbox is the fid. Essentially a slender wooden (or whalebone) cone, it is used in a similar fashion to the marlinspike – but never with a hammer. Fids come in a range of sizes, from 75mm (3in)

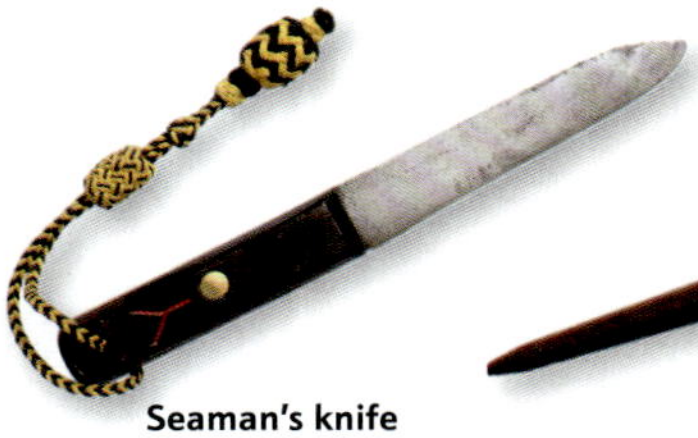

Seaman's knife  **Wooden fid**  **Marlinspike** 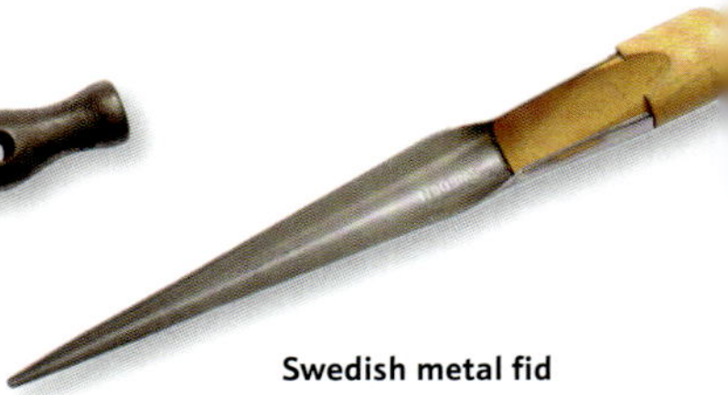 **Swedish metal fid**

Serving mallet  **Heaving mallet**  **Palm** 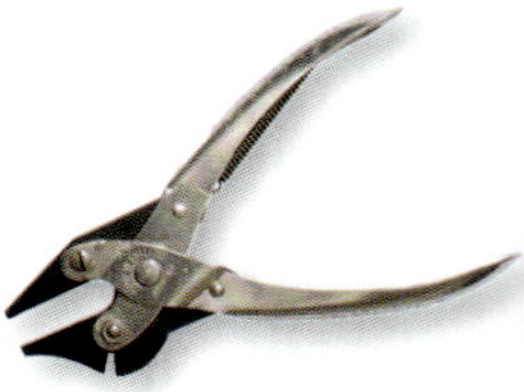 **Parallel pliers**

Waxed twine  **Various twines** 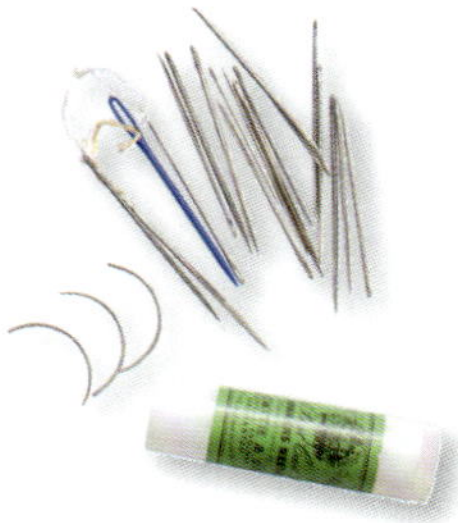 **Sailmaker's needles** 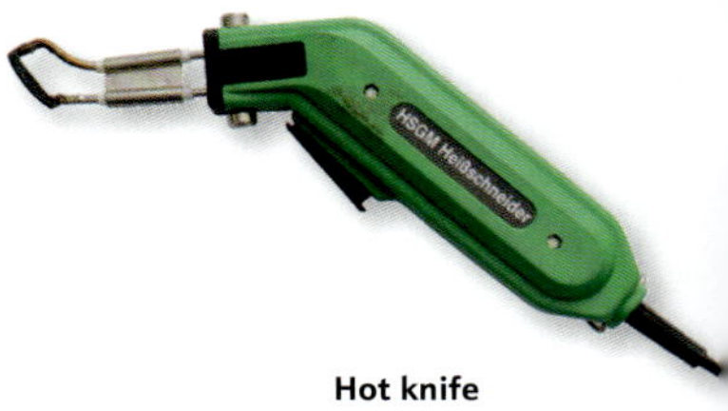 **Hot knife**

THE BASICS • 19

Above: A rigger's knife and marlinspike (or, strictly, a fid). You don't need much else for 90 per cent of the knots in this book.

upwards, depending on the type of work being done. As a rough rule of thumb, the length of the fid should be 21 times the diameter of the rope, eg the fid for working with 10mm (3/8 in) rope would be 10 × 21 = approx 210mm (8in). Nowadays, the so-called Swedish fid – with its hollow metal blade and wooden handle – has mostly supplanted the marlinspike and is often the only dedicated rigging tool that is stocked by chandlers.

Non-essential tools

An ingenious modern invention, once the province of the professional but now increasingly targeted at the amateur, is the hot knife. Essentially just an electrically heated blade mounted on a gun or stand, it has the advantage of sealing the ends of the rope as it cuts it, thereby preventing the strands from unravelling. Use only with synthetic ropes, never with traditional hemp.

Unless you've got strong hands and impervious skin, a pair of long-nosed pliers will make life much easier when it comes to tightening a knot, particularly the later, more fiddly knots in Chapters 4 and 7. The regular type available from most DIY stores will do the trick nicely. If you're worried about damaging the rope, wrap it with a piece of cloth before using the pliers.

For the finer detail work, such as whipping, you'll need a set of three-sided sailmaker's needles and some waxed whipping twine. The twine comes in many colours, which can be useful to create fancy effects. It can also be used to make miniature knots for jewellery, such as monkey's fist earrings or pendants. Alternatively, a ball of tarred twine does the job very nicely, and smells wonderful too!

A palm is the sailmaker's equivalent of a thimble, except that it's held by a leather strap and is designed to sit in the palm of the hand. This means that greater pressure can be exerted on the needle as it's pushed through layers of sailcloth – or, in this case, strands of rope. Its only application within the contents of this book is for making whippings.

Beeswax is another traditional material used by the marlinspike sailor. Draw a thread through a small block of beeswax to close the pores and keep the moisture out. It can also be used as a lubricant when drawing a stitch through canvas or leather.

Essential tools
Knife
Marlinspike or fid

Additional tools
Various fids
Pliers
Mallet
Palm
Needles
Whipping twine
Ball of twine
Beeswax

Types of rope

The choice of cordage available even in a small chandler's can present a baffling obstacle to the average person going to buy a length of 'rope'. Suffice to say that, if you just want to practise a few knots, then any rope will do. Most of the knots in this book (splices and decorative knots excepted) can be tied using two 1.8m (6ft) lengths of 10mm (3/8 in) rope of pretty much any classification.

Above: Modern ropes are available in a variety of colours, which makes identification of specific lines easier.

Natural vs synthetic

The most important choice when selecting rope is between natural and manmade fibres. By and large, people tend to fall into one camp or the other and will develop a slightly different set of tools and techniques accordingly. Even if both are used, you are strongly advised not to mix the two in one piece of work, as the materials will move differently and the manmade fibres will tend to abrade the natural ones.

Natural fibre

For thousands of years, rope has been made by teasing apart the fibres of plants, such as cotton, flax, coir, sisal, manila and hemp, and spinning them into yarns. The yarns are then twisted into strands, which are then twisted into rope. Each section is twisted in the opposite direction to the previous one, which is what holds the rope together.

Most natural fibre rope is made up of three strands, which is called plain- or hawser-laid. Four-strand rope is called shroud-laid. If three or more lengths of three- or four-strand rope are twisted together to make an even larger rope, it is called cable-laid.

Generally, the more strands there are, the weaker the rope. Therefore a 10mm (3/8in) four-strand rope is 10 per cent weaker than a three-strand rope of the same diameter, while a nine-strand rope is 40 per cent weaker. The best way to increase the strength of the rope is to increase the size of the strands, not the number of strands. Natural fibre rope has several disadvantages. When wet, it swells and makes knots difficult to untie and, unless carefully stored, it tends to attract moisture and rot. It's proportionally less strong than synthetic ropes, so a thicker diameter rope is needed for the same purpose. Also, when new, it's stiff and unmanageable and rough on the hands. For all these reasons, it's rarely

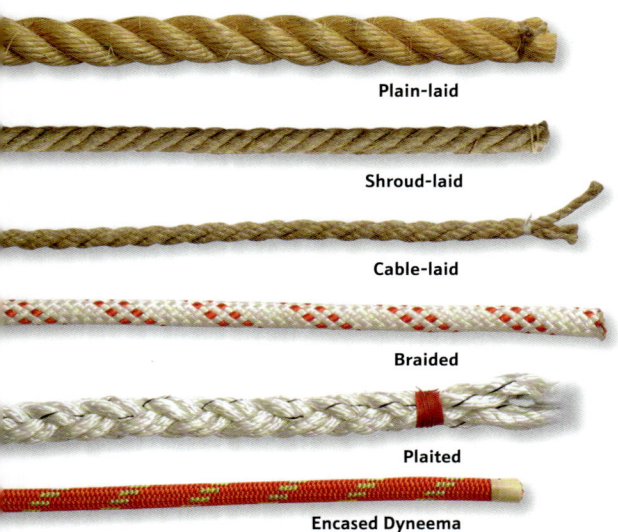

Plain-laid

Shroud-laid

Cable-laid

Braided

Plaited

Encased Dyneema

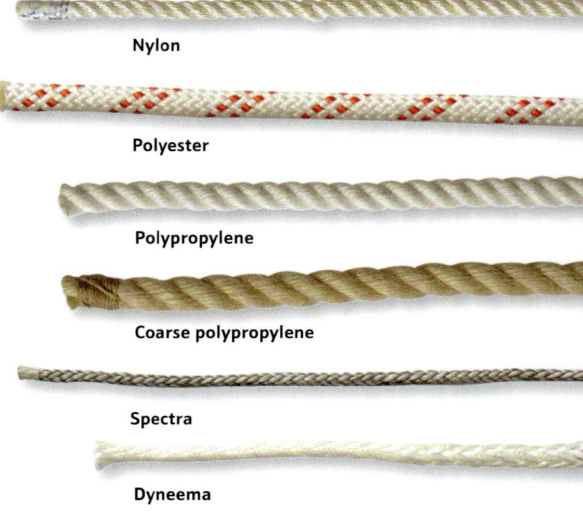

Nylon

Polyester

Polypropylene

Coarse polypropylene

Spectra

Dyneema

used on boats nowadays – although its pleasing texture and organic colours mean it's still a popular choice for decorative knots, such as the ocean braid mat (page 270).

Synthetic ropes

Since the invention of nylon in 1938, synthetic ropes have rapidly replaced natural fibre varieties. Not only are they stronger for their size, but they are also rot- and sun-resistant. What's more, they can be produced in a variety of different colours, which means the running rigging on a yacht can be colour-coded for ease of use. It's easy to get carried away with this, however, with the result that some boats can end up looking like rope pizza.

The other major drawback of synthetic ropes is that they tend to be smoother and more slippery, which is nice on the hands but means knots can come undone (or 'capsized') more easily. The solution is usually to add a half hitch or two, or even a seizing, although this is time-consuming and not as pleasing to the eye as a plain knot.

Broadly speaking, synthetic ropes divide into three categories: Nylon, Polyester and Polypropylene. Nylon is also marketed as Polyamide, Bri-Nylon and Enkalon. This is a stretchy fibre that does not float, and is suitable for mooring lines, anchor warps and towing ropes. Polyester, which is also marketed as Terylene, Dacron, Tergal and Fortrel, is not quite as strong as nylon, but it stretches less, making it ideal for halyards and other parts of the running rigging where stretch is undesirable.

Polypropylene, also known as Polyethylene, is the cheapest, and weakest, of the lot. Its main advantage is that it floats, which makes it useful for water-ski ropes, rescue lines and heaving lines.

New ropes are coming onto the market all the time, such as Dyneema, Spectra and Kevlar. Your local chandler will be able to advise you on the more specialised (and expensive!) varieties.

The weave

The other big difference with synthetic ropes is that they are woven in several different ways. As well as the usual three- and four-strand laid ropes, there are plaited ropes, braided ropes, and endless combinations of all three. You can buy a rope with a 16-strand sheath over a three-strand core, or four-strand rope laid over a one-strand core, or even a braided sheath over a braided core.

The main thing to remember, however, is that three- and four-strand rope stretches more than plaited and braided ropes. This is why it should always be used for mooring lines, where it absorbs some of the shock, while plaited and braided rope is best used for running rigging, where it maintains the tension.

Below: Salt water not only makes lines harder to handle but also degrades the fibre. Wash your lines regularly with fresh water.

Terminology

Sailors are famous for their jargon, and knot-tyers and riggers are no different. But this specialised vocabulary came about for good reason. After all, with 3,000 or so knots to choose from, it would be no good to tell a deckhand to simply 'tie a knot' when what was needed was a constrictor knot in the bight (page 43). Likewise, the different parts of a knot need naming to make their explanation that much clearer.

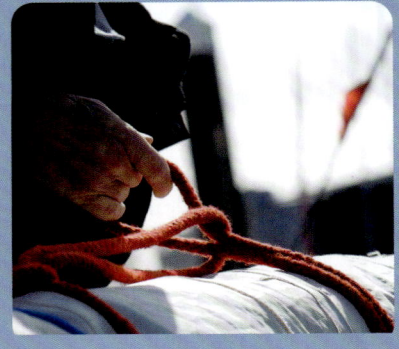

Above: Is it a bight or a loop? Knots have their own jargon which you need to familiarise yourself with.

When a knot is not a knot

First off, what is a knot? On one level, the term includes every twist and turn shown in this book, from camel hitch to Turk's head. Strictly speaking, however, when rope is tied to another object, it is known as a *hitch*. When two ends of rope are tied together, it is known as a *bend*. When the strands of a rope are unlaid and woven to another rope or onto itself, it's a *splice*. Anything else – including a loop – is simply a knot.

Working words

There are specific terms to describe the various parts of a knot while it is being tied. The active end is called the *working end*, whereas the end not in use is called the *standing end*. The inactive section of rope nearest the knot is called the *standing part*. Any part of the rope between the ends is referred to as the *bight*, and if a knot is tied in the bight it means it is tied without passing the ends of the rope through it, eg a clove hitch in the bight (page 34).

Just to confuse things, a curved section of rope within a knot-in-progress is also referred to as a *bight*. Once the rope is crossed, the bight becomes a *loop*. A loop is *overhand* when the working end is laid on top of the standing part; it is *underhand* when the working end is laid under the standing part. The place where the rope crosses to make the loop is the *crossing point*. Place two or more loops in close proximity, and they become an *elbow*.

If you use the bight, instead of an end, to tie the last part of a knot, you create a loop, which means the knot can be *slipped*. This makes untying the knot much easier, but it doesn't mean the whole knot will come undone with a single pull. That is the province of *exploding* knots, such as the exploding clove hitch (page 35).

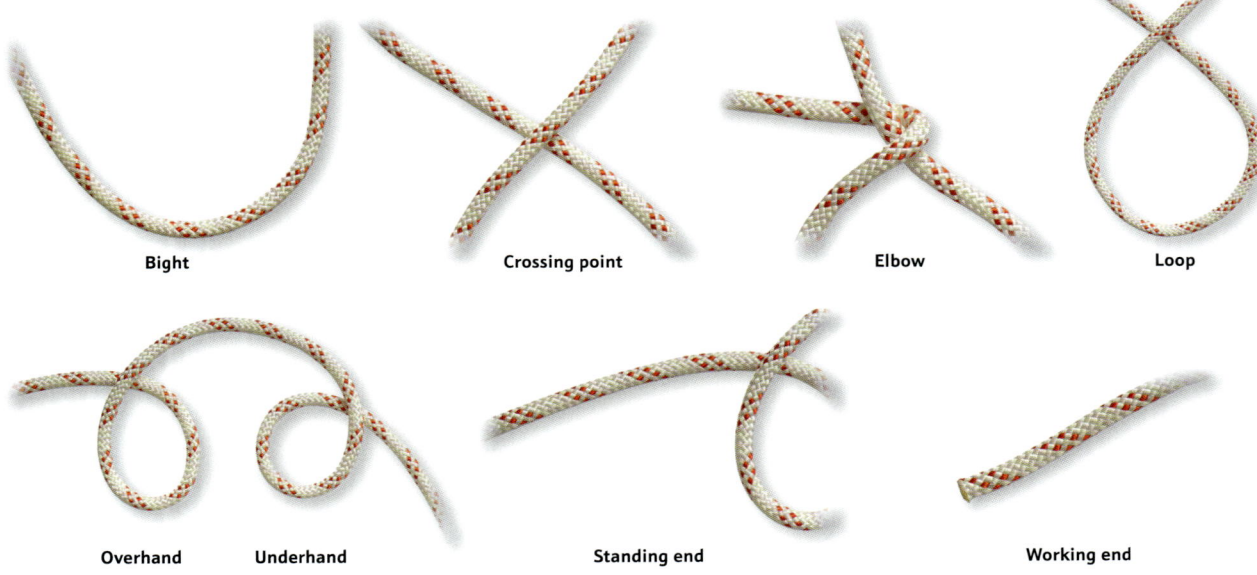

Bight **Crossing point** **Elbow** **Loop**

Overhand **Underhand** **Standing end** **Working end**

If you wrap a rope around a bollard or post, it's called taking *a turn*, or taking *a single turn*. Wrap it around once more, and it's called *a round turn*. Wrap it around again, and it's called *two round turns*.

Lines vs rope

Finally, there's the idea that there are only ever *lines* on a ship, and never *rope*. It is true that, once a piece of rope has acquired a specific function (eg raising a sail, mooring the vessel) then it becomes known as a line. A loose piece of rope with no designated purpose is, however, still a piece of rope. And there are some ropes that have specific functions that never acquire the prestige of becoming lines, such as bell ropes, bolt ropes and foot ropes.

Knot scores

All the knots in this book are awarded a five-part Knot Score, with their strength, security, ease of tying, ease of untying, and usefulness given a grade from 1–5. At first glance it might seem superfluous to treat strength and security as separate categories – after all, a knot either holds or it doesn't hold, right? There are, however, certain knots that, because of their inherent design, are liable to break the rope before they slip, while others will slip before they break.

The distinction is all the more important given the widespread use of synthetic ropes, which tend to be very strong but also rather slippery. Given a strong, slippery length of rope, you are better off using a knot that scores highly on security, but less highly on strength. On the other hand, if you are using natural fibre rope, which has good grip but is weaker than synthetic rope, then you might be better off choosing a knot that scores highly on strength but less highly on security. It's horses for courses – or turns for yarns.

It goes without saying that, just because a knot is easy to tie, that doesn't mean it's easy to untie; or that a knot that is difficult to tie is necessarily difficult to untie – hence each of those categories are scored differently. The higher the score, the easier it is to tie or to untie.

Lastly, 'usefulness' is clearly a subjective term: what might be an essential knot for one person might be regarded as frivolous by another. Equally, there's no doubt that, at some point, every knot will be just the right knot for the job – if you're dismasted at sea, for instance, there will be no better knot than the jury mast knot (page 206). There are, however, certain knots that have universal application – eg the ever-versatile one round turn and two half hitches. The 'usefulness' score is intended to suggest what would be most useful to the average sailor in normal day-to-day usage. Learn all 200 knots, and you'll be covered in almost any circumstance.

Above: A practical application of a 'decorative' knot: a turk's head is tied onto a mainsheet traveller.

Top 10 most useful knots

Not everyone has time to learn 20, let alone 200, knots. And it is true that in day-to-day life most sailors manage perfectly well using only a handful. Which knots those are, you'll only find out by practising as many as possible, but the following is a selection that should cover most eventualities – even if some come with health warnings.

Figure-eight (page 174)

It's not much more than an overhand knot with an extra turn, but that extra turn makes the world of difference. Whereas you might struggle to undo an overhand knot, generally speaking, a figure-eight will untie with relative ease. It is ideal for stopping sheets from slipping through a block or jammer. Or, for a more sophisticated (and bulkier) alternative, try Ashley's stopper knot (page 176).

Round turn & two half hitches (page 28)

The workhorse of knots. There's nothing very pretty or glamorous about a round turn and two half hitches, but it will get you out of trouble again and again. The round turn spreads the load, so it's kind on the rope, and if you want to make the knot more secure, all you have to do is throw in another hitch, or seize the end to the standing part. If you only ever learn one knot, learn this one.

Bowline (page 126)

The true sailor's friend, the bowline is quick to tie, reliable and easy to untie. It's also extremely versatile, and the number of variations it has spawned is evidence of what an ingenious knot it is. That said, it's not without its critics, who accuse it of being unreliable. They might prefer the midshipman's hitch. Yet this author has 40 years' experience of the bowline, without ever being let down.

Clove hitch (page 32)

Probably one of the most useful, and yet least reliable, knots in existence. The clove hitch can be used on posts, bollards, rings, bags, and almost anything else you can think of; it can be doubled, tied in the bight and slipped. As an instant solution for securing a line, it's almost unbeatable. But don't rely on it in the long term. There will almost always be a more reliable knot to do the job. For tying a mooring line, use a lighterman's hitch (page 62); for tying fenders, use a round turn and two half hitches (page 28); for seizing a bag, use a constrictor knot (page 38). Despite all that, the clove hitch is still a very useful knot to know.

THE BASICS • 25

Rolling hitch (page 39)
A development of the clove hitch, the rolling hitch has an extra turn that not only makes it that much more reliable but also gives it a special function: to prevent a line slipping on a smooth surface. This can be a lifesaver when securing a line to a spar, for instance, or to another line, eg a dinghy painter onto a mooring line. Use with similar caution to the clove hitch.

Reef knot (page 180)
Much-beloved of sailors and artists alike since antiquity, the reef knot holds a special place in the pantheon of nautical knots. And, used as a binding knot, it has few equals. Where it falls down is if it is used as a bend, ie to join two ropes together. Use other knots for this purpose, such as a zeppelin bend (page 86). If you want to reef your sails, however, there's no better knot than a reef knot.

Zeppelin bend (page 98)
Anyone tempted to use a reef knot as a bend, ie to join two ropes together, should learn this knot instead. Not only is it elegantly simple, it does the job thoroughly well. Despite its many merits, the zeppelin bend is relatively unknown, and even the usually infallible Clifford Ashley seems to have missed it in his encyclopaedic *Book of Knots*.

Sheet bend (page 90)
It looks like nothing at all, yet the sheet bend can hold the weight of an entire ship. Its primary purpose is joining ropes of different thicknesses, although, at a pinch, it works well enough on ropes of the same size too. If you feel nervous about entrusting your pride and joy to such a fragile-looking knot, you can secure it with a seizing – although in truth it will probably be superfluous.

Fisherman's knot (page 114)
Another deliciously simple knot. On the rare occasions where a round turn and two half hitches is not secure enough, the fisherman's knot (alias the anchor bend) will stand you in good stead. And, if you're still not completely convinced, you can always throw in a couple of half hitches for good measure. Its only minor drawback is that it's not the easiest knot to untie.

Cleat hitch (page 72)
It's certainly one of the simplest knots and wouldn't deserve to be included in this list, were it not for the frightening frequency with which it is tied incorrectly. Tie it right, and you'll sleep soundly at night; tie it incorrectly and you'll at least chafe your mooring lines or you could end up with a boat pile-up. And it's not just a matter of piling on as many turns as you can.

HITCHES 2

Round turn & two half hitches

It's one of the least glamorous knots in a sailor's inventory – yet also one of the most useful. The round turn and two half hitches is a dependable old workhorse that can be put to good use on land and at sea – and probably in the air too. It's also one of the oldest knots in existence. If you learn only one knot, learn this one.

1 Take a turn around the mooring point – in this case a horizontal pole.

Some things are so simple we tend to take them for granted. Like making a cup of tea, or riding a bike. Or, in the case of sailors, a round turn and two half hitches. But ask a non-tea drinker to make tea, or a toddler to ride a bike, or a knot novice to tie a round turn and two half hitches – and you soon realise there's more to these things than you first imagined.

The key to a round turn and two half hitches is to keep going. Once you've put in the first hitch – either clockwise or anticlockwise around the standing part – keep going in the same direction for the second hitch. It's as simple as that.

It might help to think of the knot as a clove hitch tied onto the standing part of the line. And the key to tying a clove hitch is also to keep going.

Despite its simplicity, the double hitch has some ardent admirers. Ashley quotes Admiral Stephen Luce, founder of the Naval War College in Newport, Rhode Island, as saying: 'Two half hitches will never slip.' Another anonymous source says: 'Two half hitches saved a Queen's ship.' Combined with a round turn to spread the wear, it's an even better knot.

Feel tempted to throw in a third half-hitch, just to be sure? Admiral Smyth is quoted as saying: 'Three half hitches are more than a King's yacht wants.' But no one will tell him if you do!

KNOT SCORE
Strength ❀❀❀❀
Security ❀❀❀❀
Difficulty Tying ❀
Difficulty Untying ❀❀
Usefulness ❀❀❀❀❀

HITCHES • 29

2 Take a second turn. This spreads the load, reduces wear, and prevents the line slipping.

3 Pass the working end over the standing part, and tuck it in between the two parts to create the first hitch.

4 Repeat the previous step to create a second hitch. Tighten by pulling the standing part taut and working the hitches snug against the pole.

Seized round turn & two half hitches

Tied using traditional ropes, a round turn and two half hitches will probably outlive its tyer. Modern cordage is a good deal more slippery, however, and if you want something long-lasting, a seizing will transform this modest knot into a permanent solution. For more on seizings, see page 274.

1 Tie a round turn and two half hitches in the manner described above. Make sure the knot is tightened before putting in the seizing.

2 Lay the working end next to the standing part and take several turns with some whipping twine. Tie off securely — with a round turn and two half hitches, of course!

KNOT SCORE
Strength ❀❀❀❀❀
Security ❀❀❀❀❀
Difficulty Tying ❀❀❀
Difficulty Untying ❀❀❀
Usefulness ❀❀❀❀❀

Round turn & buntline hitch

Similar to a round turn and two half hitches, the buntline has one crucial difference: the hitches are tied in the opposite direction. This means the short end becomes jammed in the knot itself, making it very difficult to untie.

KNOT SCORE

Strength
Security
Difficulty Tying
Difficulty Untying
Usefulness

1 Pass the working end over the post or ring – commonly a spar or mooring ring.

2 Take a full turn, in the same manner as a round turn and two half hitches.

3 Pass the working end over the standing part and around the back of the knot.

4 Tuck the working end between the standing part and the first hitch to create the second hitch. Tighten the knot, and then slide it until it is snug against the pole or ring.

KNOT KNOW-HOW

On square-riggers, buntlines were lines that hung from the spars on the leeward side of the sails. When the sails were being stowed, the buntlines were tightened to prevent the sail flogging. The rest of the time, the buntlines hung loose and were themselves battered incessantly by the wind. They therefore needed an extremely secure knot to attach them. Hence the buntline hitch. The same knot, in essence, is used to tie neckties.

HITCHES • 31

Innomiknot

Designed to tie down aircraft in the Pacific during World War II, this knot takes its name from the Latin word 'innominatus', ie having no name. It is said to be easy to tie in the dark, and releases quickly under tension. It can be used for tethering errant aircraft and dinghies alike.

KNOT SCORE
Strength
Security
Difficulty Tying
Difficulty Untying
Usefulness

1 Pass the line around the mooring point. If tethering an aircraft, this will need to be extremely secure!

2 Twist the loop to form first one elbow…

3 … and then another. Pass the working end around the standing part.

4 Put a bight in the working end, and tuck it into the loop.

5 Adjust the bight to form a drawloop, and tighten the knot.

 # Clove hitch

It can be tied using any size rope onto just about any object. It can be tied in the bight, one-handed, in the air, and even with your eyes closed. Essentially formed from a pair of half hitches, the clove hitch is one of the easiest and most versatile knots ever devised. And yet its one major flaw as a hitch is that it's not 100 per cent secure. That means you rely on it at your peril.

KNOT SCORE
Strength
Security
Difficulty Tying
Difficulty Untying
Usefulness

A few centuries ago, the clove hitch was known as the builder's knot, a reminder that most of these knots have been around for a very long time and have probably been through several incarnations already.

And it's not hard to see why the clove hitch might be popular. It's the simplest of knots which, once learnt, can be tied with your eyes closed. And it can be used in a wide variety of situations. Tied in the bight (page 34), it can be dropped over a bollard in a trice and still bear a mighty load. Tied with a loop (opposite), it can be slipped very easily. Tied as an 'exploding' knot (page 35), it can disappear altogether with just one tug.

Where it really excels is as a crossing knot, for tying parcels or for attaching ratlines to shrouds. Its advantage here is that, if one part of the line breaks, the clove hitch will hold and the rest of the contraption will remain unaffected.

But the clove hitch should really come with a health warning. It's such an easy knot to tie and so immediately effective that it's tempting to use it for everything. And, nine times out of ten, it will work just fine. But then, just when it matters most, it will let you down. The dinghy will come untied and float away, or, most commonly, a fender will drop into the water.

The usual reasons for clove hitch failure are excessive movement, such as the snatching of a mooring line, or being pulled at an inappropriate angle. Pull a clove hitch back on itself, and it will loosen and eventually come undone.

So, by all means make the most of the clove hitch's versatility, but if you want something for the long term, choose another knot. And always use a round turn and two half hitches for tying fenders to the guardrail.

1 Take a turn around the pole, spar, ring or other object, and lay it diagonally over the standing part.

HITCHES • 33

Slipped clove hitch

The clove hitch is really most useful as a quick, temporary attachment. Tying it with a loop means it can be untied even more easily – useful if you're trying to make a quick getaway. You can also tie the whole knot with a loop or doubled line, but this cannot be slipped in the same manner.

KNOT SCORE

Strength ❈❈❈❈
Security ❈❈❈
Difficulty Tying ❈❈
Difficulty Untying ❈
Usefulness ❈❈❈

1 Form a clove hitch in the usual manner, but when it comes to the final tuck, put a bight into the end and pull that through instead.

2 Adjust the size of the loop and then tighten the knot, being careful not to pull the loop out. To undo: simply pull the end!

2 Keep going in the same direction, passing the working end around the object and then tucking it under itself.

34 • HITCHES

Clove hitch tied in the bight

Faced with an emergency, such as a bouncing boat or bucking bronco, the fastest knot you can tie is a clove hitch in the bight. Old-time sailors and cowboys could tie the knot in the air, so it landed on the post ready-made.

KNOT SCORE

Strength ❈❈❈
Security ❈❈❈
Difficulty Tying ❈
Difficulty Untying ❈
Usefulness ❈❈❈❈

1 In this context, the 'bight' is any part of the line which does not include the ends.

2 Put a loop in the bight of the line – either overhand or underhand.

3 Put an identical loop in the line right next to the first. Make sure it 'turns' in the same direction.

4 Hold the loops together as they were formed, and drop them over the mooring point. Tighten by pulling the parts in opposite directions.

KNOT KNOW-HOW

That the clove hitch has been around for a long time is demonstrated by the number of ways that have been found to tie it. There are one-handed methods, two-handed twisting methods, a hook method, and even a two-fingered method. The four methods shown here (pages 32–35) should, however, cover most eventualities – at least until the reader becomes a professional square-rigger or cowboy.

Exploding clove hitch

KNOT SCORE
Strength ✤✤✤
Security ✤✤✤
Difficulty Tying ✤✤
Difficulty Untying ✤
Usefulness ✤✤✤

This interesting variation of a clove hitch is a recent innovation, featuring in an American yachting magazine as recently as 1999. Its main advantage is that, once the drawloop is pulled, the whole knot falls apart (or 'explodes') and there is nothing left to untie. It remains to be seen whether this knot stands the test of time.

1 Pass the working end around the mooring point.

2 Put in a couple of overhand loops in the standing part to make a clove hitch.

3 Put a bight in the working end and pull it through, first one loop...

4 ... and then the other. Note how the knot centres on the standing part.

5 Adjust the length of the drawloop to suit and then tighten the knot. To untie: simply tug on the short end, and the whole knot will collapse.

BEST FOR tying a bucket

It seems like the simplest, most obvious job in the world, yet tying a line to a bucket holds a certain challenge. That knot is going to be chucked and pulled and soaked hundreds of times, all whilst holding a small but regular load. And if it comes undone while hauling water up from the sea, the bucket will need to be rescued with a boathook, dinghy or, failing those, someone jumping over the side. So, which knot is most secure?

Sometimes the simplest challenges are the most telling. One of these is the bucket challenge. Most sailors will have tied a line to a bucket hundreds of times, usually to haul up a bucket of sea water to scrub the decks or perhaps to pass tools to someone in a dinghy or up a mast. Either way, there's always that niggling feeling of, 'Did I tie it right? Is it going to come undone?' There is a perfect knot for this job, and it's not necessarily the one you might think.

If you have all the time in the world and are using old-fashioned three-strand rope, then you can't go wrong with a soft eye splice (page 297), either in a running loop as shown or, if you're feeling fancy, spliced straight onto the bucket handle. Assuming the eye splice is done well, it will probably outlast the bucket by a long time. A quicker way of achieving much the same thing but in a fraction of the time is a bowline (page 126), again either as a running bowline (page 150) or tied straight onto the bucket handle. That would probably be the default knot for most sailors in this situation. But read on. There is a better way.

What you definitely don't want here is a clove hitch (page 32), which will very soon work its way loose. That's a sure way to lose a bucket. A round turn and two half hitches (page 28) is a reasonable choice, especially if you seize the tail with a piece of twine to stop it coming undone. Another strong contender is a constrictor knot (page 40) or, better still, a double constrictor knot (page 42), which will surely grip that handle come hell or high water. Yet in our (admittedly brief) trial using moderately slippery modern cordage, it didn't feel particularly secure. Something about the size of rope relative to the size of the handle didn't quite work.

Sometimes a knot just feels right, and in this case the fisherman's bend (page 50) just fell into place – or more specifically the fisherman's bend and bowline (page 51). A fisherman's bend is a favourite for mooring dinghies, and it might be an obvious choice here too. Combining it with a bowline takes it to another level, however, combining the reliability of a loop with the grip of a hitch, ensuring the line doesn't flop around or come undone.

So there you have it. The winner of the bucket challenge is the fisherman's bend and bowline. Now, where's that scrubbing brush…

SPLICED LOOP: If you have time to make one – or happen to have an old piece of rope with one already made – a soft eye splice (page 297) will almost certainly outlast the bucket.

BOWLINE: Everyone's favourite knot and a fantastic all-rounder, a simple bowline (page 126) will do nicely. But is there something better?

HITCHES • 37

CLOVE HITCH: A clove hitch (page 32) is the worst possible option. Don't do it.

ROUND TURN: Another adaptable and reliable knot, a round turn and two half hitches (page 28) worked well enough – though a whipping on that tail would make it more secure.

CONSTRICTOR: The constrictor knot (page 40) is famous for its unshakable grip, but in this case failed to impress.

DOUBLE CONSTRICTOR: Likewise the double constrictor (page 42). If anything, the extra bulk of rope on a relatively thin handle seemed to make it less secure.

FISHERMAN'S BEND: Snug and secure, the fisherman's bend (page 50), not to be confused with the fisherman's knot, is a great option.

FISHERMAN'S BEND AND BOWLINE: The fisherman's bend and bowline (page 51) was even better, creating a knot that was both secure and didn't slide around.

Camel hitch

A clove hitch is all well and good, but it will tend to come undone if pulled sideways. What to do if you need to hoist a spar, for instance, or tow a tree trunk? The answer is surely the camel hitch, which must be one of the best anti-slip knots yet invented. Essentially a clove hitch with some extra turns thrown in to give more grip, it's secure enough to keep any camel in its place.

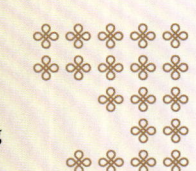

KNOT SCORE
Strength
Security
Difficulty Tying
Difficulty Untying
Usefulness

1 Take at least two or three turns around the object, depending how slippery it is.

2 In this case, three turns have been put in, before the working end is crossed over the standing part.

3 Changing direction, take another turn around the pole or spar, and tuck the working end under itself.

4 Pass the working end around the pole once more and tuck it under itself again to finish the clove hitch.

5 Tighten the knot, ensuring there is plenty of length left on the working end, in case the knot slips while tightening.

HITCHES • 39

Rolling hitch

Another variation of the clove hitch, which resists sideways pull and is much easier to tie than the camel hitch, is the rolling hitch. One of the most common uses of this knot is to tie a small line to a larger one, eg a dinghy painter onto a mooring warp, or a burgee halyard to the shrouds. It's a handy knot, almost as versatile as the clove hitch, and more secure.

KNOT SCORE

Strength ❁ ❁ ❁ ❁
Security ❁ ❁ ❁ ❁
Difficulty Tying ❁ ❁
Difficulty Untying ❁ ❁ ❁
Usefulness ❁ ❁ ❁ ❁ ❁

1 Take a turn around the pole or ring. As with the clove hitch, it doesn't matter which way you go, as long as you keep going in the same direction.

2 Take another turn around the mooring point, on the same side of the standing part.

3 Take another turn in the same direction, this time coming up on the other side of the standing part. Tuck the working end under itself.

4 Tighten the knot by pulling the working end and standing part in opposite directions.

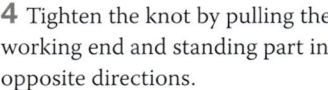

KNOT KNOW-HOW

Up until 1841, the rolling hitch was known as the Magnus or Magner's hitch, and the two round turns and two half hitches was called a rolling hitch. The knots were renamed by RH Dana in his 1841 book *The Seaman's Friend*, and have kept his nomenclature ever since. Who Magnus or Magner were is unknown, but it would have been a very rare case of a knot being named after a person.

Constrictor knot

Despite the popularity of the clove hitch in its many forms, in almost every case there are other knots that can do the job better. One of these is the constrictor knot. Although only very slightly more complicated than the clove hitch, it is infinitely more secure. If anything, it is too secure and may have to be cut off rather than untied. Like the clove hitch, it lends itself to being tied in several different ways.

You know you've got a special knot when it's one that's been prescribed to surgeons some 2,000 years ago. The constrictor knot is one of 18 knots recorded by the Greek physician Heraklas in a list of surgeons' knots published in the first century AD.

Described by one writer as 'probably the world's best seizing knot', the constrictor has a wide range of applications, apart from surgery. It can be used as a clamp while woodworking, or as an improvised hose clamp or cable tie. More commonly, it can be used to tie the neck of a canvas bag.

Tied with thin twine, it can be used to bind the end of a piece of rope to prevent it fraying, prior to applying a permanent whipping (see Chapter 9).

1 Pass the working end around the item to be bound – rope, bag, hose, body part, or whatever.

As a temporary seizing, it is more durable than either a reef knot or a strangle knot, the other two candidates for the job.

The constrictor knot was one of the knots studied by Dr Harry Asher as part of his *Law of Loop, Hitch & Bight* published in 1986. Dr Asher made the point that some knots, when removed from their point of attachment (eg pole, ring, or whatever) will collapse completely, while others will retain their shape and have to be untied manually.

He then showed that the knots that collapsed (eg the constrictor knot) were those that were able to be tied in the bight, while those that kept their shape were not tie-able in the bight. Strange but true.

KNOT SCORE

Strength
Security
Difficulty Tying
Difficulty Untying
Usefulness

HITCHES • 41

2 Cross the working end diagonally over the standing part, and go around the item again.

3 Now pass the working end over the standing part, and tuck it under both parts of the original turn.

4 Pull the working end through and tighten the knot. If using thin twine, wrap the ends around something (eg a couple of bolts) to give a better purchase.

Constrictor knot with loop

The constrictor knot might be a vicious beast in its original form, but it can be tamed by the addition of a simple drawloop. It's still more secure than a clove hitch, and you won't need a knife to remove it. The perfect compromise?

KNOT SCORE

Strength
Security
Difficulty Tying
Difficulty Untying
Usefulness

1 Tie a constrictor knot as above, but, after tucking the working end under the first part of the original turn, put a bight in the end.

2 Tuck the bight under the remaining turn to create the drawloop. Adjust the size of the loop and tighten the knot.

Double constrictor knot

There are times when even the mighty constrictor knot is liable to slip – particularly when using slippery modern cordage or waxed string. The solution is to put in an extra turn across the standing part. Don't be tempted to put in any more turns, however, as this won't increase the knot's security and will only make it more difficult to tighten evenly.

KNOT SCORE

Strength
Security
Difficulty Tying
Difficulty Untying
Usefulness

1 Take a turn around the object, and pass the working end diagonally over the standing part.

2 Take a second turn around the object and over the standing part, fitting the line snugly next to the first diagonal.

3 Take a third turn around the object, this time passing over the standing part from the other side. Tuck the working end under both diagonals and the original turn.

4 Tighten the knot by pulling the working end and the standing part in opposite directions.

KNOT KNOW-HOW

Although given its current name by Clifford Ashley in 1944, the constrictor knot is much older than that. In his 1866 *Book of Knots*, Tom Bowlings refers to the gunner's knot which 'only differs from the builder's knot [ie clove hitch], by the ends of the cords being simply knotted before being brought from under the loop which crosses them.' A constrictor knot by any other name.

Constrictor knot tied in the bight

Why tie a knot in the bight when you can tie it by the ends? The answer is that it's usually quicker to tie it in the bight. It also looks impressive and will give you extra knotting kudos – providing you get it right!

KNOT SCORE
Strength
Security
Difficulty Tying
Difficulty Untying
Usefulness

1 Take a bight out of the line and pass it over the object to be seized.

2 Pass one part over the other to form a loop.

3 Pull a bight from the upper part, so that it passes under and over the lower part of the knot.

4 Twist the bight to form a loop, and place it over the object being attached.

5 Tighten the knot by pulling the two parts in opposite directions.

Strangle knot

An alternative to the constrictor knot, the strangle knot is preferred by some because it lies flatter once tightened. It's less versatile than the constrictor knot or the clove hitch, and cannot be tied in the bight, but it's certainly neat looking. Use it to bind the end of a piece of rope to prevent it fraying, or for tying off the neck of a sack – as was originally intended.

KNOT SCORE
Strength
Security
Difficulty Tying
Difficulty Untying
Usefulness

1 Take a turn around the object to be seized, and pass the working end diagonally over the standing part.

2 Take a second turn, and pass the working end over the standing part again.

3 Tuck the working end under both turns – effectively making a double overhand knot.

4 Tighten the knot by pulling the working end and standing part in opposite directions. A drawloop can be inserted for ease of untying.

HITCHES • 45

Ground-line hitch

There's not a lot of difference between a ground-line hitch (also known as the spar hitch) and a clove hitch – except that the ground-line hitch is much more secure. Like the clove hitch, it suffers from being easily dislodged if the standing part is jerked excessively. It is, however, a better knot for most purposes, including tying fenders to a guard rail.

KNOT SCORE

Strength ❀❀❀❀
Security ❀❀❀❀
Difficulty Tying ❀❀
Difficulty Untying ❀❀
Usefulness ❀❀❀❀

1 Place the line over the mooring point – typically a wire or large line or possibly the neck of a bag.

2 Take a turn around the mooring point, in the same way you would for a clove hitch.

3 Pass the working end diagonally over the standing part, and around the mooring point.

4 Pass the working end over itself and tuck it under the original turn. Tighten the knot. The addition of a drawloop at this stage turns it into a slip knot.

> **KNOT KNOW-HOW**
>
> The ground-line hitch was the knot of choice of the cod fishermen, who used it to fix the ganging lines – the lines that held the hooks – to the trawl. The hooks themselves were attached to the ganging lines at a later stage, when the trawl was ready to be baited. The knot is also thought to have been used by the US Cavalry to tether their horses to a line at night.

Ossel hitch

Another knot much-favoured by fishermen – this time the Scottish seine netters. The ossel hitch was used to suspend driftnets in the sea. As such, it had to cope with a great deal of underwater movement, without coming undone. It also had to be tied quickly, as there were hundreds of these tied to each net. The ossel hitch answered the cause.

KNOT SCORE

Strength
Security
Difficulty Tying
Difficulty Untying
Usefulness

1 Pass the working end around the mooring point – in the case of a seine netter, this would be the float line (see Knot Know-How, below).

2 Take a turn, and pass the working end around the standing part and back on itself.

3 Take another turn around the anchoring point, but this time going the other way.

4 Pass the working end back over itself and under the original turn. Tighten the knot.

KNOT KNOW-HOW

An 'ossel' is the length of line that connects a gill net to its float line, so that the net can hang at a certain distance below the surface of the sea. The word is thought to be a regional variation of 'norsel'. The ossel hitch is therefore useful in any situation where a small line is being attached to a larger line.

HITCHES • 47

Ossel knot

Despite its misleading name, this is another hitch, also used by seine fishermen. Its structure is more similar to a ground-line hitch than an ossel hitch, and it's a little more time-consuming to tie than either of them, but it is also more robust. Use it when you need a secure knot that won't slide easily.

KNOT SCORE
Strength
Security
Difficulty Tying
Difficulty Untying
Usefulness

1 Take a turn around the pole or spar, and pass the working end diagonally over the standing part.

2 Take a second diagonal turn next to the first one and in the same direction.

3 Take a third turn, this time on the other side of the standing part.

4 Pass the working end over itself and the two diagonal turns, and tuck it under the original turn. Tighten the knot.

BEST FOR tying a fender

It's one of the most common jobs on board any boat that is kept in a marina or cruising between harbours: tying the fenders. Get it wrong and the boat is liable to suffer considerable damage. Yet there's notuniversal agreement on which knot to use for this most basic of tasks. So which is best?

Tying fenders on the side of a boat isn't the most glamorous job on board so it's usually assigned to a junior member of the crew. That's fair enough, but just make sure they know what knot to tie and can tie it quickly and securely. Losing fenders over the side is not only expensive, if you have to buy a replacement, but can result in serious damage to the boat's topsides.

For most of my childhood growing up on boats in the Mediterranean, I was the junior crew tasked with tying the fenders each time we came into harbour, and untying them when we left. And for most of that time I relied on that old favourite: the clove hitch (page 32). It's quick and easy, and you'll see it recommended for that purpose in countless books/websites.

That all changed in my late 30s when I read a critique of the clove hitch, suggesting that it was fine as a temporary fix but was fundamentally unreliable in the long term. That author recommended a round turn and two half hitches (page 28), which takes slightly longer but is infinitely more reliable. I was convinced and haven't looked back since, using a round turn and two half hitches for all my fender-tying activities. Is it more secure? Almost certainly, but just as important is the fact that it does take a bit longer to tie, forcing you to concentrate and make a better job of it. The sheer ease of tying a clove hitch encourages a more slapdash approach, which is as much of a problem as the lack of security of the knot itself. And don't even get me started on a slipped clove hitch (page 33)…

A step up from the clove hitch is a rolling hitch (page 32), which will prevent the fender sliding down a stanchion, though it still has the same reliability issues as its near-sister. If you want to get fancy, you could try the ground-line hitch (aka spar hitch) (page 45), a noble knot which is more secure than a clove hitch but a bit more of a fiddle to tie.

If you'll take my advice, stick with a round turn and two half hitches. You'll be grateful each time you find your fenders tied where you left them and your topsides still in good order. You're welcome.

HITCHES • 49

CLOVE HITCH: Slipped or not slipped, the clove hitch (page 32) is usually the recommended knot for tying fenders. Don't be tempted!

ROLLING HITCH: A rolling hitch (page 39) is slightly more secure than a clove hitch but is not to be entirely trusted.

GROUND-LINE HITCH: Another option is the ground-line hitch (aka spar hitch) (page 45), which is more fiddly than a clove hitch but more secure.

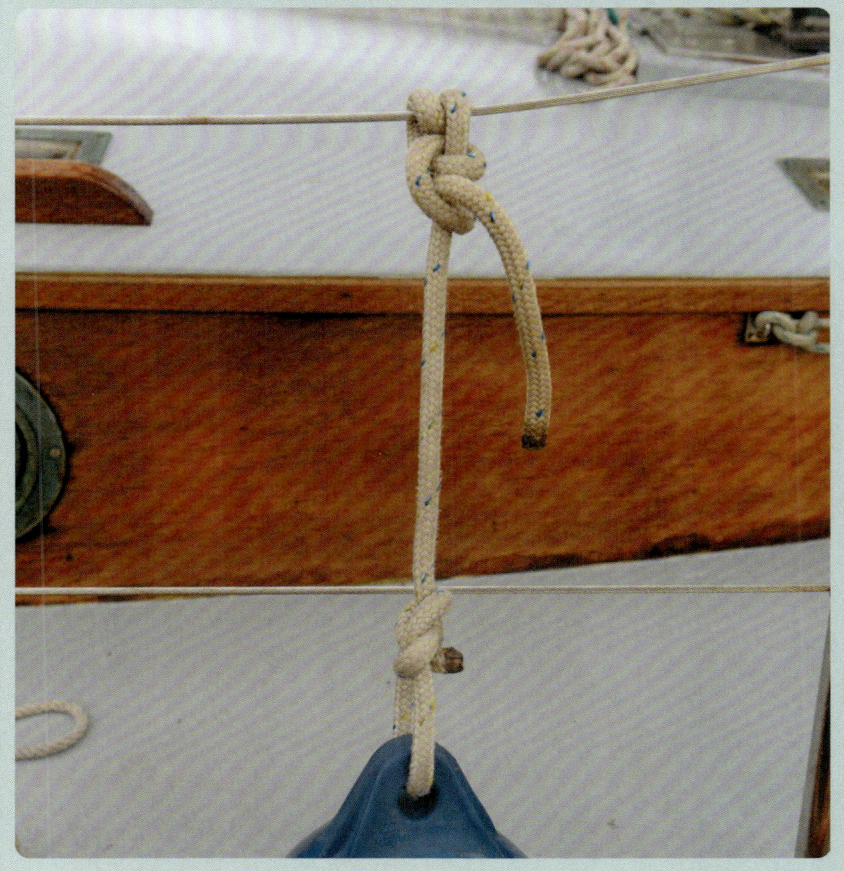

ROUND TURN & 2 HALF HITCHES: The best knot for tying fenders is the round turn and two half hitches (page 28): simple, reliable and an all-round good friend.

50 • HITCHES

Fisherman's bend

Another hitch with a misleading name, the fisherman's bend is really an improvement on the round turn and two half hitches. Because the first half hitch is locked in the turn, it's less liable to slip. Use it when you need an extra secure hitch – eg attaching an anchor warp – and seize the end to the standing part for additional peace of mind.

KNOT SCORE

Strength
Security
Difficulty Tying
Difficulty Untying
Usefulness

1 Take the working end around the post or ring twice, to make a complete round turn.

2 Pass the working end around the standing part and feed it back through the turn.

3 Pass the working end around the standing part again, and tuck it under itself to make a hitch.

4 Tighten the knot, sliding the hitch so that it sits snugly against the rest of the knot.

HITCHES • 51

Fisherman's bend & bowline

Just when you thought it couldn't get better than the fisherman's bend, along comes the fisherman's bend MkII. It's the same knot really, just with the addition of a bowline (page 126) at the end, instead of the suggested seizing.

KNOT SCORE
Strength
Security
Difficulty Tying
Difficulty Untying
Usefulness

1 Pass the working end around the post or ring. Note that this sequence is shown from the reverse side of the previous fisherman's bend sequence.

2 Pass the end around again to make a complete round turn.

3 Pass the working end around the standing part and then back through the turn.

4 Instead of putting in a hitch at the end, make an underhand loop in the standing part to start the bowline. Feed the working end down through the loop.

5 Pass the working end around the standing part and back into the loop to complete the bowline. Adjust the bowline so that both 'arms' are the same length, and tighten the knot.

Marlinspike hitch

No point in using a sledge hammer to crack a nut. Sometimes, you only need a simple, easy knot to make a temporary fastening. And it doesn't get much simpler or easier than the marlinspike hitch. Use it as a crossing knot (see Knot Know-How below), or with a marlinspike to tighten another knot. Bear in mind it may collapse once the load is off.

KNOT SCORE

Strength ❊❊❊
Security ❊❊
Difficulty Tying ❊
Difficulty Untying ❊
Usefulness ❊❊❊❊

1 Make an underhand loop.

2 Place the loop over its standing part, without altering it.

3 Pass the post (or marlinspike) under the standing part visible through the loop, and draw it up.

4 Tighten the knot by pulling both parts in opposite directions.

KNOT KNOW-HOW

It may seem strange to create a knot that only holds under tension, but many crossing knots work on this principle. And their applications are many. From tying up parcels, to making lifelines, fences, and even ladders. In most of these cases, a secure knot is required to attach the line at either end, while a quick, easily adjustable knot is needed for the points in between.

HITCHES • 53

Cow hitch

Another knot which is liable to collapse once the load is released, the cow hitch can be very effective when used in the right context. The most common application aboard ship is on deadeyes and lanyards, to attach the lanyard to the shroud. An identical knot is used on baggage labels, although there it is tied in the bight and called a bale sling hitch or ring hitch.

KNOT SCORE
Strength ❈❈❈
Security ❈❈
Difficulty Tying ❈
Difficulty Untying ❈
Usefulness ❈❈❈❈

1 Pass the working end around the mooring point – the base of the shroud, in the case of deadeyes and lanyards.

2 Pass the working end over the standing part.

3 Pass the working end around the shroud or post, in the opposite direction to the original turn, and tuck it under itself.

4 Tighten the knot by pulling both parts simultaneously. Note that this knot will only hold if tension is maintained on both parts.

Transom hitch

A compact but secure knot for holding together two objects, such as posts or cordage, at right angles to each other. It can be tied individually (eg for kite sticks) or as a series of knots in a single length of rope (eg for wooden ratlines). Similar to the constrictor knot, it is, if anything, more secure and therefore even more difficult to release.

KNOT SCORE

Strength
Security
Difficulty Tying
Difficulty Untying
Usefulness

1 Pass the working end diagonally across the two posts, around the vertical post, and then diagonally across both posts again, so that it crosses the standing part.

2 Take a turn around the lower post, on the other side of the intersection.

3 Pass the working end over the standing part, and tuck it under the initial two turns.

4 If you are tying a row of knots, make sure you have enough slack to tie the rest of the series.

5 Tighten the knot. If you are tying a single knot, you can trim the ends closely without any loss of security.

HITCHES • 55

Knute hitch

Some knots impress by their sheer ingenuity and complexity; others by their simplicity. The knute hitch definitely falls into the latter camp. A loop, a stopper knot and a ring. Who would have thought a knot could be so simple? Commonly used to tie a lanyard onto a knife, the knute can also be used for attaching a halyard to a sail, instead of a shackle.

KNOT SCORE

Strength ❀❀❀
Security ❀❀❀
Difficulty Tying ❀
Difficulty Untying ❀
Usefulness ❀❀❀

1 Tie a stopper knot (eg figure-eight, page 176) at one end of the line, and form a bight. The cord should be slightly less than half the diameter of the hole.

2 Pass the bight through the hole, leaving enough slack in the working end to pass around the knife (or in this case the marlinspike).

3 Pass the stopper knot through the bight.

4 Get rid of any excess slack in the working end, before you tighten the knot.

KNOT KNOW-HOW

Like many knots, the knute hitch had been around for years before it was deemed worthy of a name. It wasn't until 1990 that American rigger and author Brian Toss gave it its current title. What does it mean? Knute is Scandinavian for Canute and comes from the Old Norse word for 'knot'. So the knute hitch is really the knot hitch – appropriately enough for a hitch tied with a knot.

Studding sail halyard bend

A modern yacht has little use for studding sails nowadays – even in the age of sail they were something of an optional extra. But the knots devised to haul these sails hundreds of feet in the air without crashing down on someone's head must have been pretty good. Certainly good enough to hold a spinnaker pole when the shackle fails, or to crane that new propeller shaft into the engine room. A good old knot never dies.

KNOT SCORE

Strength	❁ ❁ ❁ ❁ ❁
Security	❁ ❁ ❁ ❁ ❁
Difficulty Tying	❁ ❁ ❁
Difficulty Untying	❁ ❁ ❁ ❁
Usefulness	❁ ❁ ❁ ❁ ❁

It's no secret that many of today's knots were developed aboard the mighty vessels that circled the world during the Age of Sail. And they had need for good knots. A conservatively-rigged four-masted barque set more than 30 sails, including topgallants. If the crew was being daring, they might also set skysails above the royals, and perhaps moonsails above the skysails.

There are even tales of ships setting heaven pokers, angel pokers and cloud disturbers – all above the topgallant.

The only way of increasing the sail area outwards, rather than upwards, was to extend the yards with temporary jackyards. Smaller sails could then be set outside the other sails. These were the studding sails.

The spars for most of these sails were attached with hefty permanent fittings, but the jackyards were often attached with a temporary lashing, which could be removed when the spar was stowed. Hence the studding sail bend.

In fact, there is a small family of knots named after specific parts of the ship's rig, including the topsail halyard

HITCHES • 57

1 Take two turns around the spar or post (and if you're up the mast, then hold on tight!).

2 Pass the working end around the standing part.

3 Tuck the working end under the two turns.

Gaff topsail halyard bend

This is a simplified version of the studding sail bend, omitting the final tuck under the first turn. Like its more secure sister, it cannot be tied while the standing part is under load. It is, however, an exceedingly compact and quickly tied knot.

KNOT SCORE

Strength	❁ ❁ ❁ ❁ ❁
Security	❁ ❁ ❁ ❁
Difficulty Tying	❁ ❁
Difficulty Untying	❁ ❁ ❁
Usefulness	❁ ❁ ❁ ❁

Follow the instructions above, stopping at Step 3. Note that the working end is pulled well away from the standing part.

4 Pass the working end over two turns and under the next one. Tighten the knot.

bend and the gaff topsail halyard bend – though how many of these were used for their designated purpose is open to question. The topsail halyard bend, for instance, is the same knot as the studding sail bend, with the addition of an extra turn, something which, Ashley warns, 'like the second tablespoon of castor oil, savours of redundancy'.

For the modern sailor, these knots provide a useful alternative to the ubiquitous running hitch and can be tied safe in the knowledge that today's aluminium spars are a good deal lighter than the wooden spars for which these knots were originally intended.

Topsail halyard bend

A variation on the theme of the previous knot, the topsail halyard bend has an extra turn. In theory, this should make it less liable to slide up the jackyard of the aforementioned topsail. In practice, it may just be an extra complication. Either way, if you've got an exceptionally slippery jackyard, it's certainly worth giving it a try.

KNOT SCORE

Strength
Security
Difficulty Tying
Difficulty Untying
Usefulness

1 Take three turns around the spar. It doesn't matter which direction, as long as they all go the same way.

2 Pass the working end around the standing part, and tuck it under all three turns.

3 Pass the working end over two turns and under the next one.

4 Tighten the knot. Ideally, the extra turns should be in the direction that slippage is most likely.

HITCHES • 59

Horse dealer's hitch

This is one of many 'new' knots published in recent years by the International Guild of Knot Tyers – although it has no doubt been in existence a lot longer. It seems rather fussy compared to most of the simple-but-effective knots elsewhere in this book, but is said to be extremely secure. Use it to tether a dinghy, or to impress friends.

KNOT SCORE

Strength
Security
Difficulty Tying
Difficulty Untying
Usefulness

1 Take a turn around the mooring point – originally a hitching rail on a ranch, presumably.

2 Put an overhand loop in the standing part.

3 Pass the working end clockwise around the loop.

4 Put a bight in the working end and pass it under the standing part…

5 … and through the loop. Tighten the knot by pulling on the standing part. To undo: simply pull the end!

Timber hitch

A handy knot for craning spars or dragging a post along the ground, the timber hitch uses the weight of the object to jam its own end. Once the tension is released, the knot practically falls apart on its own. Although once used by the London river police to haul bodies out of the Thames, a more common use nowadays might be to hoist spars aboard ship.

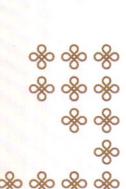

KNOT SCORE

Strength
Security
Difficulty Tying
Difficulty Untying
Usefulness

1 Take a turn around the spar or body, and pass the working end around the standing part.

2 Tuck the working end back under itself. The turns should follow the lay of the line. If they don't, start again with the working end on the other side of the standing part.

3 Put in as many turns as required. Three turns are usually ample, but a slippery line might require more.

4 Tighten the knot, pulling out any slack in the noose with the working end, and tightening the loop with the standing part.

KNOT KNOW-HOW

The timber hitch has many mentions in knotting literature. RC Anderson mentions it in his *A Treatise on Rigging* (c.1625); Denis Diderot draws it in his *Encyclopedie* (1762); David Steel features it in *The Elements and Practice of Rigging & Seamanship* (1794); the Admiralty includes it in its *Manual of Seamanship* (1891); and Clifford Ashley gives it the thumbs up in his *Book of Knots* (1946).

HITCHES • 61

Stopped half hitch

No matter how many turns you put in some lines – particularly thicker lines which are less likely to lie flat – they will always slip. The solution is to 'stop' the end with a piece of twine. Combined with a half hitch or two, this makes a very secure attachment and was often used to attach blocks in the standing rigging of large sailing ships.

KNOT SCORE

Strength ✦✦✦✦✧
Security ✦✦✦✦✧
Difficulty Tying ✦✦✧✧✧
Difficulty Untying ✦✦✧✧✧
Usefulness ✦✦✦✧✧

1 Place the standing end of the line on the spar or rigging and 'stop' it with a length of twine. This can simply be a few turns tied with a reef knot (page 180).

2 Take a turn with the working end and tuck it under itself to form the first half hitch.

3 Add another half hitch. Leaving a gap between the hitches will spread the load and prevent the line slipping. Tighten the knot.

BEST FOR lashing things down

If you're going to sea in a yacht, you're likely to need to lash something down at some point. It might be fenders onto the coachroof, or a dinghy to the foredeck, or perhaps a gas bottle in a locker. The principles are broadly the same as lashing something down to a roofrack on a car, except you can't pull over and restow things once you're at sea.

Lashing something down, be it fenders, a dinghy or an inflatable donut, might seems like an easy job while you are safely within the shelter of a harbour or mooring. As soon as you hit any bad weather and the boat starts to crash into the waves, however, you might wish you'd spent more time securing those random items that have found their way onto your coachroof. Having to lash things down while the boat is heeling over and you're being drenched in sea water can be good, exhilarating fun – or it can be a terrifying ordeal.

The simplest way to give yourself a little purchase is to tie a loop in the end of a line and, having passed it through two secure points on either side of the object, pass the other end through the loop. Pull back on the working end until the rope is taut, and tie off with a couple of half hitches. The obvious loop to use for this purpose is the bowline (page 126), but you could just as well use a figure-eight loop (page 125), or any of the other eminently suitable knots in the Loops section.

If you want to generate some serious tension to prevent things moving then you can't do much better than a trucker's hitch. This will give you a 3:1 mechanical advantage, compared to the 2:1 of the preceding method – in theory, at least.

An elegant way of tying a trucker's hitch is shown on page 82. This method has the huge advantage that the loop will never jam. On the other hand, it's slightly more tricky to get right, and if tied wrongly it will easily come undone. The down 'n' dirty version of the same knot, using a simple overhand loop (page 124), is also shown opposite. It's quick and easy to tie, will cinch up as tight as you like (possibly too tight, so beware!) – but it's also very likely to jam.

If the lashing is to be used regularly, an adjustable bend (page 108) can be used instead. This can be released whenever the item is needed and quickly tightened again when things need to be stowed. It also means the line is less likely to be lost or purloined for another purpose. A similar effect can be achieved by combining a loop with a tautline hitch.

HITCHES • 63

BOWLINE: A simple lashing formed of a bowline (page 126) with the working end tied off with two half hitches (page 28).

FIGURE-EIGHT LOOP: The same setup using a figure-eight loop (page 125).

TRUCKER'S HITCH: The classic trucker's hitch (page 82) is elegant but not very secure.

TRUCKER'S HITCH v2: The down 'n' dirty version of the trucker's hitch is more secure but liable to jam.

ADJUSTABLE BEND: The adjustable bend (page 108) is a good permanent solution but doesn't generate as much tension as a trucker's hitch.

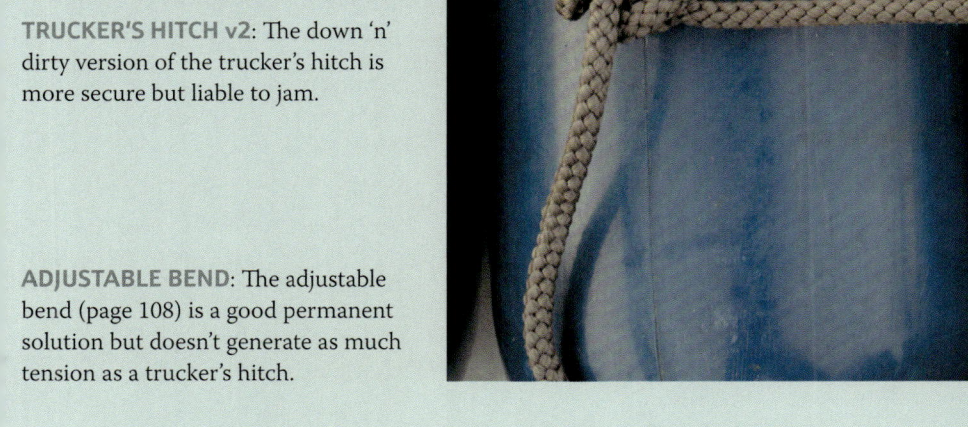

Killick hitch

Any long object that is hoisted from one point is liable to be unstable. The killick hitch is the timber hitch plus a half hitch, to give it more directional stability. The extra hitch also helps spread the load over any irregularly-shaped or top-heavy objects, making craning a little safer.

KNOT SCORE

Strength
Security
Difficulty Tying
Difficulty Untying
Usefulness

1 Take a turn around the spar and pass the working end around the standing part, as with the timber hitch.

2 Put in the required number of turns (usually three, although two may suffice).

3 With the timber hitch in place, use the standing part to tie a half hitch around the post, at least 0.6m (2ft) from the main part of the knot.

4 Tighten the knot by pulling the standing part in the direction the post is to be hoisted. Add more half hitches as required.

KNOT KNOW-HOW

Although there is little agreement about exactly how it's made, the general consensus is that a 'killick' is an improvised form of anchor. It may be made from wood and rocks, or even just rocks lashed together. Either way, the killick hitch is used to tie a warp to the resulting structure, spreading the load of the line along its length and giving greater directional stability.

Lifting hitch

They say there's more than one way to skin a cat, and there's certainly more than one way to lift a spar. If the timber hitch and the killick hitch don't appeal, try this simple but effective lifting hitch. The extra turns prevent slippage, particularly on varnished or metal spars, and it can be cast off quickly. Plus, it looks good – always something to bear in mind.

KNOT SCORE
Strength
Security
Difficulty Tying
Difficulty Untying
Usefulness

1 Wrap the working end tightly around the object to be lifted – six to eight turns should do the trick.

2 Pass the working end over and then under the standing part.

3 Take another turn around the spar, and finish off with a securing hitch.

4 Tighten the knot, making sure the turns are all sitting tightly together.

Queen clara hitch

In 1986, Dr Harry Asher published three knots with clara in their names: the clinging clara, the queen clara and the great queen clara hitches. All were designed to be tied either on spars or large ropes. The queen clara was a development of the clinging clara hitch and is said to be stronger and more secure. It remains to be seen which, if any, of these knots catch on.

KNOT SCORE
Strength ✿✿✿✿
Security ✿✿✿✿
Difficulty Tying ✿✿✿
Difficulty Untying ✿✿✿
Usefulness ✿✿✿

1 Take two turns around the spar or line. In the latter case, make sure the turns go in the same direction as the lay of the line.

2 Pass the working end over both turns and under the spar or line, going in the opposite direction.

3 Pass the working end over the first turn and under the second, still going against the lay of the line.

4 Tighten the knot. Ideally, the first two turns should lie in between the strands of the line being tied.

KNOT KNOW-HOW

New knots are being invented all the time – although usually they turn out to be either a copy or a slight variation of an old knot. Harry Asher was a genuine innovator, and his *Alternative Book of Knots* contains many new developments, including the three claras mentioned above, the simple simon (page 104) and the vice versa (although this too is said to be a variation of an earlier knot).

HITCHES • 67

Great queen clara hitch

The multiple turns contained in the bigger sister of the queen clara hitch (opposite) are designed to withstand a longitudinal pull, particularly on a varnished or metal spar. The knot was apparently demonstrated by its creator, Dr Asher, at the 1986 London Boat Show, when it resisted being pulled towards the narrow end of a billiard cue. Respect.

KNOT SCORE

Strength ✤✤✤✤
Security ✤✤✤✤
Difficulty Tying ✤✤✤
Difficulty Untying ✤✤
Usefulness ✤✤✤

1 Take a turn around the spar with the standing part, leaving plenty of slack in the working end.

2 Keep going. A minimum of six turns is recommended.

3 If the knot is to be towards the end of the spar, tuck the working end in the last but one turn.

4 Twist the resulting bight into an overhand loop, and slip over the end of the spar. Tighten the knot.

5 If the knot is not near either extremity, after Step 2, pass the working end around the spar, in the opposite direction to the previous turns. Then pass it over itself and tuck it under the last but one turn.

Lighterman's hitch

Cleats are for sissies! Or that's certainly what generations of working boat sailors seemed to think. They were quite content with a single samson post or a couple of bitts, and they devised some crafty knots to attach a line to them. Nowadays, cleats are ubiquitous, but the old knots still have their uses – not least for attaching a mooring line to the occasional canon buried in the quayside for that purpose.

KNOT SCORE
Strength
Security
Difficulty Tying
Difficulty Untying
Usefulness

It's easy to forget that cleats on a yacht are a relatively recent innovation. For centuries, vessels relied on 'bitts', or posts sunk into the deck, to attach mooring and tow lines. Even now, most docks are fitted with single bollards, rather than the convenient cleats found in many marinas.

Most commercial ships have loops spliced into their mooring lines which can be dropped over a bollard, while many larger yachts employ chains running through an eye at the end of their mooring lines. For smaller yachts, a bowline (page 126) will usually suffice.

The drawback with all these is that there is little or no room for adjustment. Which is when you need a decent mooring knot.

Most of the hitches mentioned so far can't be tied or untied while there is tension on the standing part – ruling them out as mooring knots. A notable exception is the clove hitch, which can start off as a single turn around a bollard and then be transformed into a knot. Its disadvantage is that it's liable to jam once a lot of tension is applied to it.

A round turn and two half hitches can also be tied under stress, and will work well in most instances.

There is something very appealing, however, about a knot that can simply be dropped into place with no fussy hitches, which gets stronger as more force is exerted, and yet which can be undone (or just eased) with a few flicks. Such a knot is the lighterman's hitch (also known as the tugboat hitch).

You can see the attraction for working men, such as lightermen and tug crews, who had to make fast and unfasten mooring lines all day long. The only real drawback is that the lighterman's hitch will slip when tied with light or slippery lines. In which case, get some heftier rope!

1 Take a turn around the post or bollard.

2 Take another turn, then take a bight out of the working end and pass it under the standing part.

3 Pass the bight over the top of the post or bollard.

HITCHES • 69

4 Take a turn around the standing part with the working end.

5 Finish off with a turn around the post or bollard. If you think the line might slip, don't be tempted to put in a half hitch which is liable to jam: simply add more turns.

Pile hitch

The pile hitch follows the same broad principle as the lighterman's hitch in using the weight of the object to jam the turn against the post. Like the lighterman's hitch, it can be tied with a load on the line – although untying it will be somewhat harder. This is a temporary knot, however, and should be replaced with something more secure for the longer term.

KNOT SCORE
Strength
Security
Difficulty Tying
Difficulty Untying
Usefulness

1 Put a bight in the line – if close to an end, place the standing part under the working end.

2 Pass the bight around the mooring point and under the standing part.

3 Loop the bight over the top of the post or bollard.

4 Tighten the knot. If the bight is placed near the top of the post, the knot can be undone with a well-placed kick, even while under load.

KNOT KNOW-HOW

It's impossible to tell how many knots exist. *The Ashley Book of Knots* claims to contain 3,800 – although this includes many repeats as well as illustrations of related tools and equipment. The true number of knots in the book is much less than that. On the other hand, hundreds of 'new' knots have been invented or rediscovered since Ashley's time, so the real life total may well be much higher.

HITCHES • 71

Crossing knot

Another alternative to the ubiquitous clove hitch, the crossing knot is a slightly more complex animal. Once mastered, it can be quickly tied in the bight and dropped over a post or bollard. More secure than a clove hitch and not as vicious as a constrictor knot, it's well worth adding to your repertoire of regularly used knots.

KNOT SCORE

Strength
Security
Difficulty Tying
Difficulty Untying
Usefulness

1 Put a bight in the line and twist it to make two elbows, the top one larger than the lower one.

2 Lift the larger, upper bight and fold over the smaller, lower crossing point.

3 Pass the lower bight under the knot before placing over the post.

4 Pass the post through the centre of the knot and tighten by puling both parts in opposite directions.

Cleat hitch

Samson posts and bitts have long been superseded by cleats, but, if the evidence on display in Europe's marinas is anything to go by, the majority of sailors still don't know how to tie a cleat hitch correctly. Getting it right could make the difference between sleeping soundly at night or seeing your beloved yacht being pounded on a beach. So why do so many people still get it wrong?

KNOT SCORE

Strength ❈❈❈
Security ❈❈
Difficulty Tying ❈
Difficulty Untying ❈
Usefulness ❈❈❈❈

Walk around any marina and almost every boat will have at least half a dozen cleat hitches tied in various parts of its anatomy: mooring lines, flag halyards, sail halyards, sheets, etc. That adds up to hundreds – if not thousands – of examples of the knot in every marina.

Yet, amazingly, the majority of these will be incorrectly tied (or 'belayed', to use the traditional terminology). This author's, admittedly unscientific, survey suggested only one in eight cleat hitches in his local marina were correctly tied.

Luckily, the cleat hitch is a forgiving knot, so few of these incorrectly tied knots actually come undone or cause any damage – although it could be a different story in less sheltered waters.

One of the most debated issues about the cleat hitch is how many turns to make. In former times, when ropes were coarser and generally thicker for an equivalent strength, a couple of turns around a cleat were enough. Nowadays, with thinner, smoother and more stretchy rope, more turns are needed to prevent the line slipping.

On the other hand, a common mistake is to keep on adding turns until the rope runs out, creating an unholy pile that will take a dangerously long time to undo in an emergency. The general consensus is that at least two crossing turns are required, perhaps one or two more in extremis. Any more than that just get in the way.

Another area of contention is whether to put in a half hitch at the end or not. The general rule is that, if the boat might be put in immediate danger by not being able to untie the knot, then don't put one in. So, don't put a half hitch in tow lines, sheets and sail halyards. Do put a half hitch in just about everything else.

In cases where no half hitch is used, a couple of extra turns should be added instead.

1 Take a turn around the cleat, starting at the end furthest away from you.

2 Make sure you take a full turn before crossing the cleat diagonally and passing the working end under the opposite horn.

3 Keep going in a figure-eight, until you've made at least two crossing turns. Small, slippery line will require more turns than large, coarse line.

HITCHES • 73

Slipped cleat hitch

The jib sheets of most dinghies nowadays run through jammers, which can be released with a single, sharp jerk. Halyards are often cleated, however, and here a quick, easily released knot is advisable. You'll be grateful for it when the boat is capsized, and you're trying to get the mainsail down in a hurry.

KNOT SCORE

Strength ❀❀❀❀
Security ❀❀❀❀
Difficulty Tying ❀
Difficulty Untying ❀
Usefulness ❀❀❀❀

1 Take a round turn around the base of the cleat, and a single diagonal turn across the top of it.

2 Put a bight in the working end and tuck it under the diagonal. Tighten the knot. To release: just pull the end!

4 Tighten the knot and finish off either with a simple turn or a half hitch around one of the horns (as shown), depending on usage.

Cleat hitch on a bollard cleat

Is this the best of both worlds? A cleat on a bollard might seem like the ideal compromise. In practice, it can be awkward to use as a cleat, while the pin catches on the line when tying a traditional bollard knot (page 68).

KNOT SCORE	
Strength	✿✿✿✿✿
Security	✿✿✿✿✿
Difficulty Tying	✿✿✿
Difficulty Untying	✿
Usefulness	✿✿✿✿

1 Take a full turn around the base of the bollard.

2 Pass the working end diagonally over the pin on the opposite side. Add more diagonal turns in the same way as the cleat hitch (page 72).

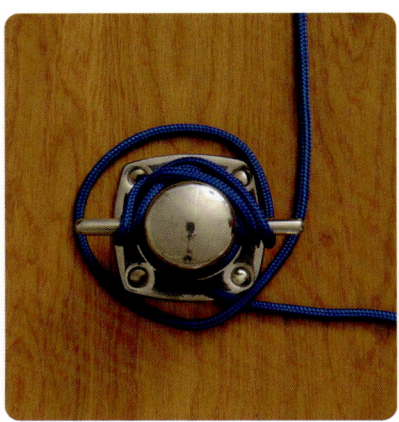

3 The number of turns will depend on the type and size of the line, but should include at least two crossing turns.

4 Finish with a half hitch – and, if you're feeling smart, cheese the leftover line! (See page 222 for cheesing methods.)

A bollard cleat works like a normal cleat – just tipped sideways.

HITCHES • 75

Cleat hitch on a pin

Before there were cleats, there were pins. Most of the running rigging on a traditional square-rigger was tied off on pin rails fixed to the bottom of the shrouds or on fife rails located on deck around the bottom of the masts. Although rarely used on modern sailboats, the principle is the same as a cleat fastened to a mast.

KNOT SCORE
Strength
Security
Difficulty Tying
Difficulty Untying
Usefulness

1 Take a turn around the bottom of the belaying pin (or cleat).

2 Pass the working end diagonally across and around the top of the pin (or cleat).

3 Take a couple more diagonal turns to make a figure-eight shape. Make sure there are at least two crossing turns.

4 If tying off a flag halyard, finish with a half hitch on the top part of the pin.

KNOT KNOW-HOW

Before the invention of cleats, belaying pins were used to tie off nearly all of a ship's running rigging. On a square-rigger, that might mean upwards of 50 belaying pins on each side of the ship. Not only did each line have to be 'belayed', but any leftover line had to be coiled and hitched on the pin too (page 213). In the case of the upper sails, that might mean hundreds of feet of line. Not a job for the faint-hearted.

BEST FOR tying a mooring line to a ring

Rings come in all shapes and sizes, from giant rusty circles embedded in docks intended for big ships to neat stainless-steel hoops on a bulwark or marina pontoon. Choosing the right knot to tie the painter of your dinghy could mean the difference between getting safely back on board ship or having to swim home.

It's a common scenario. You go ashore in the dinghy and find a suitable place to tie up. Everyone piles ashore and, in the excitement to buy some fresh pastries, the painter is quickly tied to a ring. Too quickly. Two hours later, everyone comes back with nice full tummies, but the dinghy is missing and drifting out to sea. Uh-oh.

There are any number of good knots that could prevent this happening. The most obvious is a round turn and two half hitches (page 28), and, if tied correctly, this will serve as well as any knot. It has the advantage that most people know how to tie it; the flip side of that is that familiarity breeds contempt which can result in sloppy knot-tying technique.

In this occasion, a bowline (page 126) is probably not the best option either, simply because it has to be tied at the end of the line, which may or may not be the right length for that particular situation. The chances are you'll need to tie the boat off on a shorter tether.

If you love your round turn and two half hitches but want a variation on a theme, then a buntline hitch (page 30) might be the answer: similar to a round turn and two half hitches but tied slightly differently. Be warned that it is harder to untie too, though that's unlikely to be an issue with a dinghy painter.

A better variation of the round turn and two half hitches theme is the fisherman's bend (page 50), aka the fisherman's friend. This can be happily used to moor any size boat, though again it's harder to untie in the long term.

Other options include the constrictor knot (page 40) – almost always a better option than a clove hitch, though more likely to jam. This won't be an issue tying a dinghy painter but is probably best avoided when mooring a larger vessel, as you might end up having to cut the line away to release it. The same might be said of the strangle knot (page 44).

Which brings us back to where we started. If you're in a rush to go ashore to buy your fresh pastries, you don't want to be fiddling around with a knot you're not completely sure of. In which case, stick with your tried-and-test round turn and two half hitches – but just make sure you tie it well!

HITCHES • 77

ROUND TURN & 2 HALF HITCHES: The round turn and two half hitches (page 28) has the advantage that it can be tied in the bight.

BOWLINE: The bowline (page 126) is limited to being tied at the end of the line, which means the other end has to be adjusted for length.

BUNTLINE HITCH: Similar to the round turn and two half hitches, the buntline hitch (page 30) is much harder to untie.

FISHERMAN'S BEND: The fisherman's bend (page 50) is just as strong as a round turn and two half hitches but less likely to slip.

CONSTRICTOR KNOT: The constrictor knot (page 40) is always an attractive option and will untie more easily if a loop is inserted.

STRANGLE KNOT: Likewise the strangle knot (page 44) is rated as more secure than a round turn and two half hitches but also much harder to untie.

Blackwall hitch

You don't have to be a stevedore to lift cargo on and off ships. Many yachts are fitted with davits to hoist their tenders on board, while others use their sail halyards for the same purpose. And, if you're stocking up for a long passage, you might want to 'crane' your shopping aboard ship. In any of these situations, the blackwall hitch will prove an instant (if not altogether trustworthy) friend.

KNOT SCORE
Strength ❋❋❋
Security ❋❋
Difficulty Tying ❋
Difficulty Untying ❋
Usefulness ❋❋❋

'Sunday came again while we were at Monterey, but as before, it brought us no holyday. The people on shore dressed themselves and came off in greater numbers than ever, and we were employed all day in boating and breaking out cargo, so that we had hardly time to eat...'

The above is an extract from *Two Years Before the Mast* by RH Dana. Dana was an American lawyer who, before his graduation, took a two-year sabbatical to experience life on the high seas. Despite his upper class background, he signed up as an ordinary sailor, and spent much of his time in California, loading hides onto his ship, the *Pilgrim*.

Sadly, he makes no mention of which knots were used for this work, but the blackwall hitch, or the double blackwall hitch, must be at the top of the list of contenders. Other so-called 'hook hitches' include the marlinspike hitch (page 52), the stunner hitch, and the bill hitch. But the blackwall hitch is probably the most common.

The main characteristics of a good 'hook hitch' is that it should be quick and easy to tie, it should hold a substantial load securely, and it should 'spill', or come undone, once the load is released, without any additional effort. The blackwall hitch scores on the first and last points, but is only secure if the rope used is thick enough to fill the jaw of the hook. The double blackwall hitch (opposite) is a little more secure, but both should be used with caution.

Its name is thought to originate from the Blackwall Shipyard on the River Thames which, in the latter part of the 18th century, was the largest private shipyard in the world. Its output included ships for the Royal Navy and the East India Company. The knot may have been used to carry timber around the yard and load equipment onto the ships.

1 Pass the working end around the back of the hook...

2 ... and across its mouth, to form a complete turn.

3 Pass the standing end over the working end so that it jams the latter against the hook.

HITCHES • 79

Double blackwall hitch

The blackwall hitch isn't the most reliable of knots, so the double blackwall was created to make it more secure. There are two ways of tying a double blackwall: with the extra turn in the hook itself (as shown), or with the extra turn in its shank. Try both, and see which one works best for you. Both are temporary knots intended for immediate use.

KNOT SCORE

Strength ✦✦✦
Security ✦✦✦
Difficulty Tying ✦
Difficulty Untying ✦
Usefulness ✦✦✦

1 Take a turn around the hook, as for the single blackwall hitch.

2 Pass the working end around the hook to make a second turn.

3 Pass the standing part over the two turns so it jams them against the hook.

Double cat's paw

Slings are commonly used for lifting heavy objects, and can be simply hitched onto a hook for lifting. Alternatively, a double cat's paw can be put into the bight to ensure the line doesn't slide off the hook. The knot's main credentials are that it won't slip or jam – both key characteristics for any hook hitch.

KNOT SCORE
Strength ❖❖❖❖
Security ❖❖❖❖
Difficulty Tying ❖❖
Difficulty Untying ❖❖
Usefulness ❖❖❖❖

1 Attach the sling to the cargo using a suitable hitch (a cow hitch will do the trick, see page 53).

2 Tuck the bight under itself to create two loops.

3 Twist both loops towards the centre of the knot – one clockwise, the other anticlockwise.

4 Put in two or three twists, depending on how slippery the rope is and how heavy the load is.

5 Bring the loops together and place them over the hook. Tighten the knot by pulling on both legs.

HITCHES • 81

Bubble knot

Here's one you won't find in Ashley's *Book of Knots* – or in many other books, for that matter. The bubble knot was first published in the British magazine *Practical Boat Owner* in July 2000, and may be one of the few genuinely new knots to have appeared in recent years. Use it to tie a sheet to a sail, or any situation where a line is too large for the designated hole.

KNOT SCORE
Strength
Security
Difficulty Tying
Difficulty Untying
Usefulness

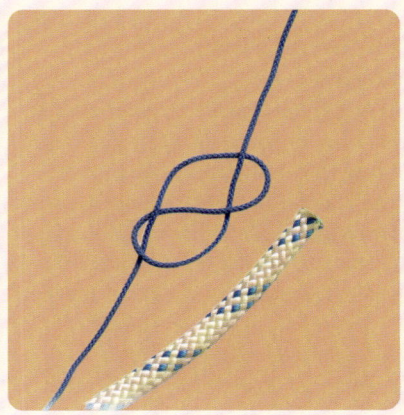

1 Tie a figure-eight (page 174) in the thinner line.

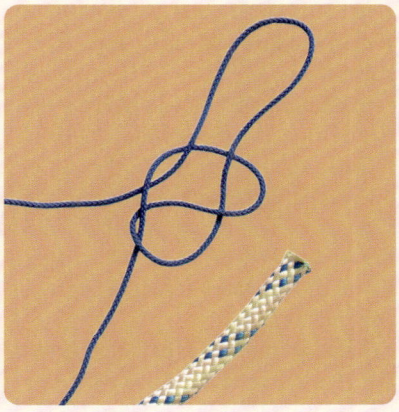

2 Pass the working end back through the top of the knot...

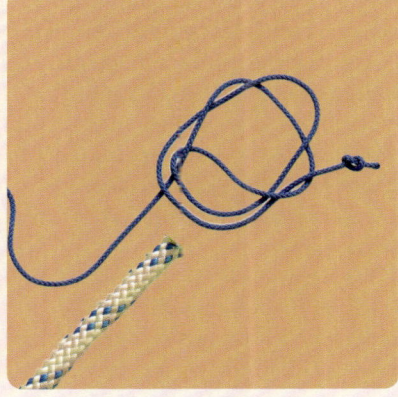

3 ... over the standing part and back into the loop, following the path of the initial knot. Tie a stopper knot (pages 174–179) in the working end to make the button.

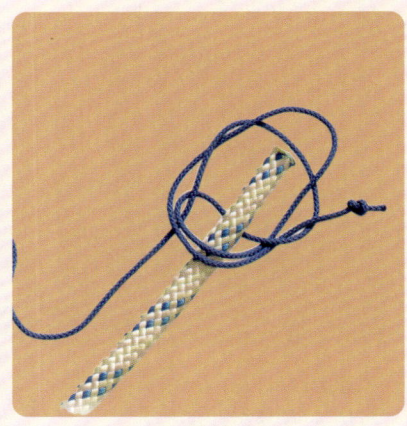

4 Pass the thicker line (eg jib sheet) under the first two turns.

5 Create an underhand loop, passing the working end through the central loop. The upper loop then becomes the button loop which will be used to attach the object (eg sail).

6 Tighten the knot, feeding the button loop and the button through the underhand loop. To use: insert the button loop through the hole and insert the button on the other side.

Trucker's hitch

Once used to lash down the covers on horse-drawn carts, the trucker's hitch has many nautical applications. Use it where you would normally use a block and tackle, if that isn't available, or if you just want to add some additional purchase. But don't underestimate its strength. It has been known to crush small craft lashed to the roof of a car. You have been warned.

KNOT SCORE
Strength
Security
Difficulty Tying
Difficulty Untying
Usefulness

It's not often that a knot arouses genuine excitement outside knot-tying circles, but the trucker's hitch is so ingenious it rarely fails to impress. It's certainly popular on the internet. One website voted it 'the most awesome knot ever', while another claims it is the second most requested knot, after the bowline.

Formerly known as the wagoner's hitch, the knot is thought to have originated among hawkers and carters who used it to tension and lash down the covers on their horse-drawn carts.

There are multiple uses aboard ship, from lashing things down on the coachroof, to craning heavy objects, or even providing a purchase on a halyard.

Essentially a block and tackle made out of rope, the trucker's hitch gives a mechanical advantage of either 2:1 or 3:1, depending which way round it is used. If the fixed point is on the side of the working end, it's a 2:1 advantage; if it's on the side of the standing part, it's a 3:1 advantage.

Typically of many older knots, there are several different ways of tying a trucker's hitch – the name being an umbrella term for a general approach. The one shown is based on a sheepshank (page 188) and, while not the most secure, is the most easily released.

A more permanent arrangement can be made by using a figure-eight loop (page 125) or even a bowline (page 126), but both these knots are likely to jam under the loads exerted. Plus, any permanent knot is likely to suffer from chafe where the line runs over the loop.

Either way, the force exerted is enough to damage even quite substantial objects if applied in the wrong way. So proceed with caution, and remember: not for nothing is it also known as the cinch knot.

1 Put a bight in the standing part and cross over the working end.

2 Take a turn around both parts of the bight, passing the working end through the loop.

3 Tighten the turn to create a 'sheepshank' style loop.

HITCHES • 83

Double trucker's hitch

There are two ways of 'doubling' a trucker's hitch. One makes it more secure, and the other increases the amount of leverage, or 'purchase', in the pulley system. Or, for a more secure pulley with extra purchase, do both!

KNOT SCORE

Strength ❀❀❀❀❀
Security ❀❀❀❀❀
Difficulty Tying ❀❀❀❀❀
Difficulty Untying ❀❀❀❀❀
Usefulness ❀❀❀❀❀

1 To create a more secure knot, simply add an extra turn to the 'sheepshank' part of the loop. Recommended for slippery lines.

2 To give extra purchase, insert a bight into the middle loop to create a new loop. Pass the working end through the shackle or ring, then back up through the extra loop.

4 Put another bight into the standing part and pass it through the loop.

5 The working end and the loop can now be attached to the fixed point and the moving object (or vice versa). To haul or hoist the object, pull the standing part.

BEST FOR tying an anchor snubber

Some people grind their teeth at night; some boats grind their anchor chains. The effect is similar to the person lying next to them: a sleepless night. The solution for most boats is to fit a snubber to the anchor chain, to transfer the load from the chain to a rope, which is less likely to grind at night and keep everyone awake. Unfortunately, a knot hasn't been invented yet to stop people grinding their teeth at night.

You can of course buy ready-made snubbers from the chandlery, or you can make up your own by splicing a suitable metal hook onto the end of a short length of rope. There was one of these on my boat when I bought it, and it's been sitting in the cockpit locker taking up valuable space ever since. On the few occasions when I have deployed it, I might just as well have used a random length of rope and tied one of the knots below.

The name of the game when it comes to snubbers is grip – or 'nip', as Clifford Ashley calls it. In other words, you don't want the line to slide up the chain. This is the very opposite of a loop, where it doesn't matter how much the knot slides around as long as it doesn't come undone. Getting maximum grip usually involves taking several turns around the object, combined with a knot that gets tighter the more force is applied to it.

One of the most common knots in that category is the evergreen rolling hitch (page 39), which would probably be most sailor's default knot in this situation. Tests have shown, however, that it performs surprisingly badly as a snubber knot, slipping much more easily than most other knots tested. The only way to improve its performance was to combine it with other hitches, such as a couple of half hitches, or even doubling up with a second rolling hitch.

Another knot that performed badly was the cow hitch (page 53). 'This knot is best left on the farm,' said one study. Clearly a knot designed to tether cows to a farmyard fence isn't so great at tethering boats to a lurching anchor chain.

Camels, however, are another matter. One of the best performing knots in this category was the humble camel hitch (page 38). There's nothing particularly clever or special about this knot, but by sheer dint of combining several turns with a clove hitch, it manages to exert exceptional grip on an anchor chain. The other winner was the prusik knot (page 194), which is essentially a double cow hitch. Those extra turns make all the difference, however, and turns it into a great snubber knot.

Another option is the double constrictor knot (page 40), which certainly has the grip required, though whether it can cope with a slippery anchor chain is open to question.

ROLLING HITCH: The rolling hitch (page 39) is the obvious, but not necessarily best, choice for a snubber knot. Think again.

COW HITCH: Only the cow hitch (page 53) performed worse than the rolling hitch. Think again.

DOUBLE CONSTRICTOR: The double constrictor knot (page 42) is a good choice, though it might suffer the same limitations as the rolling hitch.

CAMEL HITCH: The camel hitch (page 38) isn't the obvious choice but performed best out of the hitches tested here.

PRUSIK KNOT: Another good mountaineering knot, the prusik knot (page 194) tied using a rope loop performed best of all.

BENDS 3

Overhand bend

It's the mother of all bends; a knot so simple that even Bronze Age man used it 5,300 years ago. Yet it's still ranked as more secure than many later, more fancy inventions. That said, it's only recommended for use with the small stuff, such as whipping twine and similar. There are better knots for 'bending' two mooring lines together or for extending the painter on that pesky dinghy later in this chapter.

KNOT SCORE

Strength
Security
Difficulty Tying
Difficulty Untying
Usefulness

Sheet bends, carrick bends, alpine butterflies, Spanish hawser bends, zeppelin bends, simple simons – there are more ways of tying two bits of rope together than you can shake a blunt marlinspike at. The skill is in choosing the right one.

Context is everything. If one line is larger than the other, then a double sheet bend is the obvious solution. On the other hand, if two lengths of similarly-sized, slippery modern rope are being joined, then a carrick bend might be a better option.

Despite this, people tend to have their favourites and stick with them come what may. This author used a double sheet bend to lengthen a mooring line which held good for three winters and, when the time came to untie it, came apart as if it had been tied the day before. Others consider the knot unsafe, and swear by the zeppelin bend.

The overhand bend might look a bit basic compared to some of the more elaborate knots included in this chapter, but Ashley rates it above the sheet bend for security – though not for strength. This means that it's great for tying thin, slippery rope together (eg twine), but not to be trusted with the big stuff, such as mooring lines.

High security usually (though not always) means a knot is also difficult to untie. This doesn't matter in certain instances, such as tying cheap lengths of twine together, but might be a consideration if you're working with Dyneema or Spectra.

And more turns don't necessarily mean a better knot. Add an extra turn to the overhand bend and you get the figure-eight bend, which might look a little more reassuringly complicated but is in fact less secure than its more elementary sister.

Arguably the 'mother of all bends', the overhand bend has been around for millennia. A sample was found with the body of Europe's oldest man: the 5,300-year-old Ötzi the Iceman, a natural mummy found in the Italian Alps.

1 Place the two lines to be joined side by side and make an underhand loop.

2 Tuck the ends in the loop to make the bend.

3 Tighten the knot by pulling the two parts in opposite directions.

BENDS • 89

Figure-eight bend

If the overhand bend (opposite) isn't as secure as you'd like it to be, you might think adding another turn would improve matters. But you'd be wrong. The reason the figure-eight is so useful as a stopper knot is that, unlike a simple overhand knot, it can almost always be untied. Use the figure-eight bend if you want a quick, easy way of tying two lines together which definitely won't jam.

KNOT SCORE

Strength
Security
Difficulty Tying
Difficulty Untying
Usefulness

1 Tie a figure-eight (page 174) in one of the lines, and insert the working end of the other line through the end loop.

2 Take a turn around the other line's standing part and tuck the working end under itself.

3 Carry on around, following the lead of the first figure-eight. The working end should come out next to the other line's standing part. Tighten the knot.

Sheet bend

One of the most useful all-round bends, the sheet bend is equally effective for joining ropes of the same size as those of different sizes. It scores better on strength than on security, which means it holds well under a constant load, but is liable to collapse if jerked repeatedly. One way of making it more secure is to seize the end of the loop to its standing part.

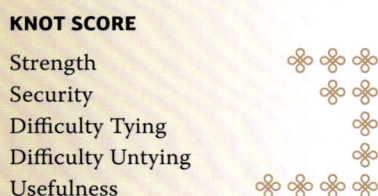

KNOT SCORE
Strength
Security
Difficulty Tying
Difficulty Untying
Usefulness

1 The sheet bend can be used for joining lines of the same size or for attaching small lines to large.

2 Put a bight in one of the lines – the larger (or stiffer) of the two, if they are different sizes.

3 Pass the working end of the other line through the bight and then under both its legs.

4 Tuck the working end under itself. The two ends should be on the same side of the knot. Tighten the knot by holding both legs of the bight, and closing the hitch.

BENDS • 91

Double sheet bend

In practice, the double sheet is almost always used on boats, in preference to the single version (opposite). It takes hardly any longer to tie, and is considerably more secure. Use it for almost any situation where there is a constant load and not too much snatching, eg halyards or lashing a tender to the coachroof – but not sheets or a tow line.

KNOT SCORE

Strength ❀❀
Security ❀❀❀
Difficulty Tying ❀
Difficulty Untying ❀❀
Usefulness ❀❀❀

1 Put a bight in the end of one line. Pass the end of the other line through the bight and around the legs.

2 Tuck the working end under itself, and pass it around the legs again.

3 Tuck the working end under the standing part, making sure not to cross the previous turn Tighten the knot.

Triple sheet bend

We've already warned against adding extra turns to try to strengthen a knot (page 88) – the result can often be quite the opposite. But if you're tying a sheet bend in thin, slippery rope, a third turn can help.

KNOT SCORE

Strength ❀❀
Security ❀❀❀
Difficulty Tying ❀
Difficulty Untying ❀❀❀
Usefulness ❀❀

1 Tie a double sheet bend as shown above.

2 Take another turn with the working end and tuck it under the standing part.

Alpine butterfly bend

Another relatively recent addition to the canon of knots, the alpine butterfly bend is essentially a butterfly loop (page 142) with the loop cut off. Although it probably isn't everyone's favourite knot, its performance compares well with that of its better-known cousins such as the zeppelin bend and carrick bend. Use this knot for joining ropes of the same size.

KNOT SCORE

Strength	✦✦✦✦✦
Security	✦✦✦
Difficulty Tying	✦✦
Difficulty Untying	✦✦
Usefulness	✦✦✦✦

1 Put a bight in the end of each line, and interlock them together.

2 Pass the working ends under their respective standing parts to create two interlocking underhand loops.

3 Pass the working ends through both loops.

4 Tighten the knot by pulling on both ends simultaneously.

KNOT KNOW-HOW

Neither the alpine butterfly bend nor the alpine butterfly loop appear in *The Ashley Book of Knots*, which suggests they may have appeared after 1944. Ashley does however feature a lineman's loop, which is essentially the same thing as an alpine butterfly loop. Both knots are also known by their abbreviated names: butterfly bend and butterfly loop.

Lapp knot

Although this looks like a temporary knot, Laplanders apparently use it to tie lanyards onto their knives and hitch their reindeer to sledges. Its main advantage is that it can be slipped with one tug of the drawloop, and the line can be pulled free without any further effort. Use it to attach a line that might need to be released at short notice – and not just reindeer.

KNOT SCORE
Strength
Security
Difficulty Tying
Difficulty Untying
Usefulness

1 Put a bight in the end of one of the lines, and pass the end of the other line under it.

2 Put a bight in the working end of the second line, and pass it over its standing part...

3 ... and through the first bight. Allow enough line to create a generous loop and long tail.

4 Tighten the knot by pulling on both parts of the first line, and the standing part of the second line.

94 • BENDS

Rigger's bend

A neat method of joining two lines, the rigger's bend is really a variation on the theme of the alpine butterfly bend (page 92) and the zeppelin bend (page 98). Although it's more prone to jamming than either of them, it's also marginally more secure. It must be one of the few knots to have made it to the front page of *The Times* (see Knot Know-How, opposite).

KNOT SCORE

Strength
Security
Difficulty Tying
Difficulty Untying
Usefulness

1 Put an overhand loop in the end of one line (on the left here), and an underhand loop in the end of the other line, and interlock them as shown.

2 Pass the working end of the overhand loop under and through the centre of the knot.

3 Pass the working end of the underhand loop over and through the centre of the knot.

4 Tighten the knot, being careful not to lose its shape.

BENDS • 95

Barrel knot

Also known as the blood knot, this bend is highly rated for joining thin, stiff, slippery lines, hence its popularity among anglers. Another key feature is its compact form, which creates minimal drag when towed through the water – a potentially useful characteristic for yachtsmen. It also has a tendency to jam, so be prepared to have to cut the rope free.

KNOT SCORE
Strength
Security
Difficulty Tying
Difficulty Untying
Usefulness

1 Put a bight in the end of each line, and place one over the other.

2 Tuck the working end of each line around the standing part of the other.

3 Pass the working end of each line over itself and around the standing part of the other line again.

4 Tighten the turns, and then pull the standing parts to tighten the knot.

KNOT KNOW-HOW

The rigger's bend achieved worldwide fame when it (allegedly) featured on the front page of *The Times* in 1978. Although already known in the US as the rigger's bend, it became known as the hunter's bend after its British co-creator Dr Edward Hunter. According to Ashley, the knot was tested by the Royal Aircraft Establishment who reported it was 'not as strong as the blood knot [...] and stronger than the fisherman's bend, sheet bend or reef knot'.

BEST FOR tying an ensign

Using the correct knots to tie an ensign is another of those subjects that seems to get people all hot under the collar. Everyone seems to have a definite opinion which they will defend unto the death. Some of the options are offered below – though needless to say I have my own way of doing it, which I too will defend unto the death…

Growing up on my parents' boat in the Mediterranean, it was my job to raise the ensign at 8am and lower it at sunset, every day. My father was a retired Royal Navy officer and was a stickler for this kind of old-fashioned etiquette. I got very used to tying and untying the flag in a certain way which I presume was also handed down from the Navy. It's not the way I would necessarily do it now, if I was coming to it fresh, but it stood us in good stead for 13 years, so it must have something going for it.

Most flag halyards are a continuous loop, with the top and bottom of the flag tied at either end of the line. The flags themselves are made with a variety of fittings, including toggles, ropes and eyes. Our ship's ensign had a toggle at the top and a line at the bottom. According to my father's instructions, I tied one end of the halyard to the toggle using a figure-eight. Although generally used as a stopper knot, the figure-eight (page 174) is sometimes used as a hitch, not least by fishermen tying their lines to a hook. The beauty of using it here was that it allowed the flag to be drawn right up to the pulley at the top of the staff, without a bulky knot getting in the way. It was also easy to untie and held remarkably well, perhaps partly due to being jammed up against the pulley once hoisted.

For the other end, I tied the halyard to the loop in the flag line with a simple pair of half hitches, without the round turn (page 28). Again, this was less bulky than other options and seemed to hold perfectly well. Once the flag was hoisted, the line was tied off on a cleat with a cleat hitch (what else?) (page 72).

Other options might include a (small) bowline (page 126) for the toggle, which would allow it to be slipped on and off without having to retie the knot, though it won't sit as snugly against the pulley as the figure-eight. A clove hitch (page 32) is also a neat solution, though it will be harder to untie than a figure-eight.

For the line, I'm a great fan of the sheet bend (page 90), so I would probably opt for that these days. I've also seen a rolling hitch (page 39) and a prusik knot (page 194) suggested for this purpose, though I wouldn't recommend either of those.

For flags fitted with eyes instead of toggles, you can't really go wrong with the ubiquitous bowline (page 126), or even a round turn and two half hitches (page 28). Or you might try out any of the loops described in the Loops chapter (page 122), most of which would be suitable for this purpose.

ENDS • 97

FIGURE-EIGHT: The author uses a figure-eight (page 174) to tie the halyard to the toggle with excellent results.

BOWLINE: A carefully sized bowline (page 126) also works well and can be left tied in the halyard when the flag is taken down.

CLOVE HITCH: There are a number of hitches to choose from, including the ubiquitous clove hitch (page 32).

SHEET BEND: For the line, you can take your pick of bends, though the trusty sheet bend (page 90) is hard to beat.

CLEAT HITCH: There's only one good knot for cleating off the halyard: the cleat hitch (page 72) of course!

Zeppelin bend

Said to have been used to secure zeppelins in the 1930s, this bend is equally handy at sea. Like the rigger's bend (page 94), which it closely resembles, it's based on nothing more than a pair of interlocking overhand knots. But if it's good enough for the US Navy, it should be good enough for the rest of us (see Knot Know-How, opposite).

KNOT SCORE

Strength
Security
Difficulty Tying
Difficulty Untying
Usefulness

1 Put a bight and a loop in one line, as if preparing to tie an overhand knot, and pass the working end of the other line through the bight.

2 Pass the working end of the first line through the loop to complete the overhand knot. Pass the working end of the other line under its standing part to make a second loop.

3 Pass the working end of the second line through the first loop and then its own loop, to create the second interlocking knot.

4 Tighten the knot on each line individually, then tighten the whole knot by pulling the standing parts in opposite directions.

BENDS • 99

Broach bend

Another Harry Asher special, this knot is clearly inspired by the approach of the zeppelin bend (opposite) and others – except that it uses interlocking figure-eights (page 174) instead of overhand knots. Think of it as a pair of figure-eights with the final tuck made in the opposite knot. A secure way of joining medium-sized lines without risk of jamming.

KNOT SCORE

Strength ✿✿✿
Security ✿✿✿✿
Difficulty Tying ✿✿
Difficulty Untying ✿✿✿
Usefulness ✿✿✿

1 Interlock a pair of overhand loops.

2 Take an additional turn around the standing part of each line, as you would for a figure-eight.

3 Tuck the working end of each line into the other line's original loop.

4 Tighten the figure-eight on each line individually, before tightening the whole knot by pulling the standing parts in opposite directions.

KNOT KNOW-HOW

Legend has it that the American aeronautic hero Charles Rosendahl insisted that the airships he commanded were tethered using the knot on the opposite page. It was subsequently used by the US Navy for all lighter-than-air craft operations, until the Navy's airship programme ended in 1962. The knot was christened the zeppelin bend by *Boating* magazine in 1976.

Carrick bend

It's been described as 'the nearest thing we have to a perfect bend', and indeed the carrick bend has most of the characteristics required of a perfect knot. No one is sure how it got its name, but the most likely inspiration must be the Carrick Roads in Falmouth, UK, which was a major port during the Age of Sail. Use it to tie large mooring lines together – or to make a decorative lanyard or mat.

Knot-tyers love the carrick bend. This is probably because it's a good example of a knot that combines aesthetics with functionality. It's aesthetically pleasing because of its simple, repetitive, symmetrical pattern. And it's utterly functional because it's the best and easiest knot to tie in thick, unwieldy ropes that can't be twisted into any other bend. Not only that, but it's extremely secure, yet does not jam, and only gets stronger when wet.

No wonder the carrick bend was described by Ashley as 'the nearest thing we have to a perfect bend'. Its only drawback is that when tightened in its 'capsized' form (as shown), it's quite bulky compared to other bends. This can be overcome, however, by seizing both the ends while the knot is still in its initial shape. The resulting knot slips more easily through hawsers and retains all the positive characteristics described above.

Apart from being used on ships to tie mooring lines together, the carrick bend has many decorative uses. It can be extended longways to make a lanyard, or it can be expanded 'in the flat' to make a mat. It also features in various logos, including Carrick District Council in the UK, which includes the natural harbour known as the Carrick Roads.

1 Put an underhand loop in the end of one line, and place it over the other line.

KNOT SCORE

Strength
Security
Difficulty Tying
Difficulty Untying
Usefulness

BENDS • 101

2 Pass the end of the second line over the standing part and under the working end of the first line.

3 Tuck the working end under its own standing part and over the other loop.

4 Tighten the knot by pulling the standing parts in opposite directions.

Open carrick bend

As ever, some knot-tyers just can't resist adding that extra turn to create a 'new' knot. The open carrick bend is similar to the plain carrick bend, apart from the addition of an extra turn. It's less liable to jam, so will be easier to untie, and may be slightly stronger. On the other hand, it's more bulky and somewhat clumsy-looking.

KNOT SCORE

Strength
Security
Difficulty Tying
Difficulty Untying
Usefulness

1 Put an overhand loop in one line (this one has been stopped). Pass the other line through the loop, between both parts, and back up through the loop.

2 Go around again, to form the second turn.

3 Tighten the knot, and 'stop' both ends – or just the loose end if the other has already been stopped.

Spanish hawser bend

It's easy to assume that the tighter you tie a knot, the better it will be. But over-tightening a knot, while making it more secure, will also weaken the line. The Spanish hawser bend cleverly takes an untightened carrick bend (page 100) and adds some seizings to give it security. This makes for a stronger, more streamlined knot. For more on hawser bends, see page 102.

KNOT SCORE
Strength
Security
Difficulty Tying
Difficulty Untying
Usefulness

1 Tie a carrick bend in the usual manner, by making an underhand loop with one line, and placing it over the other line.

2 Pass the working end of the second line over the standing part of the first line.

3 Pass the working end of the second line under the end of the first, then tuck it under its own standing part, visible inside the loop.

4 At very least, the two ends should be seized to their own standing part. For a more permanent and streamlined knot, add two further seizings on each side, as shown.

BENDS • 103

Surgeon's knot

Like its close cousin the reef knot (page 180), the surgeon's knot is strictly speaking a binding knot rather than a bend. As it is most often used to tie two pieces of rope (or thread) together, however, it's been included in this section. Use it mostly to tie small stuff together – or with heavier ropes as a binding knot. Either way, it's more secure than a reef knot.

KNOT SCORE
Strength
Security
Difficulty Tying
Difficulty Untying
Usefulness

1 Cross the ends of the lines.

2 Wrap the ends of both lines around each other's standing parts.

3 Wrap the ends around the standing parts one more time.

4 Cross the ends the opposite way to Step 1, and tie a half knot. The ends should emerge next to their own standing parts. Tighten the knot.

Simple simon

Another 'new' knot from the hands of the prolific Harry Asher, the simple simon is only 30 years old. Like most of the best knots, it has an elegant simplicity – although the double version (opposite) is more secure. Use it to tie two lines of different thicknesses as an alternative to the sheet bend (page 90) and others.

KNOT SCORE
Strength
Security
Difficulty Tying
Difficulty Untying
Usefulness

1 Put a bight in the thick line and pass the thin line through the bight and under the standing part.

4 Tighten the knot by pulling both pairs of legs in opposite directions.

2 Take a turn around the legs of the bight with the thin line.

3 Pass the working end diagonally across itself, and tuck it under and over the original bight. It should emerge next to its own standing part.

Double simple simon

Sometimes adding an extra turn to a knot can do more harm than good. But in the case of the simple simon, the extra turn definitely improves the knot's security. For a more permanent knot, tie a seizing (eg a constrictor knot, page 40) around both parts of the bight.

KNOT SCORE
Strength ❀❀❀
Security ❀❀❀❀
Difficulty Tying ❀❀
Difficulty Untying ❀❀
Usefulness ❀❀❀

1 Put a bight in the thick line and pass the thin line through the bight under the standing part.

2 Pass the working end of the thin line across the bight...

3 ... and around both legs for the first full turn.

4 Pass the working end around the bight again and across itself.

5 Pass the working end diagonally across itself and around the original bight. It should emerge next to its own standing part.

6 Tighten the knot by pulling both pairs of legs in opposite directions.

Slackline bend

Like the single stopper (page 118), the slackline bend can also be used as a hitch. In practice, however, it tends to be used to tie a thin line to a much larger line, hence its inclusion here. Use as an alternative to the heaving line bend (page 117), particularly on heavy lines which can't be bent easily to take a regular bend.

KNOT SCORE
Strength
Security
Difficulty Tying
Difficulty Untying
Usefulness

1 Take a turn with the thin line around the thick line (or, in this case, a spar), so that it passes over the standing part.

2 Take another turn with the working end, crossing back over itself and under the standing part.

3 Tuck the working end under the bight of the first line. Take another turn next to the other two, and tuck the working end under the standing part.

4 Tighten the knot by pulling the end first, before applying a sideways force with the standing part.

KNOT KNOW-HOW

While writing his *Book of Knots*, Clifford Ashley conducted an experiment to see which bends were the most secure. Ignoring a complicated knot of his own, the results were:

1. Barrel knot (p95)
2. Ring knot (not shown)
3. Carrick bend (p100)
4. Fisherman's knot (p114)
5. Double sheet bend (p91)

BENDS • 107

Jamming bend

Occasionally, you might want to attach a line to the bight of another line using a proper bend, rather than just a hitch-bend (eg the slackline bend, opposite). That might sound impossible, as most bends are formed using the ends of both lines. The jamming bend gets around that problem with a rather ingenious twist – quite literally!

KNOT SCORE
Strength
Security
Difficulty Tying
Difficulty Untying
Usefulness

1 Take two turns with the working end of one line around the bight of the other line.

2 Pass the working end under its own standing part, in the same direction as the two turns.

3 Pull the working end and twist the other line simultaneously to create a pair of interlocking loops.

4 Tighten the knot. Although the end of the blue line is visible here, the knot has been tied in the bight, without using the end.

Adjustable bend

Here's a clever way of making a bend that can be adjusted without untying a single knot. Use it to secure something that is in regular use instead of a bungee (eg a binocular case or washboards) or as a preventer to stop halyards frapping. And, if you think it just looks like a pair of rolling hitches (page 39), then you're not wrong.

KNOT SCORE

Strength ❀❀❀❀
Security ❀❀❀❀
Difficulty Tying ❀❀❀
Difficulty Untying ❀❀❀
Usefulness ❀❀❀❀

1 Take a turn around one line with the other line.

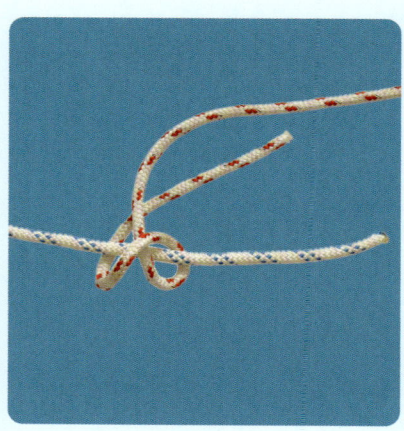

2 Pass the working end diagonally over its own standing part and take another diagonal turn, so it ends up on the same side as before.

3 Pass the working end diagonally over its own standing part again, and take a turn on the other side. Tuck the end under itself to complete the first rolling hitch (page 39).

4 Take a turn around the standing part of the line you've just tied with the other line.

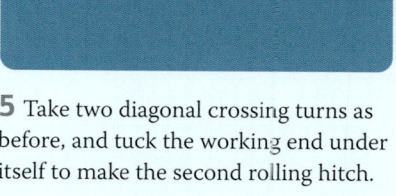

5 Take two diagonal crossing turns as before, and tuck the working end under itself to make the second rolling hitch.

6 Tighten the hitches on each line individually, before tightening the whole knot by pulling the standing parts in opposite directions.

BENDS • 109

Twin bowline

If you're a fan of the bowline (and who isn't?), this 'bowline bend' might appeal. It's not the quickest knot to tie and it can be fiddly to get the legs just the right length, but there's something very appealing about its simple symmetry. Tie it in white and black lines, and you've got yourself a perfect yin-yang bowline!

KNOT SCORE
Strength
Security
Difficulty Tying
Difficulty Untying
Usefulness

1 Put an overhand loop in the end of one line.

2 Pass the working end of the other line up through the loop.

3 Pass the end around the standing part of the first line and back through the loop to make the first bowline. Put an overhand loop in the second line and pass the end through it.

4 Complete the second bowline, and adjust it so the legs are equidistant. Tighten the knot. All the usual cautions concerning bowlines apply (page 126).

Reeving line bend

Usually, our main concern when tying a knot is to make it as secure as possible. The reeving line bend is a little unusual in that it makes a virtue of its apparent lack of security to create a long, streamlined knot that will slip through fairleads easily. A couple of seizings around the ends give it the necessary security. The result is a very useful knot which is almost certainly stronger than its more complicated counterparts.

KNOT SCORE
Strength
Security
Difficulty Tying
Difficulty Untying
Usefulness

There's little doubt the best way to join two lines together is to splice them (see from page 288). A knot such as a bowline reduces the line's strength by about 40 per cent – whereas a spliced line retains 95 per cent of its original strength.

That said, the time and level of skill required for splicing rope means that, in practice, most lines on most boats tend to be joined using knots (or, to use the proper terminology, bends). Bending lines together also has the advantage of allowing you to 'unbend' them should you no longer need such a long length of line.

Probably the most common method of joining lines together is to tie a pair of interlocked bowlines (page 126). A slightly more sophisticated method is to tie the twin bowlines shown on page 109. There are even special knots for large lines which are reluctant to twist into a loop or bight, such as the carrick bend (page 100).

The trouble with all these is that, unlike a splice, the knots tend to bulk up the line, which then snags on fairleads and winches. It also creates additional drag on a tow line or any other line being dragged through the water.

This has led to the creation of a whole sub-category of bends called hawser bends. The main feature of these knots is that, instead of being tightened into a dense ball, they are left 'open' and the ends are seized to the standing parts. This not only makes for a longer, more streamlined knot, which can slip through fairleads and around winches more easily, but it also exerts less stress on the line, making for a stronger join.

The carrick bend (page 100) can be tied in this way, as can the sheet bend (page 90). But the reeving line bend is probably the best knot for the job.

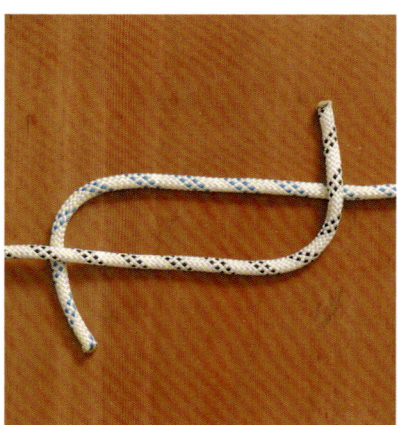

1 Overlap the ends by about 0.5–0.6m (18–24in). Place one end over, and one end under, each other's standing part.

2 Tuck the ends under themselves to create a pair of hitches.

3 Allow at least 75–100mm (3–4in) slack in the ends to make the seizings.

BENDS • 111

Double reeving line bend

Although the seizings in the reeving line bend should provide all the security you need, there are occasions when an extra hitch on each part might be needed. Mainly, this will be when using extremely slippery line – eg high modulus rope such as Dyneema and Spectra. A traditional knot for modern lines? Why not!

KNOT SCORE

Strength
Security
Difficulty Tying
Difficulty Untying
Usefulness

1 Tie a pair of hitches in the standing part of each line, as for the reeving line bend, then add a second hitch in each line. Allow enough spare line to make the seizing.

2 Seize each end to the other line's standing part, either with a temporary seizing, such as a constrictor knot (page 40), or a permanent seizing, such as those shown on pages 284–285.

4 Adjust the hitches so the legs are the same length, and secure the ends with a seizing, as specified in the panel above.

BEST FOR joining two mooring lines

Anyone who has anchored a boat in a secluded bay and tried to run a long line to the shore to hold the stern in position will have experienced the frustration of the line not quite reaching the shore. To stop that happening I usually carry an extra 'just-in-case' line in the dinghy, but which knot is best to tie the two lines together?

It usually happens when there's a strong sidewind. The boat is being blown away from the position in which you carefully lined her up. You need to get a line ashore to stop her drifting off any further – and quick! This isn't the time to mess around with fancy knots: you want an instant solution that will be strong and secure enough to hold the weight of the boat as she's hauled back into position.

Most people will instinctively tie two, interlocking bowlines (page 126). It's not the fastest option, but it's secure and it's a knot most people know and trust. The downside is that the line is likely to chafe where the two loops rub against each other, but perhaps that's a price worth paying. If you do have a bit more time, you might try tying the twin bowline (page 109), which is not only much nicer to look at but doesn't cause as much chafe as the interlocking bowlines.

If you've got slippery mooring lines, then your best bet by far is the fisherman's knot (page 114) – double or triple (page 115), depending on how slippery the line is. This should be in the standard knot repertoire of any modern sailor, so if you haven't learnt it by heart yet, then do it now.

If you are in a real hurry, however, you can't beat the king of bends: the double sheet bend (page 91). It's so simple and so quick to tie, yet so secure. With a little practice, you'll be able to tie this knot in half the time it would take to tie your those interlocking bowlines. You'll get a few funny looks from people on neighbouring yachts who will be amazed that you're entrusting the safety of your yacht to such a flimsy-looking knot. And yet, I moored a 12-ton yacht for two years with a double sheet bend on one of the bow lines, and never had an issue.

What's more, when you want to leave the anchorage, you can release the line and the knot will come apart without any trouble. And what more could you ask for than that?

TWO BOWLINES: The usual solution to tie two lines together in a hurry: a pair of interlocking bowlines (page 126).

TWIN BOWLINES: A more elegant version: twin bowlines (page 109) create less chafe but are quite fiddly to get exactly right.

FISHERMAN'S KNOT: A fisherman's knot (page 114) is the ideal solution for joining two lines made from slippery modern cordage.

SHEET BEND: The sailor's best friend: the double sheet bend (page 91) is simple, secure and easy to tie.

SHEET BEND ON LOOP: A double sheet bend can just as easily be tied using a line with a spliced loop.

Fisherman's knot

The very opposite of the reeving line bend (page 110) is the fisherman's knot. Effectively a pair of overhand knots tied onto the opposing standing part, the knot bulks up excessively and is almost impossible to untie. On the other hand, it is surprisingly secure (especially in its double and triple versions, opposite) and very easy to tie, even with cold hands.

KNOT SCORE

Strength
Security
Difficulty Tying
Difficulty Untying
Usefulness

1 Take a turn with one line around the standing part of the other line, and tie an overhand knot (page 172).

2 Do the same with the other line to create the second overhand knot.

3 Tighten both overhand knots individually before tightening the whole knot.

4 Slide the two overhand knots together. Tighten the knot by pulling the standing parts in opposite directions.

KNOT KNOW-HOW

Convention has it that if a knot attaches a line to a mooring point it's called a hitch, and if it attaches it to another line it's called a bend. That is, except when using small stuff (ie twine, fishing line, etc), in which case it's simply called a knot. This probably explains why the fisherman's knot is called a knot rather than a bend. Originally used to join fishing line, it now has many other uses.

BENDS • 115

Double fisherman's knot

If you're using the fisherman's knot, then you're probably not worried about bulk, so you may as well use the more secure, double version. The same warnings apply about untying the knot. Tie this knot in a mooring line, and after a few days the only way to get rid of it will be to cut it out. If you're joining slippery rope such as Dyneema, this could be a godsend.

KNOT SCORE

Strength
Security
Difficulty Tying
Difficulty Untying
Usefulness

1 Take two turns with the ends of each line around the standing part of the other.

2 Tuck the working ends through both turns to make a pair of double overhand knots.

3 Tighten both overhand knots individually, and then tighten the whole knot by pulling the standing parts in opposite directions.

Triple fisherman's knot

This knot is billed as the ultimate solution for slippery ropes such as Dyneema (shown) or Spectra. It's also popular with climbers, so use it to make a sling that you can trust to hold together – and which you won't need to untie in a hurry.

KNOT SCORE

Strength
Security
Difficulty Tying
Difficulty Untying
Usefulness

1 As above, but this time take three turns around both standing parts, before tucking the ends through all three turns.

2 Tighten both overhand knots individually, and then tighten the whole knot by pulling the standing parts in opposite directions.

Racking bend

Most bends are intended to join lines of roughly similar size and won't work if they are of dramatically different sizes. A typical case is tying a heaving line to a mooring line, when even a sheet bend will struggle to cope. The racking bend is designed for this purpose and can also be used if a loop is already spliced into the end of the mooring line.

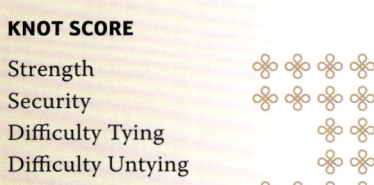

KNOT SCORE

Strength
Security
Difficulty Tying
Difficulty Untying
Usefulness

1 The racking bend can be used with a loop spliced into the thick line, or not (as shown here).

2 Put a bight into the end of the thicker (or stiffer) line. Pass the working end of the thin line through the bight and around the standing part of the thick line.

3 Take a turn around the bight and back over the standing part.

4 Weave the thin line through and around the bight to create a series of figure-eights.

5 Tuck the working end under itself to make a locking turn. Tighten the knot by pulling both parts of the thick line and the standing part of the thin line in opposite directions.

Heaving line bend

If you haven't got time to tie a racking bend (opposite), this quick and easy knot will probably do the job. Unlike the racking bend, however, the heaving line bend should only be regarded as a temporary measure. One exception to this rule is on a Japanese three-stringed shamisen, where it is used to attach the strings to silk eyes at the base of the instrument.

KNOT SCORE
Strength
Security
Difficulty Tying
Difficulty Untying
Usefulness

1 The heaving line bend is used to join two lines of very different diameters, eg heaving line and mooring line – or shamisen string and silk eye.

2 Put a bight in the end of the thick line, and place the working end of the thin line over it.

3 Pass the working end of the thin line around the standing part of the thick line, and tuck it over itself.

4 Tuck the working end under the initial turn. Tighten the knot by pulling both parts of the thick line and the standing part of the thin line in opposite directions.

Single stopper

The end of a really large line may be too stiff to bend around to make a proper bend. In this case, one of the pole hitches from Chapter 2 might work instead (eg studding sail bend, page 56, or either of the claras, pages 66–67). Alternatively, this 'stopper', traditionally used to attach a block to a shroud, will also do the job rather well.

KNOT SCORE
Strength
Security
Difficulty Tying
Difficulty Untying
Usefulness

1 Take a turn with the thin line around the standing part of the thick line.

2 Take another turn, this time around the working end of the thick line.

3 Pass the thin line around its standing part, so that it changes direction, and take two or three turns around the thick line.

4 Tuck the working end under itself, and tighten the knot. Note that the thin line should follow the lay of the big line. If it doesn't, tie the knot again the other way round.

Sansome bend

A neat development of the sheet bend (page 90) is the sansome bend, which apparently originated in the weaving trade in the 19th century. An extra locking turn cleverly inserted at the start of the knot counters the lack of security that is a common complaint about the sheet bend. Use it to tie together bungees, or any other slippery, non-compliant cordage.

KNOT SCORE
Strength
Security
Difficulty Tying
Difficulty Untying
Usefulness

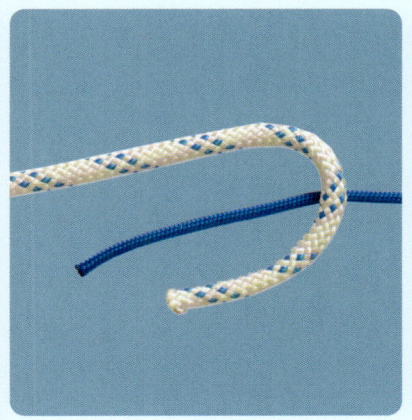

1 Put a bight in the end of the thick line, and pass the end of the thin line under it.

2 Take two turns around the working end of the thick line.

3 Take a turn around the standing part of the thick line, always going in the same direction.

4 Tuck the working end of the thin line through both turns.

5 Tighten the knot by pulling both parts of the thick line and the standing part of the thin line in opposite directions.

Braided splice

Now for something completely different. The braided splice is essentially just a schoolgirl's plait, with the clever addition of a loop at the end to secure the loose end. Like its close sister, the braided loop (page 146), it has an inherent elasticity which allows it to absorb shock, making for a stronger knot. Best used with small, slippery lines.

KNOT SCORE
Strength ❀❀❀❀
Security ❀❀❀❀
Difficulty Tying ❀❀
Difficulty Untying ❀❀❀
Usefulness ❀❀❀

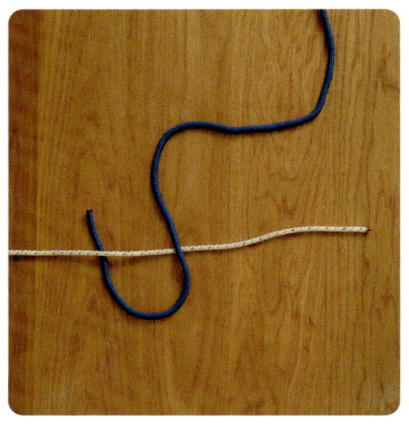

1 Put a bight in one line and pass the other line through it.

2 Pass the working end of the first line over its standing part to make an overhand loop.

3 Cross the working end of the second line to lie over the end of the first line.

4 Cross the lines, alternating from one side to the other, as if plaiting hair.

5 Keep going until you have about 0.3m (1ft) of the second line left.

6 Put a bight in the end of the second line, and carry on plaiting the lines as before.

BENDS • 121

7 When you come to the end of the bight, tuck the other working end through it and cut off any excess.

8 Tighten the knot by pulling the standing parts in opposite directions.

LOOPS 4

Overhand loop

Overhand knots are generally avoided at sea because they are so hard to untie. There are times, however, that a simple overhand loop does the job very effectively – particularly if it's a permanent installation. It also has the advantage of being tied in the bight, which can save a lot of time when tying a series of loops in a line.

KNOT SCORE

Strength ❁ ❁ ❁
Security ❁ ❁ ❁
Difficulty Tying ❁
Difficulty Untying ❁ ❁ ❁
Usefulness ❁ ❁ ❁

1 Put a bight in the line. This can be at either end of the line or any point in between.

2 Put an underhand loop in the bight.

3 Tuck the bight into the loop.

4 Adjust the size of the bight to suit, and tighten the knot.

KNOT KNOW-HOW

There is another way of tying a figure-eight loop (opposite). Simply start tying an overhand loop but take an extra turn around the standing part, as you would with a regular figure-eight. Use the bight to make the loop, and tighten the knot. Also called the Flemish loop, this version of the figure-eight loop is slightly easier to untie than the overhand loop.

LOOPS • 125

Figure-eight loop

There's a definite advantage in basing a knot on an established favourite – particularly when it's a simple knot such as the figure-eight. If all else fails, and you can't see the rabbit for the trees (see bowline, page 126), the figure-eight loop will see you out of a tight spot. Use it for just about everything you'd use a bowline for.

KNOT SCORE
Strength
Security
Difficulty Tying
Difficulty Untying
Usefulness

1 Tie a figure-eight in the standing part. Pass the working end back through the last loop, leaving plenty of slack behind.

2 Feed the working end back through the knot, passing first under itself and the standing part...

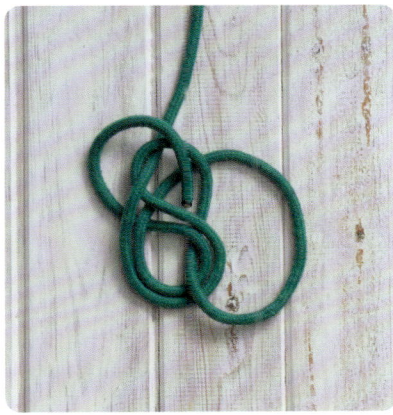

3 ... then over the standing part and back round again.

4 The working end should emerge next to the lower leg of the loop.

5 Adjust the loop and tighten the knot.

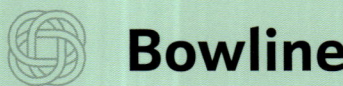# Bowline

It's known as the King of Knots, and for at least 500 years the bowline has been the indisputable loop of choice for sailors. Secure, strong and easy to untie, it seems to have everything going for it. Its reign is under threat, however, not from modern sailing techniques or a newly invented knot, but from modern ropes. So slippery are some high-tech materials, that even the mighty bowline is struggling to hang on to them.

KNOT SCORE

Strength	❁ ❁ ❁ ❁
Security	❁ ❁ ❁
Difficulty Tying	❁ ❁
Difficulty Untying	❁ ❁
Usefulness	❁ ❁ ❁ ❁ ❁

'The devil himself would make a good sailor, if he could only tie a bowline and look aloft.'

So iconic is the bowline, it's become instantly associated with sailors and the sea. Even the most land-bound landlubber knows that sailors drink rum and tie bowlines.

And the reputation of the so-called 'king of knots' is not undeserved. Unlike the clove hitch (page 32), which has become ubiquitous despite being fundamentally flawed, the bowline really is as good as they say it is. Granted, it's not perfect, and in some circumstances it can slip or 'capsize'. But tied correctly, it's not only strong and secure but also, thanks to an inbuilt breaking mechanism (see opposite), guaranteed to come undone when required. For many sailors it's the only loop they'll ever use.

The knot was originally used to attach the 'bow line' of a square sail to prevent it being taken aback, ie being filled by wind on the wrong side of the sail. It was then known as the bowline knot, or even the bowling or boling knot.

As far back as 1627, Captain John Smith wrote in *A Seaman's Grammar & Dictionary*: 'The Boling knot is also so firmly made and fastened by the bridles into the creengles of the sailes, they will breake, or the saile split before it will slip.' That said, there are occasions when a bowline will slip – particularly when using modern ropes, which are far more slippery than their traditional counterparts. Even the later, more secure versions of the knot (pages 129–130) may not prove adequate for these materials. In some cases, such as Dyneema and Spectra, the only sensible option is to splice the rope (page 306).

It's just possible that, after at least 500 years of rule, the king of knots is finally being eclipsed. Who its successor will be is currently being decided on wind-swept decks around the world.

1 Put an overhand loop near the end of the line. (Using the rabbit-around-the-tree analogy, this is the rabbit hole and the standing part is the tree.)

2 Pass the working end through the loop. (This is the rabbit coming out of its hole.)

3 Pass the working end around the standing part. (Now the rabbit is running around the tree.)

LOOPS • 127

4 Tuck the end back into the loop and tighten the knot. (The rabbit runs back into its hole, safe and sound.)

Breaking a bowline

You have to love a knot that has an inbuilt mechanism to untie it, and which will come undone almost no matter how hard it's tightened. Essentially a sheet bend (page 90) which is tied onto itself to form a loop, the bowline can usually be 'broken' in a matter of seconds. Its main drawback is that it cannot be untied (or tied) while there is a strain on the standing part. But it's a small price to pay for such a useful knot.

To 'break' a bowline, clasp the turn and ease it up the standing part. The whole knot will then loosen and can be easily untied.

Fast bowline

The rabbit-around-the-tree method is the most common way of tying a bowline (page 126), but it's not the fastest. The twist method is not only faster, but it can also be tied one-handed – particularly useful if you fall over the side and manage to catch hold of a line, and then have to tie a bowline around yourself while hanging on for dear life.

KNOT SCORE

Strength
Security
Difficulty Tying
Difficulty Untying
Usefulness

1 Form a large loop, and cross the working end over the standing part.

2 Hold the working end in place, while you twist the standing part into an overhand loop. (The rabbit hole!)

3 Pass the working end around the standing part, in the usual manner. (Rabbit goes around tree.)

4 Pass the working end back through the overhand loop and tighten the knot. (Rabbit back in its hole, safe and sound.)

LOOPS • 129

Tucked bowline

Despite all the eulogies to the bowline (page 126), not everyone loves it. Captain Alfred Henry Alston was a dissenter and in 1871 claimed that, 'With a heavy strain a bowline knot often capsizes.' He devised this variation to make the knot more secure, and it's certainly worth getting into the habit of tying it this way when using modern ropes.

KNOT SCORE
Strength
Security
Difficulty Tying
Difficulty Untying
Usefulness

1 Make your loop using either the rabbit-around-the-tree method (page 126) or the fast method (opposite).

2 Pass the working end through the loop, around the standing part and back through the loop, to make your classic bowline.

3 Pass the working end around the nearest leg of the loop and tuck it back under itself, as shown.

4 Tighten the knot by pulling the end and the standing part in the opposite direction from the loop.

Seized bowline

Belts and braces never hurt anyone, and if adding a seizing means you sleep better at night, then it's worth doing. This can be done either with a tucked bowline (as shown) or the regular version of the knot.

KNOT SCORE
Strength
Security
Difficulty Tying
Difficulty Untying
Usefulness

Tie a bowline, then fasten the end to the standing part with either a knot (eg constrictor knot, page 40) or a proper seizing (page 284).

Water bowline

This development of the bowline (page 126) is designed to be used with wet, slippery lines. It also lends itself to use with modern ropes, which tend to slip when tied with a regular bowline. The main difference is that the loop in the standing part is replaced with a clove hitch (page 32), greatly increasing the knot's security.

KNOT SCORE	
Strength	❀❀❀❀
Security	❀❀❀❀
Difficulty Tying	❀❀❀
Difficulty Untying	❀❀
Usefulness	❀❀❀❀❀

1 Make a loop, so that the working end lies on top of the standing part. This is called an overhand loop.

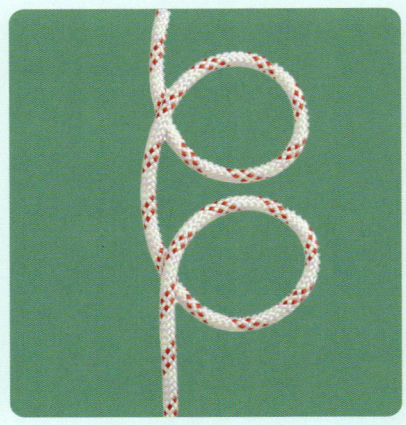

2 Make another loop right underneath, again making sure the working end is on top.

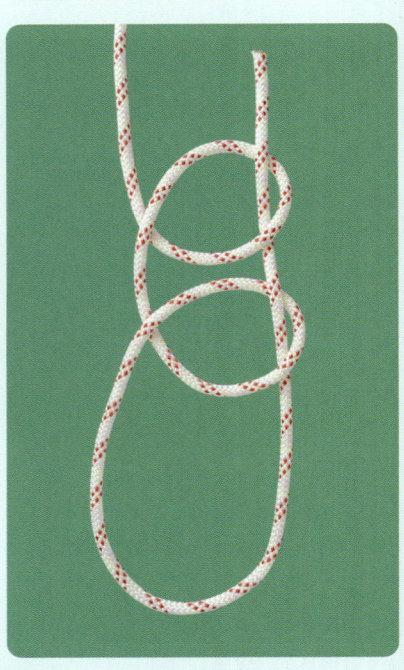

3 Pass the working end up through both loops, making sure it enters each loop from underneath.

4 Take the working end around the standing part and back down through the loops, going back the same way you came up.

5 Hold the standing part firmly and tighten first the first loop and then the second. See Knot Know-How to the right for advice about tail length.

KNOT KNOW-HOW

Make sure your bowline has a long tail. The tail should be at least 100mm (4in) long to prevent the knot from slipping. For added security, seize the end of the tail to the standing part with a piece of whipping twine.

LOOPS • 131

Bowline in the bight

A double loop spreads the load and was, in the past, used as a harness. This version has the advantage that it can be tied in the bight if, for any reason, the ends of the line are not available. Either way, you have to admire the neat way the loop replaces the turn around the standing part. There's no way that's going to slip.

KNOT SCORE

Strength
Security
Difficulty Tying
Difficulty Untying
Usefulness

1 Using the doubled-up line, tie an underhand loop and pass the bight through the loop.

2 Open the bight and pass the big loop through it.

3 Pull the bight over the standing part, and take the slack out by pulling the appropriate leg of the loop.

4 Tighten the knot by pulling the leg and the standing part in opposite directions.

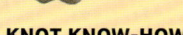

KNOT KNOW-HOW

Double loop knots such as the bowline in the bight and the Spanish bowline (page 161) were originally devised to work as improvised bosun's chairs. No one is allowed to recommend them for this purpose nowadays for fear of litigation, but it's useful to know why a knot was created. You never know when such knowledge might come in useful.

Midshipman's loop

Here's an old friend in a new guise: the rolling hitch (page 39) tied onto its standing part to create a loop. The hitch can then slide up and down the line to adjust the loop, and be tightened once it's the right size. Recommended on land for tent guys and the like, while at sea it can be usefully employed on awning lines, where there is liable to be some stretch.

KNOT SCORE

Strength
Security
Difficulty Tying
Difficulty Untying
Usefulness

1 Take a turn around the mooring point, if appropriate, or put a bight in the end of the line.

2 Pass the working end around the standing part and through the loop.

3 Take a turn around the standing part, outside the loop.

4 Pass the end through the loop. Take another turn around the standing part, outside the loop, and tuck the working end under itself.

5 Tighten the hitches on the standing part, and slide up or down to adjust the size of the loop. Once the loop is the correct size, tighten the knot again.

Angler's loop

If you're looking for a tenacious loop that will hold even slippery line, such as bungee rope, then this might just do the trick. Traditionally used by anglers to tie loops in gut fishing lines, it's got a mighty grip and will probably jam in regular rope. So avoid using it on mooring lines, unless you want a permanent loop, and use it with the small stuff instead.

KNOT SCORE
Strength
Security
Difficulty Tying
Difficulty Untying
Usefulness

1 Form an overhand loop and pass the working end under it.

2 Pass the end through the loop to make an overhand knot, and form a large bight.

3 Pass the working end back through the loop and over the standing part.

4 Tuck the end between the bight and the original loop.

5 Tighten the knot, keeping the end at right angles to the knot as far as possible.

BEST FOR tying a rope harness

Climbing up a mast is always a nerve-wracking experience. You only have to read about round-the-world sailor Ellen MacArthur climbing her boat's mast while sailing across the Atlantic to realise how scary it can be. While most bosun's chairs are 100% secure, it can be reassuring to have a second harness on a second halyard as a back-up. What you need is a good loop or two – or even three.

Did you ever wonder what the point was of tying double and triple loops? Like most knots, they had various practical uses before being becoming part of a hobby. One of these was as harnesses for the poor souls who had to climb up and down the rigging several times a day. It was dangerous work, and being able to tie a good knot could mean the difference between life and death.

Nowadays there's less need to climb the rigging, and those who do usually have a sturdily-made bosun's chair hooked to a reliable modern halyard. It still makes sense to have a second harness as a back up in case the first one fails – even the best modern shackle can break unexpectedly and without warning. Which is where those double and triple loops come in handy.

The classic knot for this purpose is the Spanish bowline (page 161), and there is something very satisfying in the way two interlocked loops which look very much like bowlines emerge from a few cunning twists and tucks. The end result is much more elegant than the process itself. In practice, however, this was the least comfortable option of the harnesses we tried out. As well as feeling unbalanced, the knot had a tendency to slide up one's bottom, which could get quite painful if you had to stay up the mast for any length of time.

A better option was the bowline in the bight (page 131). This was easy to tie – basically like a regular bowline but with a twist at the end – and in practise felt solid and comfortable. It's important to note that the two loops need to be adjusted to size, with a bigger loop at the bottom and a smaller loop to go around the waist.

But the best back-up harness was the simplest of them all: the triple loop bowline (page 164). This really is just a regular bowline tied in the bight to create the first two loops; the third loop is created by the tail end of the knot, which hangs next to the first two loops. In practise, we found it best to pass the legs through the first two loops, and place the third (the original bight) around the waist. This way, the three loops could easily be adjusted to get a good fit.

Last but not least, if you need a harness in an emergency (for example, you've fallen over the side) then a line passed under the armpits and tied with a one-handed bowline (assuming you're using the other hand to hang on for dear life) might just sort you out.

SPANISH BOWLINE: A classic harness knot from the Age of Sail, the Spanish bowline (page 161) is actually quite uncomfortable and unsafe.

BOWLINE IN THE BIGHT: Easy to tie and extremely secure, a bowline in the bight (page 131) is a good option if you want a simple double loop harness.

FAST BOWLINE: The knot of choice if you are being dragged through the water and need to tie a harness in a hurry.

TRIPLE BOWLINE: More is definitely better when it comes to harnesses, and this triple bowline (page 156) is not only secure and comfortable but easy to adjust too.

Honda knot

This is the knot that conquered America – or at least tamed a few of its wild animals. The honda knot (also known as the bowstring knot) was used by cowboys for their lassos, as it can be tied in stiff material. Its use aboard ship is rather more limited, but it should keep the kids entertained and might even come in useful if you're ever stranded on a desert island.

KNOT SCORE

Strength
Security
Difficulty Tying
Difficulty Untying
Usefulness

1 Tie an overhand knot (page 172) in the end of the line, allowing plenty of slack to form the loop.

2 Pass the working end back through the initial loop.

3 Tie a figure-eight (page 174) in the working end.

4 Tighten the overhand knot. The size of the loop can then be adjusted by pulling the figure-eight, and then tightening the overhand knot.

LOOPS • 137

Carrick loop

After the success of the carrick bend, it's not surprising that the same form has been transposed into a loop. The result is a compact knot which, after a little practice, is quickly and easily tied. Use it as an alternative to the bowline (page 126), particularly with traditional cordage, which is less likely to slip.

KNOT SCORE

Strength
Security
Difficulty Tying
Difficulty Untying
Usefulness

1 Make an overhand loop and a bight, as you would for a bowline.

2 Pass the working end through the loop and around the standing part.

3 Pass the working end through the bight and tuck it between itself and the original loop.

4 Tighten the knot.

KNOT KNOW-HOW

The honda knot (opposite) was not the only knot cowboys tied in their lassos. When not out corralling wild animals, they entertained people with lasso tricks, such as the pretzel knot – basically a pair of loops which, when spilled, turned into a figure-eight. Try doing that with your heaving line next time you're stuck in the Doldrums.

Harness loop

A quick and easy knot to tie in the bight, the harness loop should only be used for non-critical purposes. A load needs to be maintained on the loop, or the knot will pull out of shape. Also known as the artillery loop, it's thought to have been used by soldiers for moving guns over hilly or boggy ground. Use it for towing – but not as a harness!

KNOT SCORE
Strength ❀❀❀
Security ❀❀❀
Difficulty Tying ❀❀
Difficulty Untying ❀❀
Usefulness ❀❀❀❀

1 Make an overhand loop in the working end.

2 Pass the end through the loop to make an overhand knot.

3 Form a bight in the loop, and tuck it between the standing part and the working end.

4 Pull the bight through to make the loop, and tighten the knot.

Double harness loop

Although more secure than the harness loop (opposite), the double harness loop is not recommended as a harness either. There are other knots better suited to that purpose, eg the butterfly loop (page 142). It does, however, make a handy loop for hanging objects from once both ends are tied off.

KNOT SCORE

Strength ❀❀❀
Security ❀❀❀
Difficulty Tying ❀❀❀
Difficulty Untying ❀❀❀
Usefulness ❀❀❀

1 Put a bight in the line and twist the standing part to make a loop.

2 Put another bight in the line and pass it through the loop.

3 Pass the first bight through the second bight.

4 Put the second bight through to form the loop.

5 Tighten the knot.

KNOT KNOW-HOW

The artillery weren't the only ones to have their own special knots. Although it's often said that nine-tenths of knots were devised by sailors, many carry the hallmark of other trades, such as the cow hitch (page 53) for farmers, the honda knot (page 136) for cowboys, the bell-ringer's knot (page 215) for bell-ringers, and the hangman's noose (page 158) for the hangman.

Broach loop

Sometimes it's hard to appreciate the beauty of what we've got until we see the alternative. For instance, what would a strong, secure, general purpose loop look like if we didn't already have the bowline (page 126)? The broach loop is one possible answer, and it is arguably at least as strong and secure as its better-known rival. An alternative for ultra-slippery ropes.

KNOT SCORE	
Strength	✽✽✽✽
Security	✽✽✽✽
Difficulty Tying	✽✽✽
Difficulty Untying	✽✽✽
Usefulness	✽✽✽

1 Put an unfinished figure-eight in the end of the line, omitting the final tuck.

2 Pass the working end up through the lower part of the figure-eight, between itself and the standing part.

3 Pass the working end up through the loop and tuck it into the lower part of the original figure-eight.

4 Tighten the knot, working out any slack in the legs and both parts.

Peace knot

A very different approach is required for this loop. Whereas the broach loop (opposite) attempts to achieve maximum strength and security, the peace knot is designed for maximum ease of untying. Pull the drawloop out, and the whole contraption disappears, with no further effort required. Use it as a temporary knot, when a quick getaway is in order.

KNOT SCORE
Strength
Security
Difficulty Tying
Difficulty Untying
Usefulness

1 Put a bight in the standing part.

2 Pass the working end over itself to form a loop, then over and under the initial bight.

3 Pass the working end over and under the standing part...

4 ... and through the loop.

5 Put a bight in the working end and tuck it through the initial bight.

6 Adjust the drawloop to suit, and tighten the knot. To untie: simply pull the end!

Butterfly loop

A much more secure alternative to the harness loop (page 138), the butterfly is popular with climbers as a way of tying a loop in the middle of a line when you don't have access to the ends. Cut the loop off, and it becomes a simple bend (page 92). Use it to create secure mooring points on a line, either for dinghies, fenders or coiled rope.

KNOT SCORE

Strength
Security
Difficulty Tying
Difficulty Untying
Usefulness

1 Twist the bight of the line to create a pair of loops, the top one larger than the lower one.

2 Fold the top loop over the lower one, and put a bight in it.

3 Pass the bight through the smaller loop.

4 Pull the bight through to create a loop, and tighten the knot.

KNOT KNOW-HOW

The butterfly loop is another knot with a long and interesting lineage. Originally named the lineman's rider in 1914, it was said to be popular with, among others, telephone men. It started its mountaineering career in 1928 as the butterfly loop, later the alpine butterfly loop, and it has become widely used ever since.

Eskimo bowline

You might think you already know every bowline variation you'll ever need, but this one has a distinct USP. Whereas the standard bowline (page 126) is likely to collapse when its legs are pulled wide open (who wouldn't?), this version takes such abuse completely in its stride. Aside from that, it's really just a bowline tied on its side...

KNOT SCORE
Strength
Security
Difficulty Tying
Difficulty Untying
Usefulness

1 Pass the line around the object being 'looped' – in this case, a sail bag.

2 Put an overhand loop in the standing part.

3 Pass the working end *down* through the loop, instead of up through the loop as you would for a regular bowline.

4 Pass the working end around *itself* (rather than around the standing part as for a regular bowline) and back *up* through the loop.

5 Tighten the knot by pulling the legs of the loop in opposite directions.

BEST FOR tying a jib sheet

Another line that gets a lot of wear and tear on a boat is the jib or genoa sheet. One moment it's being stretched taut by the sail, the next it's being shaken around like a rabbit in a dog's mouth, and then suddenly it's back to being stretched again. It's also likely to get doused in sea water regularly. It's a dog's life, isn't it?

During the great Age of Sail, sheets were subject to much less strain. There was 'give' in the cotton sail, 'give' in the rigging, 'give' in the sheets themselves, and a block and tackle spread the load and made it possible to pull the sail in by hand. There's no such leeway with modern rigs: modern sails and rigging have very little give, and the sheet usually runs directly from the sail to a winch in the cockpit, via a single turning block. The loads are immense.

The modern solution is to splice an eye into the end of the sheet, or the middle if the two sheets form a single continuous line, which is shackled straight onto the sail. Job done. But woe betide anyone who has to take that sail down in a strong wind, when the clew is thrashing around on the foredeck and the crew is hanging on to the rail for dear life. That's when you'll be grateful for the gentle strength of a knot.

Once again, the classic knot used by many (probably most) sailors in this case is a bowline (page 126). Tie the end of each sheet to the clew cringle and you've got a forgiving and adaptable setup. If one of the sheets gets tangled up, it can easily be untied, untangled, and tied back on. At the end of the day's sail, the sheets can be easily untied, coiled and stowed away.

There is some appeal however in using a single, long length of line for a sheet – not least if you have a long bit of rope you don't want to cut in half. A lot of sailors swear by a simple cow hitch (page 53), whereby the bight is passed through the cringle and the ends are passed through the bight and the line is pulled right through. It's a foolproof option, which is attractive if you're not 100% confident tying a bowline yet. It's also less bulky than two bowlines, which might be helpful to prevent the sail sagging in light winds.

An interesting variation of the cow hitch approach is to only pass one end through the bight. The line is still locked in place, but the wear from the two ropes pulling in different directions is reduced.

Another simple solution often used on dinghies is to run a long line through the cringle and, once its centred, tie a figure-eight (page 174) on each side of the sail to hold the sheet in place. You could even try a butterfly hitch (page 92).

Very occasionally, you might find that the sheet is too big to go through the cringle. In that case, you could attach a shackle to create a bigger 'hole', or you could use the ingenious bubble knot (page 81), as pictured opposite. Or you could just find a thinner line to use as a sheet.

LOOPS • 145

BOWLINES: Yes, it's that bowline (page 126) again! This is the tried and trusted way of tying jib and genoa sheets.

COW HITCH v1: If you're not confident tying a bowline, you can't go wrong with a cow hitch (page 53).

COW HITCH v2 An alternative way of tying a cow hitch which reduces the wear on the line

FIGURE-EIGHT: Another way of using a single long line to make a pair of sheets by tying a figure-eight (page 174) on either side of the sail.

BUBBLE KNOT: The bubble knot (page 81) is designed to attach a line to a cringle that's too small for it. It's fiddly and not very secure but may serve a purpose.

Braided loop

Most of the loops in this chapter have specific practical applications to which they are very well suited – but they're not necessarily the prettiest of knots. When it comes to making a lanyard for your binoculars, for instance, you might feel tempted to go for something a little more decorative. Alternatively, you might just need a good practical knot to put a loop in the end of a fishing line. Either way, the braided loop will serve.

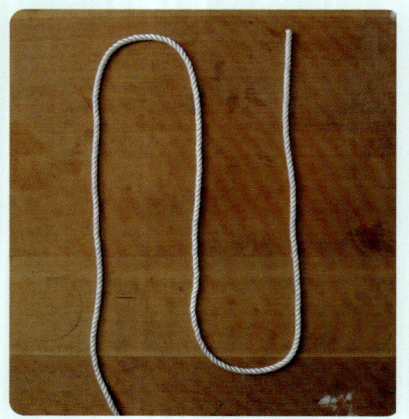

1 Form a pair of bights in the line, leaving a long working end.

2 Pass the left-hand leg over the centre leg, to form two loops.

3 Pass the working end through the lower loop.

7 Pass the working end through the lower loop.

8 Keep going like this for at least four rounds. Then pass the left-hand leg over the centre leg, to form two loops.

9 Put a bight in the working end, and pass it through the lower loop.

LOOPS • 147

KNOT SCORE
Strength
Security
Difficulty Tying
Difficulty Untying
Usefulness

4 Bring what was the left-hand leg back over the centre leg.

5 Pass the working end through the loop.

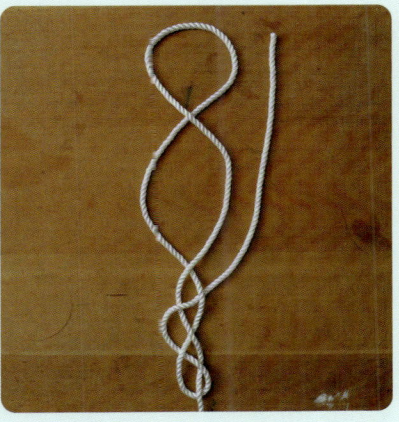

6 Pass the left-hand leg over the centre leg, to form two loops.

10 Close the lower loop, then pass the bight through the upper loop.

11 Keep going like this, weaving the loops in and out, until you run out of line.

12 To finish, pass the bight over the loop, then tighten the bight by pulling on the working end. Trim off any excess line (not shown).

Braided interlocking loop

An interesting method of joining two thin lines is this knot published by British knot-tyer and author Geoffrey Budworth in 1999. Its main advantage is that it spreads the load and therefore the wear and tear over a longer length of line. That means there's less likely to be chafe resulting in a nasty surprise. Apart from that, the knot also has some decorative merit.

1 Tie a fixed loop, such as an overhand loop (page 124), in the end of one line.

2 Put two twists in the loop, and pass the working end of the other line through it. Tie a figure-eight in the end of the second line, a few feet from the end.

3 Pass the end of the second line through the first loop.

4 Repeat until the line is woven through all three loops.

5 Weave the line through the loops again, this time from the opposite side.

LOOPS • 149

6 Make sure the figure-eight is close up under the bottom loop, and weave the working end back through the knot.

7 Tighten the knot, starting with the braid and then the figure-eight.

KNOT SCORE

Strength
Security
Difficulty Tying
Difficulty Untying
Usefulness

Running bowline

If you're trying to throw a noose over something – to recover an object that's fallen overboard, for example – and you can't quite remember how to tie a real lasso (page 136), the running bowline will probably do the job just as well. It's quick and easy to tie because, after all, everyone knows how to tie a bowline – don't they?

KNOT SCORE

Strength
Security
Difficulty Tying
Difficulty Untying
Usefulness

1 Put a bight in the end of the line...

2 ...and put an overhand loop in the working end.

3 Pass the working end around the standing part...

4 ...and back down through the loop.

5 Pass the working end around the nearest leg of the bight, and tuck it into the loop. Tighten the knot. The bowline should run free on the standing part.

LOOPS • 151

Ichabod knot

Another sliding noose, this one designed for that very purpose. Legend has it that it was used as a hangman's noose at Newcastle jail in Delaware, USA, and was also used by local farmers to tether cows. It can be used as a hitch, to a rail or spar. Or you can pass the standing part through the loop and turn it into a 'running ichabod', like the running bowline (opposite).

KNOT SCORE
Strength
Security
Difficulty Tying
Difficulty Untying
Usefulness

1 Put a bight in the end of the line, and pass the working end over the standing part.

2 Take a turn around both legs of the bight.

3 Take another turn around both legs of the bight.

4 Tighten the turns so that the first turn makes a loop at the top of the knot.

5 Tuck the working end through the loop, so that it emerges next to the standing part.

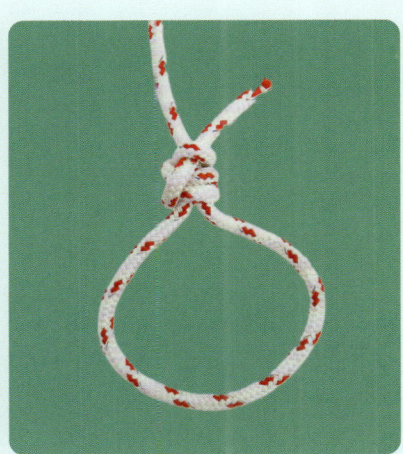

6 Tighten the knot. It should slide up and down the standing part with some resistance, depending on how you wish to use it.

BEST FOR tying a mooring line to a bollard

They say that boats are safest when they're at sea, and that the real problems start once you get close to land. It's true that a lot of damage can be caused by a bad manoeuvre into harbour and from mooring lines coming loose. Choosing the right knot to tie off the mooring lines is therefore an important safety consideration.

Whether you're coming alongside a pontoon or anchoring stern to a quay, you'll need to tie a set of mooring lines to a secure point on land. Most marinas have cleats fitted on their pontoons, in which case a cleat hitch (page 72) is the obvious solution. Elsewhere, you'll encounter a range of bollards, rings and other objects which you'll need to attach a mooring line to.

Once again, the default knot on a mooring line is the trusty bowline (page 126). You can have one ready-tied in the end of the line, or you can tie it on the spot. The advantage of having one ready-tied is that it's much quicker and, even if the loop doesn't fit over the bollard, you can pull a bight through the loop to turn it into a running bowline (page 150), which will fit over most things.

There are of course other loops which can do the job just as well as the bowline. The carrick loop is an interesting variation which is said to be more secure than a bowline (ie less likely to shake out). And if you're worried about the loop slipping off a bollard, then the midshipman's loop (page 132) might be a good option. The main part of the knot (essentially a rolling hitch) slides up and down the standing part, allowing the loop to be tightened. It's also said to be more secure than a bowline, though harder to untie once it's pulled up tight on a bollard.

Another common option is a round turn and two half hitches (page 28), which is extremely adaptable and will work in almost any situation. It's possible to use a clove hitch (page 32) too as a temporary measure, though it's not to be trusted in the long term.

The simplest option of all is a slip line: simply pass the line around the bollard and bring the end back to the boat, where it can be tied off on a cleat. The main drawback is that your mooring line will chafe right in the middle. The advantage is that you don't need to go ashore to untie the line, but can simply cast off, pull the other end in, and away you go!

LOOPS • 153

BOWLINE: A bowline (page 126) can be tied in advance and looped over a bollard or tied in situ.

RUNNING BOWLINE: If a pre-tied bowline doesn't fit, it can be quickly turned into a running bowline (page 146).

CARRICK LOOP: There's no real advantage in tying a carrick loop (page 135), though it is said to be slightly more secure than a bowline.

MIDSHIPMAN'S LOOP: This is an adjustable loop (page 132) which tightens on the bollard, which might be useful, though it is harder to untie.

ROUND TURN & 2 HALF HITCHES: A round turn and two half hitches (page 28) will probably do the trick too, though a loop will cope better if there's a lot of movement.

CLOVE HITCH: The least desirable and least secure option (page 32). Only for temporary use.

Gibbet knot

A 'gibbet' is any device used for public execution, eg gallows, guillotine or executioner's block. This suggests that this knot, like the ichabod (page 151) was used for such purposes, although there is no real evidence to back this up. The gibbet is very similar to the ichabod, but one may suit a certain type of line better than another. Try them both and see.

KNOT SCORE

Strength
Security
Difficulty Tying
Difficulty Untying
Usefulness

1 Make an overhand loop at the end of the line.

2 Pass the working end under the standing part.

3 Take a turn around the bight.

4 Tighten the turns, so the first turn makes a loop at the top of the knot.

5 Take a turn around the nearest leg of the bight, passing the working end through the bight.

6 Tuck the working end into the loop at the top of the knot. Pull the other leg to close the loop, and then tighten the knot.

Locking loop

A newer loop from the creative mind of Harry Asher, the locking loop was first published in 1993. It has the advantage of being easily adjusted by sliding the knot up and down the standing part, and then locking when under a load. A drawloop ensures it can be untied easily. One to try with particularly slippery lines.

KNOT SCORE
Strength
Security
Difficulty Tying
Difficulty Untying
Usefulness

1 Put an overhand loop in the end of the line.

2 Put another overhand loop in the end, crossing the working end over the first loop. Pass the end under the first loop.

3 Tuck the working end under the standing part, where it is visible through the second loop. Tighten the knot.

4 To put a drawloop in the knot, put a bight in the end before the final tuck. Adjust the drawloop to suit before tightening the knot as above.

Slip & nip loop

There's a certain deliberate logic to this knot which is fascinating to knot-tyers: the two turns act like a pair of jaws, which 'bite' the end more tightly as more weight is applied to the loop. And there's an echo of the bowline (page 126) in the way the knot can be broken by pulling the two loops apart. For the rest of us, it's just a jolly useful, all-round noose.

KNOT SCORE
Strength ❀ ❀ ❀ ❀
Security ❀ ❀ ❀ ❀
Difficulty Tying ❀ ❀ ❀
Difficulty Untying ❀ ❀ ❀
Usefulness ❀ ❀ ❀

1 Put an underhand loop in the end of the line.

2 Take a turn around the loop with the working end, in the same direction.

3 Pass the working end around the loop again, as if taking another turn, but this time tuck the end over the standing part as you go under the knot.

4 The working end should emerge between the two turns on the standing part.

5 Tighten the knot. This picture shows the other side of the knot after tightening, clearly showing the end trapped between the two 'jaws', or turns.

LOOPS • 157

Adjustable loop

Although bearing a superficial resemblance to the ichabod and gibbet knots (pages 151 and 154), this adjustable loop differs in that most of the turns are taken around the standing part alone. While this can be very effective with small stuff, such as cords and lanyards, it should be avoided when using thicker line as this will be reluctant to make such tight turns.

KNOT SCORE
Strength
Security
Difficulty Tying
Difficulty Untying
Usefulness

1 Put a bight in the end of the line, and take a turn around the standing part as if tying an overhand knot (page 172).

2 Take another turn around the standing part, in the same direction as before.

3 Pass the working end around both legs of the bight...

4 ... and tuck it under itself.

5 Tighten the knot. A drawloop left in the final tuck will make untying easier.

Hangman's knot

It's probably the most famous knot in the world, instantly recognisable to almost anyone due to its morbid associations. It has inspired films, books and songs – and there are superstitious beliefs about exactly how it should be tied. Yet the hangman's knot does have other uses, apart from hanging people. And it's up to you how many turns you put in it.

KNOT SCORE
Strength
Security
Difficulty Tying
Difficulty Untying
Usefulness

'Did you ever see a hangman tie a hangknot?/I've seen it many a time and he winds, he winds/After thirteen times he's got a hangknot.'
(Woody Guthrie, *Hangknot, Slipknot*)

There are several knots that can be used for hanging, including the ichabod and gibbit (pages 151 and 154) and the scaffold knot (page 160). Even a common running noose such as the honda knot (page 136) or running bowline (page 150) will serve the purpose. But the most iconic by far is the hangman's knot.

As Woody Guthrie suggests in his 1963 song, the number of turns in the knot is significant. One school of thought recommends 13, presumably to underline the condemned person's bad luck, while another says nine, so that 'even if a man has as many lives as a cat, there shall be a full turn for each one of them' (*Ashley's Book of Knots*).

Either way, the hangman's knot is particularly suited to the task, partly because it's difficult to untie, but also because it's more likely to break the person's neck, which is the desired result, rather than strangle them.

Aside from this morbid function, the hangman's knot does have other applications. Anglers know it as the 'uni' knot, where its multiple turns can tame even the most slippery line.

Aboard ship, it can be used to attach an eye in the end of a line, in place of a splice.

In practice, the number of turns you put in depends on how slippery the line is and also how easily you want the noose to run: the more turns there are, the greater the friction, and therefore the tighter the knot's grip. In most of the above instances, six to eight turns should usually suffice.

Back to Woody for the grand finale: 'I don't know who makes the law for that hangknot/But the bones of many a men are whistling in the wind/Just because they tied their laws with a hangknot.'

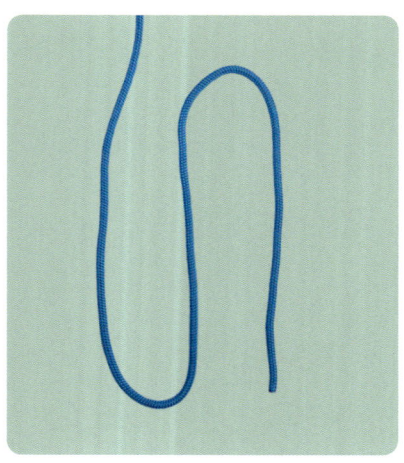

1 Put a pair of bights in the end of the line.

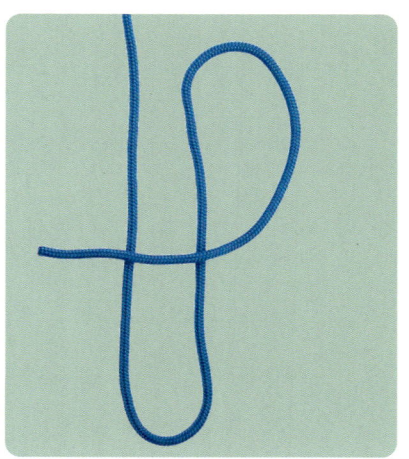

2 Pass the working end over both bights.

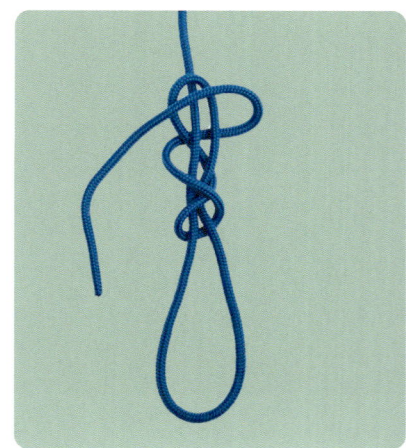

3 Keeping the bights in situ, wind the working end around both bights, working from the bottom upwards.

LOOPS • 159

4 Once the required number of turns are complete (6–8 for an eye 'splice', 9–13 for a hanging), tuck the end through the topmost bight.

5 Tighten the knot by working the slack upwards through the end.

KNOT KNOW-HOW

The hangman's noose wasn't always tied in the form of a knot. The standard executioner's kit issued in the UK until the 1960s included a running noose with a hard eye (page 296) spliced into the end of the line. The noose was traditionally placed behind the condemned person's left ear. Other items in the kit included a hood, various straps, and a bottle of whisky, to calm the prisoner's nerves.

Scaffold knot

Hangmen were once busy people and didn't always have time to tie the full hangman's knot, which is presumably why they devised this quick, easy-to-tie version with fewer turns (three for luck?). Joking aside, the scaffold knot makes a good, simple sliding noose which can also be used as a hitch on a rail or spar. And it won't give anyone the creeps.

KNOT SCORE

Strength
Security
Difficulty Tying
Difficulty Untying
Usefulness

1 Put an underhand loop in the end of the line.

2 Take a turn around the loop with the working end.

3 Take another turn around the loop – more if required.

4 Pass the working end through the turns, so it emerges next to the standing part.

5 Tighten the knot, making sure the turns stay side by side.

Spanish bowline

The ever-versatile bowline (page 126) is brilliantly developed in this classic knot from the Age of Sail. Although originally devised as a substitute bosun's chair, for health and safety reasons such usage is not recommended nowadays. Use it instead to create a double attachment point or to spread the load when lifting something heavy.

KNOT SCORE
Strength
Security
Difficulty Tying
Difficulty Untying
Usefulness

1 Find the middle of the line and make a large bight. Bend the bight behind the twin standing parts to create two loops.

2 Twist the top of both loops inwards to make two smaller loops at the top. Keep the bight big as you'll need plenty of slack there later.

3 Pass the left loop through the right loop by crossing over the right hand standing part (nearest middle).

4 Pass the large left-hand loop through the small loop directly above it (this is when you need that slack!).

5 Do the same with the other side so that you end up with a pair of 'ears' above. Make sure the knot is symmetrical.

6 Adjust the loops and tighten the knot.

BEST FOR making a rope ladder

Some long-distance cruising yachts have steps fitted to the mast. This makes life much easier when someone needs to go up in a bosun's chair, as they can carry most of their weight rather than leaving it to the person on the halyard winch to do all the work. Failing that, you can improvise a rope ladder which you can hoist up the mast with a halyard to assist in a mast hoist, as well as providing some back-up should the bosun's chair fail.

We've all been there: sweating at the bottom of the mast, winching someone up in a bosun's chair and wishing they'd help out just a little. Or perhaps you've been that person in the bosun's chair, trying to find something to hang onto to take the load off the halyard, and getting scratched and frustrated in the process. Why didn't anyone think of attaching steps to the mast? Most Tall Ships have ratlines running up their shrouds that get around this problem. But for the rest of us a simple rope ladder might offer a solution.

An obvious knot to turn a length of rope into a ladder is the harness loop (page 138) – except that not only is this knot tedious to tie, but it is extremely unstable too. We couldn't recommend it for this purpose, so we didn't bother photographing it either.

A much better option is the double harness loop (page 139), which is not only much more secure than its single cousin but, crucially, can be tied in the bight. This is extremely important if you're tying a dozen or more steps on a long length of rope. All in all, the double harness loop seemed up to the job and was moderately easy to tie.

Our preferred knot for this purpose, however, is not a boating knot but a classic mountaineering knot: the butterfly loop (page 142). Like the double harness loop, it is designed to be tied in the bight, so you can rattle out a whole series of steps with ease. Not only was it easy to tie, but it was the most secure of the lot.

Another mountaineering knot that can be useful when climbing a mast is the prusik (page 194). Make a loop out of a thin length of line about 3ft long by tying the ends together with a double fisherman's knot (page 115). Use the loop to tie a prusik knot onto the boat's rigging and you've got a ready-made grip which will assist you on the way up and act as a brake on the way down.

HARNESS LOOP: A much more secure version of its single cousin, the double harness loop (page 139) made a moderately good rope ladder.

BUTTERFLY LOOP: Trust the climbers to have the best climbing knots: the butterfly loop (page 140) made the best rope ladder.

LOOPS • 163

PRUSIK RIGGING BRAKE: A 'prusik brake' is a useful piece of equipment to have while climbing a mast. Tie the ends of a length of rope together with a double fisherman's knot (page 115), then attach the 'brake' to the rigging with a prusik knot.

Triple loop bowline

If two loops spread the load better than one, then three loops will surely spread it even better. That's the logic for this cunning triple loop. What's more, you don't even need to learn a new knot to tie it. Observant readers will note that it's nothing more than a bowline (page 126) tied not in the bight, but with the bight. Read on...

KNOT SCORE

Strength
Security
Difficulty Tying
Difficulty Untying
Usefulness

1 Put a bight in the end of the line, allowing enough slack to form the three loops.

2 Put an overhand loop in the bight, doubling up the line to do so.

3 Pass the end of the bight through the loop. (Remember the rabbit analogy: here they are peeping out of the hole.)

4 Pass the bight around the doubled-up standing part, allowing plenty of slack. (Here they are running around a pair of trees.)

5 Pass the bight back through the loop. (The rabbits are back in the hole.)

6 Pull the bight through to make the third loop. Adjust the loops to the desired sizes, and tighten the knot.

Double angler's loop

It might look like a coil gone wrong, but the double angler's loop is a very effective way of creating a double loop. Like its close relation the angler's loop (page 133), it has a sharp grip and is liable to jam. So it's best used with small stuff, such as bungee cord or fishing line, rather than mooring lines or halyards.

KNOT SCORE
Strength ❀❀❀
Security ❀❀❀
Difficulty Tying ❀❀
Difficulty Untying ❀❀❀
Usefulness ❀❀

1 Tie an overhand knot (page 172), and put a bight in the end of the line.

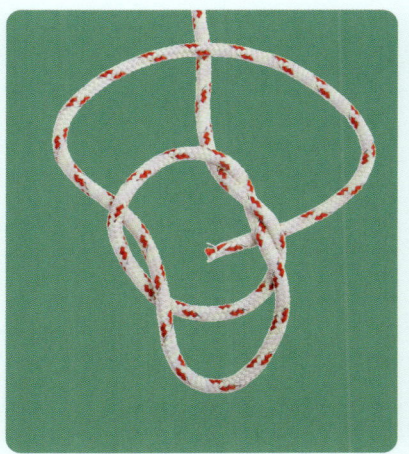

2 Pass the working end through the loop (ie the overhand knot), across the standing part, and back up through the loop.

3 Pass the working end through the loop again and over the standing part, to make the second bight/loop.

4 Tuck the working end behind both parts of the initial overhand knot/loop, so that it emerges on the other side.

5 Tighten the knot by pulling the standing part, and adjust the loops to suit the purpose.

Tom fool's knot

Although known as a handcuff knot for tying up prisoners, the tom fool's knot was probably originally intended to hobble animals when they were left to graze in the wild. It is also used by firefighters as a rescue chair, and is said to be just as effective as the more popular handcuff knot (opposite). Use it to tie a pair of oars together, or to lash them to the rails.

KNOT SCORE

Strength ❀ ❀ ❀ ❀
Security ❀ ❀ ❀ ❀
Difficulty Tying ❀ ❀ ❀
Difficulty Untying ❀ ❀
Usefulness ❀ ❀ ❀

1 Form a pair of underhand loops and place them side by side as shown.

2 Slide the lefthand loop over the righthand loop so they overlap.

3 Pull a bight from one loop through the other loop, and vice versa.

KNOT KNOW-HOW

As well as serving many functions aboard ship, the tom fool's knot is a popular 'trick' knot among sailors and landlubbers alike. The conjurer holds the line in both hands, weaving the loops in and out of each other, and challenges the audience to do the same. Despite the knot's apparent simplicity, it's surprisingly difficult to follow, let alone repeat.

4 Use the lower legs of the loops to adjust their size, and use the upper legs to tighten the knot.

LOOPS • 167

Handcuff knot

One of the problems with keeping a sailing dinghy aboard a yacht is where to store all those pesky spars. One solution is to lash them to the rail, or even to a convenient beamshelf or other anchoring point below deck. Either way, the handcuff knot is a neat way of carrying them and then lashing them down. The extra half turns give that added bit of security.

KNOT SCORE
Strength ❁❁❁
Security ❁❁❁
Difficulty Tying ❁❁❁
Difficulty Untying ❁❁❁
Usefulness ❁❁❁❁

1 Make an underhand loop...

2 ... followed by another underhand loop.

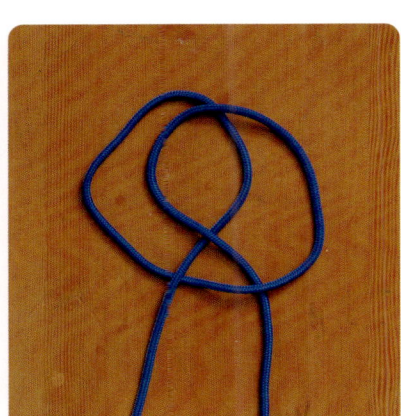

3 Overlap the loops, placing the righthand loop over the lefthand loop.

4 Pull a bight from one loop through the other, and vice versa. Adjust the loops, and tighten the knot.

5 Tie a half hitch around each loop with the adjacent standing part.

BEST FOR tying a halyard

It's one of the most important knots you'll ever tie, and it comes under enormous strain, particularly in heavy weather. So which knot should you use to tie a halyard to a sail? The obvious contenders won't always work, and it might take some lateral thinking to achieve the desired result. Might isn't necessarily king when it comes to halyard tying.

Given the important role they play on sailing yachts, it's perhaps not surprising that many halyards are equipped with dependable metal fittings, such as shackles and quick release clips, which are spliced securely into the end of the line. It's the foolproof solution surely? Yet shackles can be hard to undo, requiring you to carry a tool to open them, and even a substantial, relatively new quick release clip can snap unexpectedly. I know; it happened to me. By contrast, a knot should always untie without needing any tools, and won't break unexpectedly – providing it's correctly tied in the first place.

What we need is a secure knot that's easily untied, no matter how much strain is put on the line. No one wants to be responsible for the sail coming crashing down during a storm. The obvious contender is the ubiquitous bowline (page 126). You could tie your halyard with a bowline all day long, and I doubt it would ever come undone. Likewise a round turn and two half hitches (page 28) or even a buntline hitch (page 30), as used on the square-riggers during the Age of Sail. If you're in doubt, try a tucked bowline (page 129), as shown opposite.

The problem with all of these, however, is that they are bulky – the tucked bowline being the bulkiest of the lot – and there may not be enough space between the head of the sail and the halyard pulley at the top of the mast to accommodate them.

To find a really compact way of attaching the halyard, you might need to go back to your dinghy sailing days. Many dinghies are fitted with a plain halyard which you simply pass through the cringle at the top of the sail and tie a figure-eight (page 174) to stop it coming out. In most cases, a figure-eight will reliably untie with relative ease. On a big rig with much bigger forces at work, a better option might be to pass a bight through the cringle (assuming it's big enough) and lock it in place with a figure-eight tied in the end of the line. Either way, both approaches allow the head of the sail to be hoisted right up to the pulley, if needed.

It might sound a bit lightweight for such an important role, yet often the simplest solutions are the best. And you'll never have to worry about a shackle corroding, jamming, breaking or dropping over the side ever again!

KNOTS • 169

BOWLINE: A well-tied bowline (page 126) with a small loop should sit snugly at the head of the sail and not interfere with hoisting it.

TUCKED BOWLINE: For extra security, use a tucked bowline (page 129), though it may be too bulky for some situations.

BUNTLINE: Another valid option is a buntline hitch (page 30), though this will be much harder to release.

FIGURE-EIGHT LOOP: A figure-eight (page 174) is a delightfully simple option, often used on dinghies, though it might be hard to untie.

FIGURE-EIGHT IN LOOP: A figure-eight passed through its own bight is usually easier to release.

KNOTS 5

Overhand knot

It's so simple, the overhand knot barely deserves a place in a knot book. And it's probably one of the few knots most of us can tie with our eyes closed. But, while most sailors will tell you it should never be used aboard ship, the DNA of the overhand knot runs right through many of the more complicated knots we tie every time we go to sea.

KNOT SCORE

Strength
Security
Difficulty Tying
Difficulty Untying
Usefulness

There is an argument that the overhand knot should be the first item in any book of knots – not just because it's the easiest to tie, but also because it's the basis of so many other knots. However, due to the way knots are arranged in 'families' (ie hitches, loops, knots, etc), that would mean starting this book with a chapter that also included atypical knots such as the monkey's fist (page 186) and the prusik bottle sling (page 194). Which is why the overhand knot finds itself where it is now.

Yet there's no denying how fundamental the overhand knot is to a great many fancier and more highly ranked knots. Add another turn, and it forms the ubiquitous figure-eight (page 174). Rearrange it around a rail, and it becomes a half hitch. Rearrange it twice around a rail with a turn, and it becomes a round turn and two half hitches (page 28). The overhand knot is also evident in the structure of knots as varied as the strangle knot (page 44), the zeppelin bend (page 98), the fisherman's knot (page 114), the angler's loop (page 133) and the sheepshank (page 188).

Despite being imitated in dozens of sailing knots, the overhand knot itself is rarely used aboard ship. The reason for this is not that it isn't secure enough – quite the contrary, it's too secure. The overhand knot has a tendency to jam and can be difficult to untie without damaging the line it's been tied into. Which is why the figure-eight knot was invented. Although the figure-eight doesn't provide much extra bulk as a stopping knot, it does untie more easily. Plus it's much prettier to look at.

But, as well as providing an interesting DNA trace, the overhand knot does have a few uses at sea. You can use it to secure reefing points to the sail, one being tied on either side of the sail. As you're unlikely to want to take these out and since the figure-eight doesn't provide any more bulk, an overhand knot will do just fine here. And you can use it as stops for a rope ladder, or even as grips for a footrope.

Whoever said the overhand knot should never be used aboard ship?

1 Form an overhand loop.

2 Tuck the working end in the loop.

3 Tighten the knot. Well done, you just tied the knot that helped reef a thousand ships!

Double overhand knot

Very slightly more complicated than the overhand knot (opposite) is the double overhand knot. For all its similarities, it makes for a much more interesting-looking fixture. Perhaps that's why it was used on the ends of a cat-o'-nine tails and other whips, thereby earning itself the alternative name of 'blood knot'. Shudder...

KNOT SCORE

Strength
Security
Difficulty Tying
Difficulty Untying
Usefulness

1 Tie a 'simple' overhand knot, as shown opposite.

2 Pass the working end through the loop a second time, going in the same direction as the first turn.

3 Tighten the knot to form a neat, square 'X'.

Slipped overhand knot

The obvious solution for a jamming knot is to insert a drawloop to make it easier to untie. Contrary to expectations, a drawloop doesn't weaken a knot – if anything, the evidence suggests it makes it stronger.

KNOT SCORE

Strength
Security
Difficulty Tying
Difficulty Untying
Usefulness

1 Form a loop in the usual manner (see opposite) and put a bight in the working end.

2 Tuck the bight through the loop, adjust the size of the drawloop, and tighten the knot.

Figure-eight knot

This is the stopper knot of choice aboard most vessels, where it is normally used to prevent a line slipping through a hole, eg sheets through a block or jammer. Although not any bulkier than the overhand knot (page 172), it is much easier to untie and equally strong. Also known as the flemish knot, it forms the basis of several other, more complicated knots.

KNOT SCORE

Strength
Security
Difficulty Tying
Difficulty Untying
Usefulness

1 Put an underhand loop in the end of the line, and pass the working end around the standing part.

2 Tuck the working end under and up through the initial loop.

3 Tighten the knot by pulling the end and the standing part in opposite directions.

Slipped figure-eight knot

Although it's unlikely to get jammed, the figure-eight knot still requires a few moments to untie. The addition of a drawloop in the final stage allows it to be untied almost instantaneously. Handy if you're in a hurry.

KNOT SCORE

Strength
Security
Difficulty Tying
Difficulty Untying
Usefulness

1 Form an underhand loop, pass the working end around the standing part, and put a bight in the end of the line.

2 Tuck the bight up through the initial loop, to create a drawloop. Adjust the size of the bight, then tighten the knot.

KNOTS • 175

Stevedore knot

Stevedores were the men who unloaded the cargo from ships after they came into port. This knot was used by them in preference to other stopper knots because it's bulkier and easier to untie – although it doesn't fill a bigger hole than the overhand (page 172) or figure-eight (opposite) knots. From the dockside, the knot boarded ship and soon gained favour among seamen too.

KNOT SCORE

Strength ❁❁❁
Security ❁❁❁
Difficulty Tying ❁
Difficulty Untying ❁❁
Usefulness ❁❁❁

1 Put a bight in the end of the line, and take a turn around the standing part with the working end.

2 Take another half turn around the standing part.

3 Turn the working end through the loop.

4 Tighten the knot by pulling the end and the standing part in opposite directions.

KNOT KNOW-HOW

The figure-eight knot (opposite) also features in heraldic symbols, most notably of the Italian House of Savoy. There, it appears above the motto *Stringe ma non costringe*, ie 'It tightens, but does not constrain', which sums it up nicely. Car lovers might recognise the knot from the Alfa Romeo badge, which included two figure-eight, or Savoy, knots until 1972.

Ashley's stopper

There is a tradition in knot-tying that knots are rarely named after people – no doubt in recognition of the fact that most knots have been around for centuries before they are 'discovered' by someone and claimed as their own. One exception is the Matthew Walker knot (page 238), named after an unknown historic figure. Another is Ashley's stopper, named after the man who did more than anyone else to promote the art of knot-tying.

KNOT SCORE
Strength
Security
Difficulty Tying
Difficulty Untying
Usefulness

The weight of history hangs heavily on this knot. For this is the knot that Clifford Ashley devised when he was trying to replicate a stopper knot he'd spotted on an oyster boat on the Delaware Bay one spring around 1910.

The knot in question turned out to be nothing more than a figure-eight (page 172) tied into a swollen old length of line. But the investigation it prompted and the invention of what he named the oysterman's stopper got Ashley hooked on knots.

Over the next 30 years, he spent all of his spare time researching the history of knots used by various trades across the United States, culminating in the publication of his totemic *The Ashley Book of Knots* in 1944. More than any other publication, it was this book which revived interest in the art of knot-tying and led to the current enthusiasm for the activity. And it was all because of a misleading knot on a fishing boat that pricked Ashley's interest over a century ago.

The knot he devised may or may not be original (most knots turn out to be centuries old) but it certainly makes an effective stopper. Based on a simple overhand noose tightened on its own end, it fills a larger hole than either the overhand or figure-eight knot. And it has a pleasing, trefoil-like appearance.

In recognition of his vast contribution to the world of knot-tying, the knot is now usually referred to as Ashley's stopper.

1 Form an underhand loop in the end of the line, and place it over the standing part as shown.

2 Pull a bight out of the standing part and pull it through the loop to make a noose. Pass the working end over the standing part.

3 Tuck the working end through the noose from the back to the front. Pull the standing part to close the noose, and tighten the knot.

Quatrefoil

Literally meaning 'four leaves', the quatrefoil stopper is made up of four loops, or 'rims'. It's the next step up from the trefoil-shaped Ashley's stopper knot (page 176) and fills an even larger hole. Like all the stopper knots in this book, it can be used not only to prevent a line pulling through a hole, but also as a grip to prevent the line slipping through your hands.

KNOT SCORE

Strength
Security
Difficulty Tying
Difficulty Untying
Usefulness

1 Form an overhand loop in the standing part and a bight in the working end. Pass the end through the loop and under the bight.

2 Pass the working end over the bight, under itself, and through the initial loop, as shown.

3 Pass the working end over the bight once again.

4 Work the slack out of the knot through the standing part, keeping the end short.

5 Tighten the knot, and trim the end as required.

Cinquefoil

If a quatrefoil (opposite) is made up of four loops, or 'rims', then it follows that the cinquefoil has five. Bigger but not necessarily better than its four-leafed brother, the cinquefoil does fill an even bigger hole, but it's also less stable and has a tendency to lose its shape. Use it for more decorative rather than strictly practical purposes.

KNOT SCORE

Strength
Security
Difficulty Tying
Difficulty Untying
Usefulness

1 Form one overhand loop and one underhand loop in the end of the line, as shown.

2 Overlap the loops, so the first is contained within the second.

3 Pass the working end under the two right-hand strands. Then bring it back to the front and pass it under the two left-hand strands.

4 Tuck the working end through the first loop, so it emerges in the middle of the knot.

5 Tighten the knot, working any slack through to the standing part. Trim the end to size.

Reef knot

The reef knot is probably as old, or older, than sailing itself. And, if you want to reef a sail or tie a ligature, there's probably no better knot. But beware using it to tie two lines together, as this can be downright dangerous. There's very good reason why the knot is featured here rather than in the earlier chapter on bends.

The ancient Greeks knew it as the Heracles knot, and the Romans as the knot of Hercules. It features on ancient Egyptian sculptures and has been used in jewellery since ancient times. As the 'love knot', it is used to symbolise the union of two people, often in the form of a ring. As the 'square knot', it has been used to bind everything from parcels to ligatures. And, as the 'reef knot', it has been used for furling sails on ships for centuries.

The reef knot, then, is one of the oldest and most symbolic knots in existence. It's also fundamentally unstable and relies on being pressed against something for its security. Which is why it's brilliant for tying together packages and suchlike, but extremely unreliable for 'bending' together two unsupported lines.

Ashley goes as far as to say: 'Employed as a bend (to tie two rope ends together), the reef knot is probably responsible for more deaths and injuries than have been caused by the failure of all other knots combined.' Strong words indeed.

Another reason the reef knot is so distrusted by seasoned knot-tyers is because of its close resemblance to even less stable knots. As the saying goes: 'Right over left, left over right, makes a knot both tidy and tight.'

Tie right over right, or left over left, on the other hand, and you end up with that most despicable of things: a granny knot. Tie it with the ends emerging on different sides, and you've got another undesirable: a thief knot.

Legend has it that sailors used the thief knot to tie up their ditty bags. If someone was tempted to open the bag and steal from it, they would instinctively close it again with a reef knot. The sailor would then immediately know his bag had been tampered with.

In practice, there's little difference between the thief knot and a true reef knot – except that if you pull both ends of the thief knot it will 'capsize', whereas the same action will tighten a reef knot. But why risk it? Tie a true reef knot every time.

1 The reef knot is best used to bind objects using lines of the same size.

2 Right over left and under... overlay the two lines as shown.

KNOTS • 181

KNOT SCORE

Strength
Security
Difficulty Tying
Difficulty Untying
Usefulness

3 Left over right and under... passing the ends around each other again, but in the opposite direction to the first twist.

4 Tighten the knot by pulling both adjacent parts in opposite directions. Note that both ends should emerge on the same side of the knot.

Heaving line knot

The classic heaving line knot, used to weight the end of a line to make it easier to throw from ship to shore, is the monkey's fist (page 186). If you haven't got time to tie that, then this heaving line knot, closely based on the hangman's knot, will make an adequate substitute. You can add weight to it by wrapping a piece of lead around the initial bights.

KNOT SCORE
Strength
Security
Difficulty Tying
Difficulty Untying
Usefulness

1 Form a pair of bights in the standing part. Pass the working end through the initial bight and over the standing part.

2 Pass the working end under the initial bight and over the right-hand leg.

3 Working clockwise, take a turn around both bights, leaving the top of the initial bight exposed.

4 Take as many turns around the bights as required, working from the top down. After the final turn, tuck the working end through the bight at the bottom of the knot.

5 Tighten the turns, then pull the appropriate leg of the top bight to tighten the lower bight. Pull the standing part to tighten the upper bight.

Martha's vineyard heaving line knot

This is a neat way of making a heaving line knot using a length of old rope. You can then attach it to a throwing line as and when you need it. Use soft rope so you don't have to worry when you throw it at someone's head!

KNOT SCORE
Strength
Security
Difficulty Tying
Difficulty Untying
Usefulness

1 Form three loops in the end of the line.

2 Pass the working end through the loops, and then under itself.

3 Take a couple of turns around the initial three loops.

4 Put in as many turns as required, working from top to bottom. Tuck the working end through the initial three loops, and tighten the knot.

5 To attach to a heaving line, pass the end of the line through the initial three loops.

6 Tie a bowline, or splice the end of the heaving line to its own standing part, as shown, using a soft eye splice (page 297).

BEST FOR tying a stopper knot

We've all done it. We've all experienced that terrible moment when we release the jib sheet, the boat comes about and we go to pull the sheet on the other side – and it's not there! Someone forgot to tie a stopper knot in the end of the line and now the sail is flailing about and the skipper is shouting and you've got to scramble onto the foredeck to retrieve it. All for the sake of one little knot.

It could be worse. Imagine what it's like when, in the middle of a long passage, you go to hoist the mainsail and the end of the halyard is missing. Someone forgot to tie a stopper knot and the pulling end of the halyard is now inside the mast. The only solution is to climb up the mast, send a 'mouse' down the roller, and reroute the halyard. Not fun when you're rolling around in a nasty swell, miles away from land.

It doesn't take a minute to tie a stopper knot in the end of a line to stop that happening. Which one is best, though? According to the law of evolution, the knot that is most commonly used for this purpose (and is therefore the 'fittest') is the figure-eight (page 174). It is sufficiently bulky for most situations and easier to untie than a plain overhand knot (page 172). And that should have been that. Job done. Except there is always room for improvement, and in this case that means a bulkier knot, less likely to pull through the sheet block, or halyard pulley.

One obvious way to make the figure-eight bigger is to take an extra turn around the standing part before passing the working end through the loop and tightening up. The stevedore knot (page 175) does just that, and was soon adopted by the dock workers from which it derives its name – although in truth it's not really any bulkier than a figure-eight.

A similar approach was taken with the overhand knot to create the double overhand knot, a pretty little knot which serves well on the end of a cat-o'-nine tails but won't stop that sheet disappearing over the side.

One man who was up to the challenge of finding a better stopping knot than the figure-eight was knot guru Clifford Ashley. He stumbled across what he considered a new knot while trying to replicate a stopper knot he saw on an oyster boat on Delaware Bay. He named his knot the oysterman's stopper, but most knot-tyers now refer to it as Ashley's stopper in recognition of his invaluable contribution to the world of knots.

Ashley's stopper is undoubtedly the best stopper knot in the business and yet, the law of evolution notwithstanding, the figure-eight continues to prevail.

FIGURE-EIGHT: The winner in the stopper knot 'survival of the fittest' contest is undoubtedly the figure-eight (page 174).

STEVEDORE: Add an extra turn and you've got yourself a stevedore knot (page 175), which looks good but isn't any bulkier than a figure-eight.

DOUBLE OVERHAND: The double overhand (page 173) isn't any bulkier than a figure-eight either, but it does have a certain charm.

CINQUEFOIL: Proof that bigger isn't always better, the cinquefoil is certainly bulky but it's also fussy and, frankly, looks quite silly.

ASHLEY: The king of stopper knots is undoubtedly Ashley's stopper, discovered by the man himself. Learn it, use it, teach it.

Monkey's fist

Often imitated but never equalled, the monkey's fist is the ultimate heaving line knot and has been used as such since at least 1889. Traditionally, a ball bearing, wooden ball or marble was inserted into the middle to give the knot extra weight and help it on its way. Although mostly associated with ships, the monkey's fist was also used as a weapon called a slungshot, and was banned in some states in the USA.

KNOT SCORE

Strength
Security
Difficulty Tying
Difficulty Untying
Usefulness

1 Put three loops into the end of the line. It might help to use your hand or fingers as a 'former'.

2 Wrap the three initial loops with three more turns, at right angles to the first.

3 Pass the working end through the initial three loops, and straight out the other side.

4 Wrap the second set of turns with three more turns, at right angles to the second set. Insert the marble or ball now, if desired.

5 Tighten the knot by working the slack out through the turns. This may take some time. The end can then be cut and sealed.

6 Alternatively, if you decide not to insert a weight in the centre, you can insert the end there instead. Tie an overhand knot (page 172).

Monkey's paw

The monkey's paw is a new name for an old knot, and is nothing more than a monkey's fist with the end tied to the standing part. You can use a bowline to do this or, if you're using three-strand rope, you can finish off with a soft eye splice (page 297).

KNOT SCORE

Strength
Security
Difficulty Tying
Difficulty Untying
Usefulness

1 Tie the monkey's fist as shown opposite. Seize the line about 150mm (6in) from the end, and tease the strands apart.

2 Splice the end to the standing part, as shown on page 297.

3 Trim the strands and, if using synthetic line, seal the ends with a butane whipping (page 281).

7 Prise open the turns to make a suitably sized hole.

8 Tuck the end, followed by the overhand knot, into the hole.

9 Tighten the knot by working the slack back through to the standing part. Do not overtighten as this will reduce the size of the 'fist'.

Sheepshank in the bight

Probably the most talked about and most rarely used knot in sailing, the sheepshank was traditionally used to shorten lines without cutting the ends. It can also be used to bypass a chafed line by placing the chafed area in the middle of the knot. In practice, it's seldom used nowadays, other than for entertainment and knot-tying practice.

KNOT SCORE

Strength
Security
Difficulty Tying
Difficulty Untying
Usefulness

1 Form three overhand loops side by side.

2 Place the left-hand loop over the centre loop, and the right-hand loop under it.

3 Pull a bight from the centre loop through the left-hand loop, and another through the right-hand loop.

4 Tighten the knot by pulling on both standing parts.

Sheepshank tied with ends

A sheepshank in the bight is not particularly secure, and can be easily spilled if the two protruding loops are nudged in the wrong direction. This can be avoided by using the ends to 'lock' the knot.

KNOT SCORE

Strength
Security
Difficulty Tying
Difficulty Untying
Usefulness

1 Tie a sheepshank in the usual way (opposite). The ends here are lined up ready for the next step.

2 Pass the ends through the loops at either end of the knot.

3 Tighten the knot, and you've got something that bears more than a passing resemblance to a pair of bowlines.

Sheepshank with clove hitch

If the ends aren't available, the sheepshank can be made more secure by turning the half hitches at either end into a pair of clove hitches. This is particularly useful if extra coils are needed to shorten the line.

KNOT SCORE

Strength
Security
Difficulty Tying
Difficulty Untying
Usefulness

1 Tie the sheepshank as shown opposite. More coils can be added if the line needs to be shortened further.

2 Add another half turn at either end to create the two clove hitches. Tighten the knot.

Yardarm knot

This might look like an innocent variation of the sheepshank (page 188), and structurally that's exactly what it is. The yardarm knot, however, fulfils an altogether more sinister function than shortening lines. Tied to a yardarm with a noose at the other end, it was used to hang people. It can however be used in any situation that requires a preset amount of line to be released.

KNOT SCORE

Strength
Security
Difficulty Tying
Difficulty Untying
Usefulness

1 Put an overhand loop in the standing part. The size of the loop should be about half the distance required for the 'drop'.

2 Put a small underhand loop in the working end.

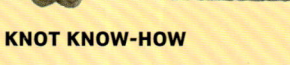

KNOT KNOW-HOW

Adventurer Bear Grylls caused a stir by using a variation of the sheepshank to scale down a cliff in the TV series *Man vs Wild*. Instead of using it to shorten a long line, he used the so-called 'kamikaze' knot to join two short lengths together. When he got to the bottom of the cliff, he shook the knot out and released the lower half of the line. Whatever you do, do NOT try this at home, folks!

3 Tuck the end of the main loop through the small locking loop.

4 Tighten the knot. The top of the main loop can be tied to the standing part with light twine. This will break once a load is applied, releasing the line in the coil.

Poldo tackle

It's hard to imagine how this knot works until you tie it, and then you realise how ingenious it really is. Use it in place of the ubiquitous bungee cord as an adjustable and quickly released tensioner, eg to lash down a liferaft on deck. Apparently named after Italian sailing instructor Poldo Izzo, it's been in use since the 18th century or earlier.

KNOT SCORE

Strength
Security
Difficulty Tying
Difficulty Untying
Usefulness

1 Form a couple of bights in the line. Pass the working end around the first bight.

2 Tie a bowline (page 126) or angler's loop (page 133) around the first bight.

3 Pass the other end of the line around the second bight.

4 Tie a bowline or angler's loop to create the second 'pulley'.

5 Ready to go! To apply tension, pull the loops apart; to release, slide the loops together.

Versatackle

All boats should carry a spare, ready-made block and tackle which can be put to immediate use without having to dismantle half the rigging. Alternatively, this rope version will make a handy substitute. It's not as free-running as its mechanical muse, but even that has certain advantages. It's distinctly cheaper, too, which means you might get tempted to set it up for all kinds of useful applications!

KNOT SCORE
Strength
Security
Difficulty Tying
Difficulty Untying
Usefulness

Mechanical advantage (otherwise known as 'purchase') is a wonderful thing. It enables you to lift or haul enormous loads with minimal effort. On boats, it's used in the form of 'tackles' to tension sails, raise centreboards, and hoist dinghies.

Such tackles are usually made up of a pair of pulleys (or 'blocks') with a continuous length of line running between them. The more turns in the line, the greater the 'purchase', and the less effort required to move the object. On the other hand, more turns also means more rope to pull in, which inevitably means that it takes longer.

Blocks are usually used to make tackles because they reduce friction at each turn. Modern blocks in particular are sometimes fitted with ball bearings which greatly reduce the effort lost in the system, which in some old-fashioned blocks can be as much as 10 per cent per sheave.

But you can make a very effective rope tackle using loops instead of blocks. The friction caused by the rope 'pulleys' will nullify some of the mechanical advantage, but it will still be considerably easier than lifting or pulling without a tackle.

The friction also has the benefit of making the system 'self-locking' – which most tackles are not. That said, it makes sense to play safe and lock the versatackle with a half hitch, if leaving it with a load.

The versatackle can be used to pull two objects together within the initial bight. Alternatively, the tail of the first loop can be made longer and be attached to an object. Either way, the contraption can be used to tension rigging, lash a dinghy down onto a deck or trailer, or even clamp wood together.

One drawback of this system is that repeated use will cause wear on the line – particularly inside the loops. If that's the case, you're probably better off with a 'proper' block and tackle.

The versatackle shown was first published by George Aldridge in 1985 and has been widely imitated ever since.

1 Tie an angler's loop (page 133) in the end of the line – leaving a long end if this is to be attached to either point (see above).

2 Tie another angler's loop in the standing part.

3 The distance between the two loops will determine the span of the versatackle.

KNOTS • 193

4 Pass the standing end of the line through the first loop. You'll need plenty of line to form all the turns.

5 Pass the standing end through the second loop.

6 Put in as many turns as needed. The more turns, the greater the mechanical advantage, but the slower and stiffer it will be to use.

Prusik bottle sling

Climbers will be familiar with the Prusik knot, invented by Austrian mountaineer Dr Karl Prusik in the 1930s. Little did the good doctor know that his ingenious sliding knot would be put to good use as a bottle sling. It's yet another natural development which goes to show that, unlike a good wine, knots never stand still.

KNOT SCORE

Strength
Security
Difficulty Tying
Difficulty Untying
Usefulness

1 Tie the ends of a line together to make a loop, and pass it around the bottle as shown.

2 Pass the line around the bottle and through the loop again, so the new strands slide between the old ones.

3 Tease the loop out and put in a twist (either clockwise or anticlockwise will do).

4 Pass the end of the sling through the twist. Tighten all the turns so the knot is snug against the bottle.

Indian jug handle

A more permanent – and complicated – attachment can be created using this strangle knot, also known as the hackamore or moonshiner's knot. The history of this knot can be traced back to the ancient Greeks who, according to the Greek physician Heraklas, used it to carry their amphorae. A variation was also widely used by American cowboys as a horse bridle.

KNOT SCORE
Strength
Security
Difficulty Tying
Difficulty Untying
Usefulness

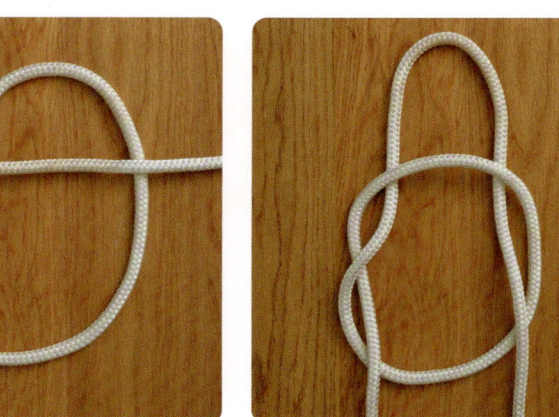

1 Make an underhand loop, and cross it with the working end as shown.

2 Pull a bight from the top strand through the loop to make a simple noose.

3 Bring the working end up to make a bight at the bottom, and tuck between the top loop and top bight.

4 Bring the working end around the knot, tucking it under the top bight, and pass it through the bottom bight.

5 Tease the top bight out to create one handle, and tighten the knot into a ring to fit over the bottle.

6 Slide over the bottle and tighten firmly around the neck. Tie the working and standing ends together to make the second handle.

LASHINGS 6

Pole hitch

Long before we had nails, screws and shackles, we had rope lashings. Once a key part of the riggers' armoury, lashings gradually gave way to mechanical fastenings and fittings. Now they are making a comeback, thanks to an unlikely saviour. The pole hitch is one of the simplest lashings. Use it to carry poles and spars, or to lash them to the rail or car roof rack.

There's something very primitive about lashings. They put us in mind of earlier societies, when basic fastenings had yet to be invented, and the only way you could hold things together was to lash them.

The *Kon-Tiki* proved that lashings could be used to build a sea-going vessel – even if it was just a 14m (45ft) glorified raft. Lashings were used not only to hold the hull logs together, but also the mast, rudder, cabin, and even the bamboo sail. In fact, the whole vessel was held together with hemp lashings and little else.

At about the same time that rafts such as the *Kon-Tiki* were being built in the Pacific, the Vikings were building their exquisite longships. They mostly fastened the vessels' strakes with iron spikes, but sometimes used lashings instead.

Lashings were widely used on sailing craft right up until the end of the 19th century, when the yards of mighty ships such as the *Cutty Sark* were held to the mast using parrel lashings. The advent of stronger and longer-lasting metal fittings and fastenings, however, meant that they gradually became outmoded and were reduced to more menial jobs – such as rigging up a temporary awning or attaching a lifering bracket to the railings.

Only in extreme circumstances, such as setting up a jury rig after dismasting or making a temporary tiller or rudder, did lashings suddenly play a rather important and often life-saving role. There aren't any hardware stores in the middle of the Southern Ocean, so if you lose your rig you have to make do with what you've got. And what most boats have got is plenty of rope to turn into lashings.

More recently, however, the durability of modern cordage has brought lashings back into vogue. Catamaran designer James Wharram has long used a figure-eight lashing instead of metal fittings to hang rudders. Now the rest of the boatbuilding world is catching onto the benefits of 'soft' fittings, and high-modulus rope lashings are increasingly being used in place of shackles and other metal fastenings.

Properly made, these attachments are not only stronger than their metal counterparts but cause less wear and tear to both the boat and its crew. A whipping genoa sheet is less likely to injure the foredeck crew if it's fitted with a 'soft shackle' (page 312) instead of a conventional metal one.

So, far from being a primitive method of attachment, the humble lashing is coming into its own again at the very cutting edge of sailboat technology. Now, who would have predicted that?

KNOT SCORE
Strength ❈❈
Security ❈❈
Difficulty Tying ❈❈
Difficulty Untying ❈❈
Usefulness ❈❈❈❈

1 Form a pair of bights in the standing part of the line.

LASHINGS • 199

2 Place the poles on the line so the bights protrude on either side.

3 Pass the ends of the line through the opposite bight.

4 Take the slack out of the bights, and tie off the two ends with a reef knot (page 180) or similar.

200 • LASHINGS

Square lashing

Whether you're lashing a yard to the mast or making some kind of improvised shelter, the square lashing is the one you'll use most often. Before you start, though, you'll need to sort out your wrapping from your frapping (see Knot Know-How, below). And you'll need to revise a couple of basic knots, namely the timber hitch (page 60) and the clove hitch (page 32).

KNOT SCORE

Strength ❀❀❀❀
Security ❀❀❀❀
Difficulty Tying ❀❀
Difficulty Untying ❀❀❀
Usefulness ❀❀❀❀

1 Tie the end of the line to the lower spar or pole with a timber hitch (shown) or clove hitch.

2 Wrap the line over the top spar, around the bottom spar, back over the top spar and then under the bottom spar again. Do this three times. These are the wrapping turns.

3 Now apply two turns around the wrapping turns themselves. These are the frapping turns.

KNOT KNOW-HOW

Most lashings are made up of turns that are either 'wrapping' or 'frapping'. The wrapping turns are applied first, and hold the poles together. The frapping turns are then put around the wrapping turns and serve to tighten them. A simple rule of thumb is: 'wrap thrice and frap twice'. Wedges may also be used to further tighten the lashing.

4 Tighten the turns and secure the end with a clove hitch (page 32).

LASHINGS • 201

Diagonal lashing

Not everything's square, however, and it's likely the poles will be crossing at a different angle, in which case a diagonal lashing will be more suitable. Use it whenever you need to brace a structure with a couple of diagonal poles – be it a wicker chair or a boat cover. An alternative method to this knot is shown on page 204.

KNOT SCORE
Strength
Security
Difficulty Tying
Difficulty Untying
Usefulness

1 Tie the poles together with a timber hitch (page 60) and pull them together hard.

2 Wrap the poles together three times where they make the widest angle.

3 Take three more wrapping turns where the poles make the narrowest angle.

4 Take two frapping turns around the previous turns, pulling as tightly as you can.

5 Tighten the knot, and finish off with a clove hitch (page 32).

202 • LASHINGS

Shear lashing

If you need to extend anything, from a spar to a boathook or maybe even a broken tiller, the shear lashing will usually do the trick. Simple yet effective, it combines wrapping and frapping turns with a couple of clove hitches to good effect. It can also be used if the spars are to be splayed out, for making a crutch or (with an extra pole) a tripod.

KNOT SCORE

Strength
Security
Difficulty Tying
Difficulty Untying
Usefulness

1 Tie the standing end of the line onto one pole with a clove hitch (page 32).

2 Wrap the line around both poles seven or eight times.

3 Take a couple of frapping turns around the lashing.

4 Tighten the turns, and tie the working end to the second pole with a clove hitch (page 32).

Figure-eight lashing

Shackles are normally used to join one eye to another. But there are situations when a shackle just isn't appropriate: if you need to adjust the distance between the eyes, or if you want to be able to cut the eyes apart quickly in an emergency, or if you just don't have the right size shackle. In these cases, a figure-eight lashing is a perfect substitute.

KNOT SCORE

Strength
Security
Difficulty Tying
Difficulty Untying
Usefulness

1 Tie one end of the line to one eye using a bowline (page 126), an angler's loop (page 133) or, as pictured, a soft eye splice (page 297).

2 Weave the twine through the two eyes in a figure-eight shape.

3 The number of turns depends on the strength required and the thickness of the line.

4 Tighten the turns and finish off with several 'frapping' half hitches.

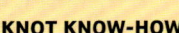

KNOT KNOW-HOW

Lashings played an important role when large ships were raising anchor. As the anchor hawser was often too thick to go around the capstan, a messenger rope was lashed to it and used to haul the hawser in. The lashings were called 'nippers', and the youngest crew members were given the job of tying and untying them. From there, the term 'nipper' for a young boy made its way into our everyday language.

Filipino lashing

This is used as an alternative to the diagonal lashing (page 201), and differs mainly in its starting and finishing points. Because it's tied in the bight, its starting point is absolutely secure and the final knot can be tied with two ends. Ultimately, the choice will probably depend on whether you prefer the reef knot (page 180) or the clove hitch (page 32).

KNOT SCORE

Strength
Security
Difficulty Tying
Difficulty Untying
Usefulness

1 Put a bight in the middle of the line, and pass it around the two poles. Pass the ends through the bight to make a cow hitch (page 53).

2 Wrap both parts of the line around the poles three times in the same direction as the first.

3 Wrap both parts of the line around the two poles three more times, at right angles to the first set of turns.

4 Separate the ends, and take two frapping turns around the lashing, with the ends going in opposite directions.

5 Tighten the lashing, and finish with a reef knot (page 180).

LASHINGS • 205

Japanese lashing

This alternative to the square lashing (page 200) is ostensibly quite similar to the Filipino lashing (opposite), although its starting point is quite different. For additional security, the knot can be started with a clove hitch (page 32), instead of the initial loop. This will stop it sliding along the spar, and will prevent the whole knot coming undone if one part is worn through.

KNOT SCORE
Strength
Security
Difficulty Tying
Difficulty Untying
Usefulness

1 Put a bight in the middle of the line, and loop it over the vertical spar.

2 Pass both parts over the top spar and around the bottom spar for the first wrapping turns.

3 Pull the poles together tightly, and put in two more wrapping turns.

4 Separate the ends, and put two frapping turns around the three wrapping turns.

5 Tighten the knot, and finish with a reef knot (page 180) or similar.

Jury mast knot

Whether you're building a jury rig after being dismasted in mid-ocean or simply setting up a mast on a dinghy, you'll need something to tie the rigging onto. The jury mast knot replaces those fancy metal bands and straps that most boats use nowadays. And it has the advantage that it doesn't rust or come unfastened.

There are many extraordinary stories of yachts being dismasted in mid-ocean and limping into port under a variety of ingenious jury rigs. Usually their crews have to make do with whatever materials they happen to have to hand – be it a spinnaker pole or boom rigged as a mast, or the top half of the mast lashed to its stump.

Whether any of these vessels used the jury mast knot (also known as the masthead knot) is open to debate. Even more uncertain is whether the knot was ever used in historic times to rig the sailing ships of yesteryear.

Most square-rigged sailing ships had a mass of shrouds and stays holding up their masts – up to 20 pairs, according to some sources. These were usually attached to the mast by means of a loop either seized or spliced into the ends – or, if they were fitted in pairs, spliced into the middle of the shrouds.

Eventually, these loops and splices were replaced by single metal fittings, with multiple tangs for the necessary number of shrouds and stays. Which is what the jury mast knot attempts to approximate.

Whatever its practical purpose, the knot has several more frivolous functions. Like the tom fool's knot (page 166), which has a similar starting point, it can be turned into an amusing party trick. Tie the ends together and drop it over a jug – with two loops tucked under the base and the other two forming a pair of handles – and you have a neat jug carrier, to rival the prusik bottle sling (page 194). Tuck one working end across the middle of the knot, going alternately under and over, and go around the whole knot again, and you've got the basis of a place mat.

So, if you do get dismasted and end up on a desert island, at least you'll be able to serve dinner in style.

KNOT SCORE
Strength ❈ ❈ ❈ ❈ ❈
Security ❈ ❈ ❈ ❈ ❈
Difficulty Tying ❈ ❈ ❈
Difficulty Untying ❈ ❈
Usefulness ❈ ❈ ❈

1 Form three overhand loops in the standing part, and place them side by side as shown.

2 Tuck the left-hand loop over the middle loop, and the right-hand loop under it.

LASHINGS • 207

3 Pull a bight from the right-hand loop over the left-hand loop.

4 Pull a bight from the left-hand loop over the centre loop, and pull a bight of the right-hand loop under it.

5 Pull the bights over and under again, until they emerge on each side. Tighten the knot.

208 • LASHINGS

Marline hitches

Most yachtsmen and women nowadays use sail ties to secure a sail once it's been lowered. There are occasions, however, when a series of large marline hitches tied in a single line, leading aft from the clew to the tack, can be a very fast and effective means of stowing a sail. And you're much less likely to lose that line overboard than all those darned sail ties!

KNOT SCORE

Strength
Security
Difficulty Tying
Difficulty Untying
Usefulness

1 Secure one end of the line either to the boat itself or around the sail using a sliding loop, eg a running bowline (page 150).

2 Take a turn around the sail about 0.3m (1ft) away from the initial turn and pass the working end under the standing part.

3 Pull the line sideways to create the first hitch, and repeat the process until you either run out of line or run out of sail.

KNOT KNOW-HOW

Marline hitches are traditionally used to stow a hammock. First, the bedding is evenly spread, leaving 15cm (6in) clear at either end so nothing falls out. The working end is passed through a soft eye splice at the standing end to form the first hitch. Seven marline hitches are then tied along the length of the hammock – one for each of the Seven Seas – before finishing with a couple of half hitches.

4 Secure the end by tying a pair of half hitches onto the standing part (page 28), or simply tie it off to one side.

LASHINGS • 209

Chain stitch lashing

Another fancier method of stowing a sail or awning is the chain stitch lashing – similar to the method used to seal some parcels. One pull of the end, and the whole thing comes undone like a zip. It's guaranteed to impress your neighbours at the marina, as they fiddle about with their endless sail ties.

KNOT SCORE

Strength ❁❁❁
Security ❁❁❁
Difficulty Tying ❁❁
Difficulty Untying ❁
Usefulness ❁❁❁

1 Secure one end of the line, using a timber hitch (page 60) or similar. Take a turn around the sail and tuck a bight under the standing part.

2 Take another turn around the sail about 0.3m (1ft) from the first. Put a bight in the working part, and tuck it through the first bight.

3 Continue taking turns and tucking each new bight into the previous bight until you run out of line or run out of sail.

4 Tighten the hitches (not too tightly, if securing a sail), and finish off with a clove hitch (page 32). To 'unzip', simply untie the clove hitch, untie the locking turn and pull on the end!

COILS 7

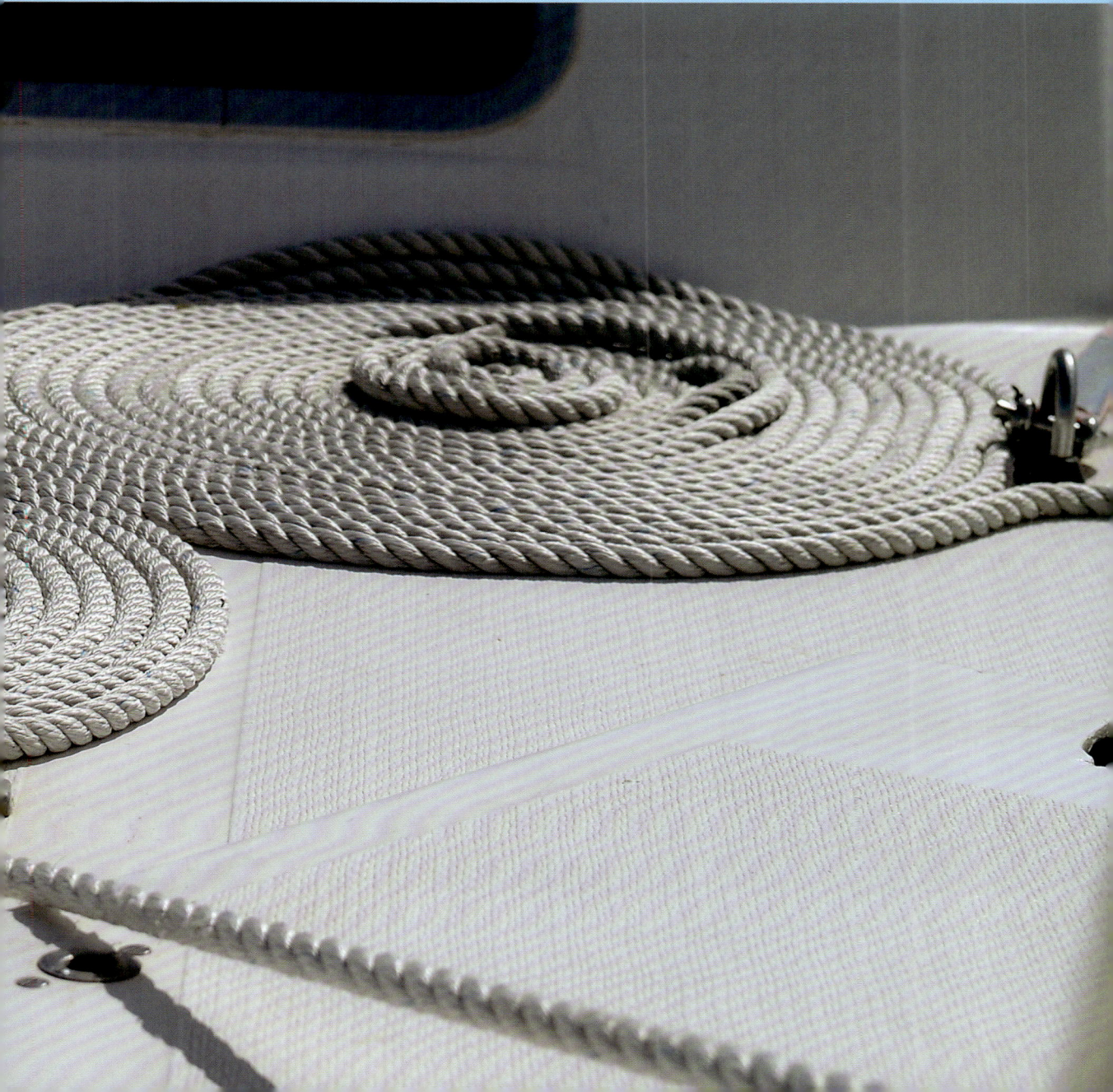

Simple coil

Keeping your lines neat and tidy is one of the secrets of happy knot-tying, and learning to coil them properly is the first step in that direction. Pretty soon you'll be able to do it with your eyes closed. First, however, you've got to decide which school of rope-coiling you belong to, because there's more to this activity than meets the eye.

KNOT SCORE
Strength
Security
Difficulty Tying
Difficulty Untying
Usefulness

You might think coiling rope is a straightforward matter. After all, it's just a matter of stacking a load of loops in a neat pile and lashing them together, isn't it? Flick through a few books and search the internet, however, and you'll see everyone has their favourite method.

Should you put a twist in each loop as you coil the rope? Should you alternate the direction of each loop? Should you twist the turns into a figure-eight? Should you finish with a gasket or a clove hitch? Butterfly coil or alpine coil?

It's enough to make you dizzy – and that's before you've tied a single knot!

As ever, the best method for you will depend on your circumstances: the type of rope you are using, whether you are left-handed or right-handed, and how the line is going to be stowed. There are, however, a few hard and fast rules.

If coiling a halyard or any line attached at one end, start from the end nearest the cleat. This means any tangles can be shaken out of the free end.

Start with the standing part of the line in your (non-dominant) hand, and slide your other (dominant) hand along the line to form the loops. If you're coiling a long length of line, use your full arm span to create each coil, and repeat the same span for each coil to keep them even. Three-strand rope is usually laid right-handed, which means it's best coiled clockwise. In practice, if the rope has already been coiled, it's usually easier to coil it the same way as before. You can help the loops lie flat by twisting each one half a turn inwards as you add them to the coil.

Modern rope is non-directional, which means it doesn't need to be twisted while coiling. To prevent any twist creeping into the line, try coiling it into a figure-eight. It's a bit more messy, but better for the line. Another method is to alternate the direction of each loop.

Various methods of tying off the coil are shown on the following pages. Try them all and decide for yourself which one is your favourite.

1 Make a coil, as described above.

2 Remove two loops from the top of the coil. Put a high waist in the coil, and wrap the working end around it.

3 Take at least three turns, leaving at least half a loop to tie off the coil.

COILS • 213

Halyard coil

If the line is attached at one end, in the case of a halyard for instance, then the coil shown opposite will be too cumbersome to untie quickly. Two methods of tying halyard coils are shown, both with their roots in the Age of Sail.

KNOT SCORE

Strength ✤✤
Security ✤✤
Difficulty Tying ✤✤✤
Difficulty Untying ✤✤
Usefulness ✤✤✤✤

1 If the coil isn't too large and the cleat horns are long, then the coil can simply be hung from the cleat or pin (as shown).

2 For a larger coil, pass the standing end through the coil, and tie it off with either a figure-eight or a single half hitch.

4 Pass the working end through the top bight. Pull the line through, and tighten the knot.

5 The coil can be stowed just like this, or the end can be used to hang it from a convenient place.

Clove hitch coil

If you're piling a whole bundle of lines together, you might need something slightly more secure than the simple coil (page 212). The method of making this coil is exactly the same, but it's tied off with our old friend the clove hitch (page 32). Leave a long enough tail, and you can tie together pairs of lines (eg genoa sheets) with a suitable bend (page 90).

KNOT SCORE

Strength
Security
Difficulty Tying
Difficulty Untying
Usefulness

1 Coil the rope in the usual way, and pass the working end around its waist.

2 Tie a clove hitch around the coil, tucking the second turn under the standing part.

3 Tighten the knot. The tail can be used to hang the coil or tie a pair of lines together.

Gasket coil

The classic method for tying off coils is ingeniously simple and not only locks the loops in place but can be used for hanging the coil up or tying them in pairs. Once you get the hang of it, you'll never use anything else.

KNOT SCORE

Strength
Security
Difficulty Tying
Difficulty Untying
Usefulness

1 Coil the line, and take at least three turns around the waist. Put a bight in the working end and pass it through the top of the coil.

2 Pass the bight over the top of the coil, then down so that it lies next to the other turns. Pull the working end to tighten the knot.

Bell ringer's knot

There are occasions when you might want to lift a free-hanging line off the deck or cabin top, in which case the bell ringer's knot will serve the purpose well. If it looks familiar, that's because it's essentially half a sheepshank (page 188), or an upside-down yardarm knot (page 190). An extra half hitch can be added if more coils need to be hung.

KNOT SCORE
Strength
Security
Difficulty Tying
Difficulty Untying
Usefulness

1 Put an overhand loop in the standing part.

2 Form a bight in the line below the initial loop.

3 Tuck the top of the bight through the loop, and pull the standing part to tighten the knot.

BEST FOR coiling a rope

With so many types of coils to choose from, how do you decide which one to use? Well, as we've seen, it's partly about the type of rope you are coiling and in what context – eg is it a halyard hanging off a cleat, a line being stored in a locker, or a mooring line sitting on deck? But it's also about personal preference.

For me, if a halyard is cleated off at the base of the mast, or even on a pin rail on the side of a traditional boat, then I would use a halyard coil every time. Simply coil the rope as described on page 213, then pull the standing part (in this case, the line nearest the cleat) through the coil and attach it to the cleat with a simple half hitch.

To make it more secure, you can tie a full cleat hitch, but that seems excessive to me. It will also slow you down when you come to release the halyard, which you might want to do in a hurry. A simple half hitch will suffice. Another option is to simply hang the coil from the cleat or pin, which is less secure but perfectly adequate if the cleat horns are long enough, and gives almost instant access to the line.

If the line is a genoa sheet which comes back to a winch in the cockpit, then a simple draped coil over the winch not only looks good but gives easy access. If it's going to be there for some time, make sure the bottom of the coil doesn't rest on the deck as that will attract moisture. If it's the end of season, then you're best off removing the sheets altogether if possible, and stowing them somewhere dry.

If it's a mainsheet, my preference is to tie a gasket coil (page 214), then feed the working end through the shackle at the end of the boom and hang the coil using a figure-eight (page 125) at the end of the line. That way it's out of the way, stays dry and looks cool.

Another common scenario is mooring lines. Nearly all the methods shown here can be used to coil the rope and hang it somewhere out of the way – eg guardrail or pushpit. That will keep the rope dry, though it might be fiddly if you need to leave in a hurry. A simple coil left lying on the deck works well enough, though it will gather moisture and dirt and get in the way if you need to scrub the decks.

The most inefficient method, which is detrimental to the deck and the rope itself in the long term, is cheesing the line (page 222). But I still can't resist doing it sometimes, just for fun. Plus, it's a great way to keep the kids entertained.

Finally, stowing lines in a locker. The point of this is to have a secure bundle which won't come undone when you're rummaging around for a line. The clove hitch coil (page 214) and gasket coil are both excellent options for this, not least because there's a loose end to pull the rope you're after out with. For bigger, longer lines, the wrapped coil is a great solution. I usually tie it off with a couple of lengths of twine, one on each side, but the method shown on page 219 is nicely self-contained.

COILS • 217

GASKET: A gasket coil (page 214) is handy for hanging mooring lines out of the way, as well as stowing random lines in a locker.

WINCH: For sheets, a plain coil draped over the relevant winch is quick, easy and efficient. Keep the coil off the deck to keep them both dry.

HALYARD COIL: A variety of different approaches are shown here, but the neatest is the second from left: a halyard coil (page 213) with a simple half hitch to hold it in place.

CLOVE HITCH: The clove hitch coil (page 214) is a reliable way to stow coils of lines in a locker, as it's less likely to come undone.

CHEESE: Cheesing a rope (page 222) looks smart but isn't great for the line or deck as moisture gets trapped underneath. But do it anyway!

Alpine coil

All the coils discussed so far have assumed a fairly malleable line that won't mind having a 'waist' put into it. This isn't the case if you're working with stiff line that needs to stay in a round coil. Fear not, help is at hand in the shape of the alpine coil, for instant access, and the wrapped coil (page 221) for longer-term storage.

KNOT SCORE

Strength ❀❀
Security ❀❀❀
Difficulty Tying ❀❀
Difficulty Untying ❀❀
Usefulness ❀❀❀

1 Coil the line in the usual way. Put a bight in one end, and take a turn around the coil with the other end.

2 Take at least three turns around the coil, working towards the end of the bight but leaving its end uncovered.

3 Tuck the working end through the bight.

4 Pull the standing end to close the bight, and tighten the knot. If the coil is to be hung, leave a tail in the working end.

Butterfly coil

This coil is traditionally used by climbers for carrying rope, but it can be equally useful afloat, eg for carrying a halyard up a mast or transporting a line ashore. To add a harness, put the coil on your back, with one end over each shoulder. Pass the ends back under your armpits, over the coil, and forward again, securing them around your waist with a reef knot (page 180).

KNOT SCORE
Strength
Security
Difficulty Tying
Difficulty Untying
Usefulness

1 Fold the line in half, and coil it in the usual way, starting with the ends and finishing with the bight.

2 Fold the coil into a U shape, and take a turn around the middle with the bight.

3 Take two or three turns around the coil, until you are near the end of the bight.

4 Pass the bight over the top of the folded coil to cinch it, and lock the loops in place.

5 Tighten the knot. To make a harness, place the ends (visible at the top of the coil) over your shoulders, and follow the instructions above.

Figure-eight flake

If you need to run a line out quickly with minimum risk of it getting tangled, forget all your fancy coils and use a flake instead. The most common use of flaking is for anchor warps and mooring lines, when a tangled line can cause disaster, particularly in heavy weather. And, if your anchor chain is prone to jamming, it might pay to flake that on deck too before you drop anchor.

KNOT SCORE

Strength
Security
Difficulty Tying
Difficulty Untying
Usefulness

1 Starting from the standing end of the line, form a couple of turns on the deck.

2 Form a figure-eight, and lay it over the previous turns so that it partly overlaps them.

3 Keep forming overlapping figure-eights, stacking them in the direction the line will be released.

KNOT KNOW-HOW

The figure-eight flake is just one of many flakes available to the eager line handler. A long flake is a series of turns laid side by side on the deck, and released longitudinally. The French flake is the same, but released at right angles to the turns. A Flemish down is the same as the French flake, but with overlapping turns. A Flemish flake is not a flake at all – it's a cheese (page 222)!

4 To release the line, pull the end at right angles to the turns.

Wrapped coil

Here is a longer-term solution for stiff lines that can't be coiled in the usual manner. If the rope is too stiff to wrap around itself as shown, stops can be made from twine and tied at intervals around the coil. Either way, this is the best way to store thick lines which aren't in regular use, to make sure they don't get twisted during storage.

KNOT SCORE
Strength
Security
Difficulty Tying
Difficulty Untying
Usefulness

1 Coil the line in the usual way, and tie the ends off with a reef knot (page 180) or similar.

2 Wrap the ends around the coil, passing them in opposite directions. If the line is too stiff for this, use short lengths of twine (or 'stops') instead.

3 Once the coil is fully wrapped, tie off the ends with another reef knot.

4 Tighten the knot. The line can now be stored without fear of it tangling or snagging on anything.

Cheesing

You can always spot a well-turned out yacht by the neatly 'cheesed' mooring lines on the aft deck. They pretty well shout out, 'look at me!'. Coil several of them one on top of the other – starting alternately at the centre and the outside – and you've got a French coil. But beware, there may be unwelcome side effects for your lines and your deck.

KNOT SCORE
Strength ❦
Security ❦
Difficulty Tying ❦ ❦
Difficulty Untying ❦ ❦
Usefulness ❦ ❦ ❦

There are few things that look more quintessentially 'yachty' than a line neatly 'cheesed' (or 'cheesed down') on a scrubbed teak deck. It's one of the rare occasions when sailors indulge in creating something that has little purpose other than to look pretty – after all, it would be quicker just to coil the rope.

But not everyone agrees that cheeses, or Flemish flakes as they are also known, are a good thing. For one thing, the line is liable to become twisted (particularly in the centre of the cheese), meaning the method is not suitable for any line that will subsequently be required to run through a block, eg sheets.

Because cheeses are usually left on deck, they get trodden on and the line may become dirty or even damaged. They also retain moisture, which is bad for both line and deck. Much better to coil the line normally and hang it out to dry, say some rope afficionados.

Despite these criticisms, cheesing remains a popular art, and is likely to remain so. Although circles are the most common form, cheeses can be made in different shapes to fit the space available, eg oblongs or even squares. Some turn them into a permanent feature, by stopping the outer end with twine to prevent them coming undone.

1 Estimate the size of cheese needed, and coil the line to fit around it.

2 Coil the working end to form the start of the spiral.

3 Three-strand rope (which is usually right-laid) should be cheesed in a clockwise direction (as shown).

COILS • 223

4 Gradually rotate the cheese to add more turns, tightening it as it grows.

5 A fully-formed cheese can be slid to its correct position, but it should not be lifted.

6 Cheesing can put twist in the line, and is not recommended for lines that need to be payed out quickly or run through blocks, eg sheets.

DECORATIVE KNOTS 8

Crown knot

Whether it was to prevent wear or stop tools falling out, sailors devised ingenious knots that not only fulfilled their purpose but looked beautiful too. The crown and its close sister the wall knot (page 228) form the basis of many of these more elaborate creations. It can also be used on its own as a stop, to prevent a rope fraying, until a more permanent solution is found. Conveniently, it's the first step for a back splice (page 294).

KNOT SCORE
Strength ❁❁❁❁
Security ❁❁❁
Difficulty Tying ❁❁
Difficulty Untying ❁❁
Usefulness ❁❁❁❁

In a world where crews were pitted against extremes of weather and had to do without home comforts for months on end, sailors were understandably proud of their macho credentials. You couldn't be a sissy if you had to climb a 100ft mast to furl the topgallants in a Force 8 gale.

Yet, when they weren't doing all manner of incredibly arduous and often filthy tasks, sailors were quite happy to spend hours on end fiddling around with bits of string to perform what was known as marlinspike seamanship. Basically, macramé.

Originally, most of the fancy knots aboard ship fulfilled strictly practical functions. It's not difficult to see, for instance, how the killick hitch (page 64) might be turned into a covering for a bottle, for the purely pragmatic reason of preventing that bottle breaking if it fell over.

Many decorative knots started as stopper knots in the ends of lines, to prevent them slipping through blocks. Others, such as the elaborate-looking turk's head (pages 260–267), were devised to prevent chafe on a rail or spar. Rope mats (pages 268–271) too were tied to protect the deck from wear, and subsequently developed into objects of art.

The popularity of fancy knotwork among the general public meant that sailors began increasingly to make rope artefacts to sell when they got into harbour. Hence the craft of macramé was born.

The trade in marlinspike seamanship continues to this day. Lanyards, which were originally created to prevent knives and other tools dropping overboard, are turned into necklaces and bracelets. Bell ropes are turned into handles for almost anything, and the monkey's fist (page 186), originally devised for hurling messenger lines ashore, is now more commonly seen on key rings than flying through the air.

Ships might not have topgallants to furl anymore, but the sailor's craft from the Age of Sail lives on.

1 Seize the line a distance 12 times its own diameter from the end, and tease the strands apart. Stop the ends of the strands with a constrictor knot (page 40) or butane whipping (page 281).

2 Pass the centre strand over the right-hand strand. The knot should always follow the lay of the rope.

3 Pass the left-hand strand over the centre strand.

DECORATIVE KNOTS • 227

4 Pass the right-hand strand over the left-hand strand...

5 ... and tuck it under the standing part of the centre strand.

6 Pull the strands through the loops, and tighten the knot.

Wall knot

The wall knot is basically an upside-down crown knot (page 226). But whereas the crown leads the strands back to the line's standing part, the wall knot leaves them pointing in the original direction. This means the line can be reconstituted to form a knot 'in the bight'. The wall and crown are often combined to make a larger stopper, known as the manrope knot.

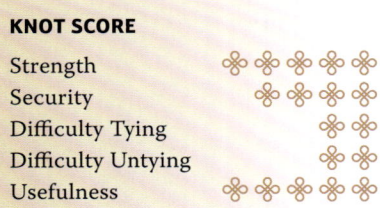

KNOT SCORE

Strength	❁ ❁ ❁ ❁ ❁
Security	❁ ❁ ❁ ❁
Difficulty Tying	❁ ❁
Difficulty Untying	❁ ❁
Usefulness	❁ ❁ ❁ ❁ ❁

1 Prepare the line as before (page 226, step 1), or tie four lengths of thin line together with a whipping and a seizing, as shown. The same principles apply for three strands.

2 Pass the ends under the standing part of its neighbour, working in a clockwise direction.

3 When the last strand is reached, pass the end through the loop formed by the standing part of the first strand.

4 Pull the strands to take out any slack, and you should see a helicoidal form following the lay of the line.

5 Tighten the knot.

DECORATIVE KNOTS • 229

Double wall knot

A larger, though slightly less stable, stopper knot is formed by following the lead around for one more tuck. According to Darcy Lever in his 1808 book *The Sheet Anchor*, the double wall was 'tied in the ends of topgallant braces, to button in the clews of topgallant sails.' And if it's good enough for the topgallant, it's good enough for most things.

KNOT SCORE
Strength ❀❀❀❀❀
Security ❀❀❀
Difficulty Tying ❀❀❀
Difficulty Untying ❀❀❀
Usefulness ❀❀❀

1 Prepare the line as for a crown (page 226, Step 1). The example shown is four strand, but the same principles apply for three strand.

2 Pass the ends under the standing part of its neighbour, working in a clockwise direction.

3 Pass the ends through the loops formed in the previous step, still working in a clockwise direction.

4 Pull the strands to remove any slack, and make sure each strand passes through two loops apiece.

5 Tighten the knot.

Diamond knot

Nothing flashy about this knot, which has been around since at least 1769. It's based on that old sailor's favourite, the carrick bend (page 100), although only the most ardent knot-tyer would recognise it in this form. Use it as a component in making a knife lanyard, or simply as an alternative stop in the end of a line.

KNOT SCORE

Strength ❀ ❀ ❀ ❀ ❀
Security ❀ ❀ ❀ ❀ ❀
Difficulty Tying ❀ ❀ ❀ ❀ ❀
Difficulty Untying ❀ ❀ ❀ ❀ ❀
Usefulness ❀ ❀ ❀ ❀ ❀

1 Seize the line a distance 12 times its diameter from the end, and tease the strands apart. If using traditional rope (as shown), the strands will need to be stopped with twine.

2 Turn down the ends, and stop them just below the seizing.

3 Select one of the strands, and pass it over the strand immediately to its right, and under the next one.

KNOT KNOW-HOW

Knots such as the diamond and (famously) the footrope knot (page 234) were tied in footropes hung below the yards, to prevent sailors' feet slipping. To do this, the line was unlaid from one end to the middle. Stopper knots were then tied at suitable intervals and the rope relaid. The process was then repeated from the other end of the line.

DECORATIVE KNOTS • 231

4 Repeat the process for the other two strands.

5 Remove the stop, and tighten the knot, working it up hard against the seizing.

6 Relay the strands to reconstitute the line.

7 Fasten the end of the line with a suitable whipping (pages 274–287).

Double diamond knot

Doubling the diamond knot (page 230) transforms it from something merely useful into a far more decorative knot – almost like a miniature monkey's fist (page 186). Don't be fooled, however. The double diamond still has an important practical application, and was once recommended by the British Admiralty to provide additional grip on bucket ropes.

KNOT SCORE

Strength ✤✤✤✤
Security ✤✤✤✤
Difficulty Tying ✤✤✤
Difficulty Untying ✤✤✤
Usefulness ✤✤✤✤

1 Seize the line a distance 12 times its diameter from the end, and tease the strands apart. If using traditional rope (as shown), the strands will need to be stopped with twine.

2 Turn down the ends, and stop them just below the seizing.

3 Pass each strand over its neighbour on the right and under the next one.

7 Repeat the process for the other strands so all the turns are doubled.

8 Relay the strands to reconstitute the line.

9 Fasten the end of the line with a suitable whipping (pages 274–287).

4 Pick a strand and pass it over and under again so it emerges below the knot.

5 Repeat the process for the other strands, working in a clockwise direction.

6 Pick a strand and pass it over and under again so it emerges above the knot this time.

Footrope knot

'First a crown, then a wall. Tuck up, and that's all.' This is the well-known mnemonic from Captain Charles W Smith for learning the footrope knot. Similar in structure to the diamond knot (page 230), the end result is rather more handsome and less liable to wear. It can be doubled by tucking the strands a second time above the first set.

KNOT SCORE

Strength
Security
Difficulty Tying
Difficulty Untying
Usefulness

1 Prepare the line as before (page 226, Step 1), or tie four lengths of thin line together with a whipping and a seizing, as shown. The same principles apply for three strands.

2 Tie a crown knot (page 226).

3 Pass each strand under its neighbour to the left, ie form a wall (page 228).

4 Tuck each strand through the loop directly above it.

5 Pull the strands through, and tighten the knot. The line can then be relaid (page 230, Steps 6 & 7) or more knots tied to make a larger piece.

DECORATIVE KNOTS • 235

Star knot

All the decorative knots so far have had a similar recognisable pattern, one building on the next. The star knot does its own thing, however, and apart from the appearance of a crown halfway through, doesn't bear much relation to any of the others. Use it as part of a decorative lanyard or, by tucking the ends down one more time, turn it into a button or toggle.

KNOT SCORE

Strength
Security
Difficulty Tying
Difficulty Untying
Usefulness

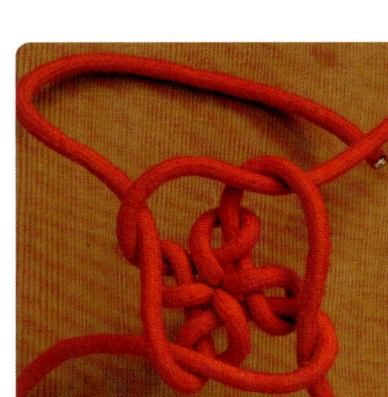

1 Prepare the line or seized lines as before (page 226, Step 1). Put an underhand loop in each strand, and tuck the end through the loop immediately to its right.

2 Work in an anticlockwise direction around the line, or seized lines.

3 Pass each strand over its neighbour to the left, working in a clockwise direction.

KNOT KNOW-HOW
The finished star knot in Step 8 can be turned into a button simply by tucking each end through the loop to its immediate left, keeping it parallel with the adjacent strand. Alternatively, you can go the extra mile and throw in a crown before you tuck the ends away. This adds a nice decorative touch to the centre of the star, as well as making the knot more secure.

5 ... and down through the nearest loop, keeping the line parallel with the adjacent strand.

6 You should now have a pattern of double interlocking strands, with the ends emerging below the knot.

4 Now tuck each strand back under itself…

7 Turn the knot over and follow the adjacent strand up and through the knot so the end emerges on the other side.

8 Pull the strands through, and tighten the knot. The line can then be relaid (page 231, Steps 6 & 7) or more knots tied to make a larger piece.

Matthew Walker knot

How times change. A hundred years ago, the Matthew Walker was one of the commonest and most important knots aboard ship; now it's rarely used other than for decoration. Yet, if you want to put a permanent stop or toggle in anything – from soft shackle to rope ladder – it's a lot more secure than a figure-eight, and nicer to look at too.

KNOT SCORE
Strength ❁❁❁❁❁
Security ❁❁❁❁❁
Difficulty Tying ❁❁❁❁
Difficulty Untying ❁❁❁
Usefulness ❁❁❁❁

It used to be said that the Matthew Walker knot was the only knot named after an individual. Clearly that is no longer the case, as this book alone contains at least two other knots named after people: the Ashley stopper knot (page 176) and the Poldo tackle (page 191).

Another sign of the times is that, a hundred years ago, the Matthew Walker was used on everything from bucket handles to deadeye lanyards. It was the knot of choice for any situation that required a permanent stop – where we might simply use a figure-eight. 'It is the most important knot aboard ship,' wrote Ashley in his *Book of Knots*. Admittedly he was referring to 'knots proper', which excludes loops, hitches and bends, but it's still a strong statement. Nowadays, it is used almost entirely for decorative purposes.

As for Matthew Walker himself, the story goes that he was a sailor sentenced to death who was offered a pardon by the judge (himself a former sailor) providing he could tie a knot that he (the judge) could neither tie nor untie. The prisoner requested 10 fathoms (60ft/18m) of line which he unravelled to its midpoint, tied a Matthew Walker knot, and relaid. He was duly acquitted, and earned himself a place in knot folklore.

DECORATIVE KNOTS • 239

1 Prepare the line or seized lines as before (page 226, Step 1). Tie a wall knot (page 228), tucking each strand under its neighbour to the right.

2 Work in an anticlockwise direction to make a helicoidal shape.

3 Pick any strand, and tuck it under the next loop to the right. Place it above the strand already in the loop.

4 Do the same for the other strands, working in an anticlockwise direction.

5 Work the strands so they emerge from the top of the knot.

6 Tighten the knot. The line can then be relaid (page 231, Steps 6 & 7) or more knots tied to make a larger piece.

Double Matthew Walker

The double (or 'full') Matthew Walker used to be the standard stopper knot aboard ship, until it was replaced by the 'single' Matthew Walker, which is somewhat neater. The double version is worth knowing, however, if only for variety's sake. The tying method is also more unusual, and can be adapted for the single version.

KNOT SCORE

Strength
Security
Difficulty Tying
Difficulty Untying
Usefulness

1 Prepare the line as before (page 226, Step 1), or tie three lengths of thin line together with a whipping and a seizing, as shown. The same principles apply for four strands.

2 Pick any strand and pass it around the line(s) and under its own standing part.

3 Do the same for the strand immediately to its right, passing the end through both bights.

4 Repeat for the third strand, passing the end through all three bights.

5 Work the lines so they emerge at the top of the knot.

6 Tighten the knot. The line can then be relaid (page 231, Steps 6 & 7) or more knots tied to make a larger piece.

Matthew Walker loop

Strictly speaking, this knot should be in Chapter 4, but we've included a few loops that are more suitable for decorative purposes in this chapter. Confusingly, there's almost certainly no link between the legendary Matthew Walker knot and this one, apart from a vague similarity in the finished item. But it's an easy 'starter' knot for making a loop on a lanyard.

KNOT SCORE
Strength ❈❈❈❈
Security ❈❈❈
Difficulty Tying ❈❈❈
Difficulty Untying ❈❈❈❈
Usefulness ❈❈❈

1 Put an overhand knot (page 172) in the bight of the line.

2 Pass the working end through the knot to form a bight.

3 Take a turn around the bight with the working end.

4 Pass the working end under itself and through the initial loop.

5 Tighten the knot.

Lanyard knot

Two types of lanyards were commonly used aboard ship: one purely practical, the other increasingly decorative. The lanyard knot could be used for either. Nowadays, it can be combined with other knots to hold a phone, or it can be tied in a line to create a rope handrail for a staircase, or any other instance where a handgrip is needed.

KNOT SCORE
Strength
Security
Difficulty Tying
Difficulty Untying
Usefulness

There are many things that sailors and ships have contributed to modern life, but one of the most ubiquitous is the humble lanyard. Once the province of salty dogs sailing the Seven Seas, it can now be found on everything from cameras to mobile phones, phones, key rings and ID badges.

Lanyards were no doubt used long before sailors discovered them, but they did take them to a new level by decorating them with elaborate knotwork. The use of lanyards to hold knives and other tools freed sailors' hands when they climbed aloft – as well as saving the crew below from being injured by a falling piece of hardware. Holed up aboard ship for months on end, sailors soon developed ever-more complicated ways of making lanyards and decorating them with fancy knots – many of which are featured in these pages.

Lanyards soon migrated to shore, where they were used to secure swords, pistols and whistles. In time, they acquired a more symbolic role, and were used on military uniforms to denote rank.

But these lanyards were not the only lanyards aboard ship. The term also refers to a line used to attach the rigging to the sides of the ship. Before the invention of bottlescrews, each shroud was terminated with a deadeye, a round block of wood with several holes drilled through it. This was reeved by means of a suitable line to another deadeye attached to the side of the ship. This line was called a lanyard.

The lanyard knot was no doubt devised for this latter usage, in order to stop the lanyard in one of the holes in a deadeye. As such, it would need to be extremely secure, as the ship's rig was dependent on it. The fact that it was decorative too, meant that it could also be used on the other sort of lanyards as well, once again combining the practical with the functional.

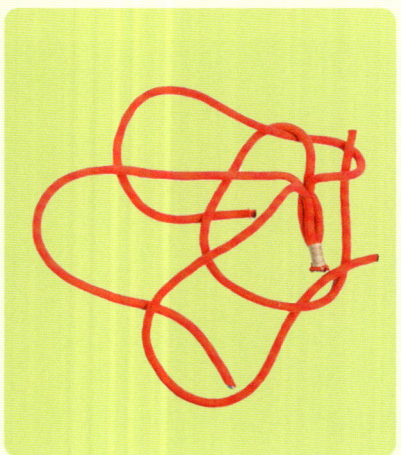

1 This knot is for four-strand rope, or four lengths of thin line tied together with a whipping and a seizing, as shown. If using three-strand rope, see page 226, Step 1.

2 Tie a wall knot (page 228) by passing each strand under the standing part of the strand immediately to its right.

3 Work the strands through in an anticlockwise direction.

DECORATIVE KNOTS • 243

4 Pass each strand through the loop to its right, so it emerges next to the standing part of its neighbour.

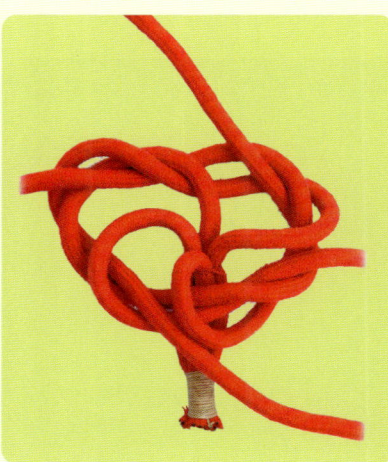

5 Work the strands so they emerge at the top of the knot.

6 Tighten the knot. The line can then be relaid (page 231, Steps 6 & 7) or more knots tied to make a larger piece.

Chinese lanyard knot

If you were a bit nonplussed by the simplicity of the Matthew Walker loop (page 238), then this knot might be for you. Also known as the plafond knot, this loop looks more complicated on the page than it is in real life. Use it for a knife lanyard, alone or as part of a series of knots.

KNOT SCORE

Strength
Security
Difficulty Tying
Difficulty Untying
Usefulness

1 Fold the line in half, and form a bight at the centre. If attaching a knife, slide the ring into the bight now. Tie a pair of overhand knots (page 172).

2 Leave a space, and then tie two more overhand knots. Fold the lower knot up into the centre loop.

3 Fold the top knot into the centre, and tuck the initial bight through the lower knot.

4 Pass one of the ends through the upper knot...

5 ... followed by the other end.

6 Take the slack out of the knot, making sure the ends remain the same length.

DECORATIVE KNOTS • 245

7 Tighten the knot to form the loop. The ends can be tied off using a suitable bend from Chapter 3.

KNOT KNOW-HOW

The Chinese have been tying fancy knots for thousands of years. According to Chinese folklore, individual knots are imbued with different characteristics, such as luck, happiness, longevity, and so forth. The craft reached its pinnacle during the Qing Dynasty (1644–1911) but was almost wiped out during the Cultural Revolution. It is now enjoying a resurgence.

Japanese loop

The Japanese have a long tradition of knot-tying that dates back centuries, if not millennia. While widely recognized in the West for its intricate designs, Japanese knots serve a variety of functional purposes. For example, this double loop is ideal for use on items like necklaces or lanyards.

KNOT SCORE

Strength
Security
Difficulty Tying
Difficulty Untying
Usefulness

1 Fold the line in half, and put a loop in the middle, as shown. If attaching a knife, slide the ring into the loop now.

2 Pass the left-hand part over the loop, and the right-hand part under it.

3 Cross the right-hand part over the left-hand part.

4 Pass the left-hand end under the initial loop, and over the opposite part. Do the same with the right-hand end, going under the initial loop and over the left-hand part.

5 Tighten the knot by pulling on both parts and teasing out both sides of the initial loop to form a pair of loops, one on either side of the knot.

Chinese crown loop

Another attractive Chinese import, this loop is based on the popular Chinese crown knot (also known as the shamrock knot). Used by sailors to decorate tools and weapons, it was brought home and incorporated into the burgeoning art of macramé. Now it is used in everything from martial arts weapons to hanging lanterns.

KNOT SCORE

Strength
Security
Difficulty Tying
Difficulty Untying
Usefulness

1 Fold the line in half, and put a loop in the middle, as shown. If attaching a knife, slide the ring into the loop now.

2 Put a bight in the left-hand leg, and tuck it under the right-hand leg.

3 Pass the right-hand end under the left-hand leg, through the initial loop, and through the bight.

4 Tighten the knot, taking care not to pull it out of shape.

Good luck knot

It seems highly unlikely that this knot was ever tied in the rigging of even the most fancy square-rigger. More likely, sailors used it to make decorative artefacts which they sold when they got to port – or possibly to decorate their own cabins. The large lobes on the good luck knot make it unsuitable for key rings or suchlike, but it can make an attractive hanging ornament.

KNOT SCORE

Strength
Security
Difficulty Tying
Difficulty Untying
Usefulness

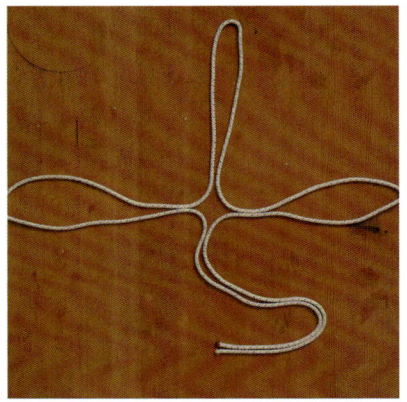

1 Fold the line in half, put in three bights, and arrange in a cross shape, as shown.

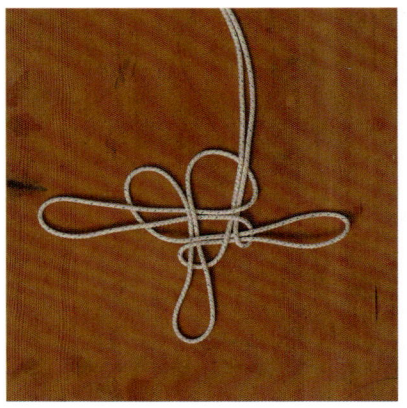

2 Pass the standing parts over the right-hand bight, the right-hand bight over the top bight, and the top bight over the left-hand bight. Tuck the left-hand bight into the first loop.

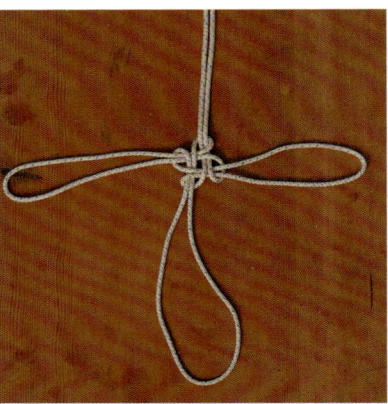

3 Tighten the resulting anticlockwise crown (page 226), making sure the pairs of strands lie parallel to each other.

4 Tie a clockwise crown, passing each bight and the standing parts over its neighbour. Tuck the final bight in the loop created by the first bight.

5 Tighten the knot, adjusting the three loops to the desired size. The knot can be used like this, or...

KNOT KNOW-HOW

Ashley simply called this knot 'a four-looped knot with a double square crown', and it seems to have remained nameless until 1981, when Lydia Chen named it the good luck knot in her book *Chinese Knotting*. The Japanese name for it is the chrysanthemum. There are dozens of variations with different numbers of petals, including a nine-petal version, and one with flowers.

6 ... an extra set of lobes (or petals) can be created by teasing out the corner loops. Tighten the knot by pulling the standing parts.

DECORATIVE KNOTS • 249

Mystic knot

This knot is said to be one of the eight treasures of Buddhism, symbolising the belief that there is no beginning and no end, but only a constant round of birth and rebirth. You'll certainly find yourself going round and round as you tie what is a far more durable decorative knot than the fragile good luck knot (page 248). Just make sure you stop before reaching infinity…

KNOT SCORE
Strength
Security
Difficulty Tying
Difficulty Untying
Usefulness

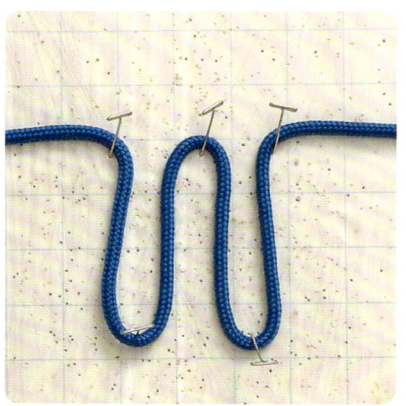

1 Centre the line and form a pair of bights, as shown. Use tacks or pins to hold the line in place, if desired.

2 Put a bight in the right-hand part and pass it under the first strand, over the next strand, and under and over again. The yellow line shows the path the blue line should follow.

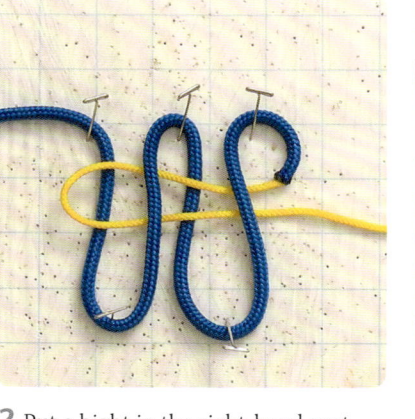

3 Put a second bight in the line, and pass it under the strands in exactly the same way as the first bight.

5 Pass the left-hand end through the top right-hand loop. Pass it behind the bights, then around the front and through the lower right-hand loop, and behind the bights again.

6 Pass the end through the bottom left-hand loop and go over three strands, under one, and over three. On the return, go under two, over one, under three and over one.

7 Repeat the process in between the initial bight, and you should end up with this shape. Use pins to hold the shape, if desired.

DECORATIVE KNOTS • 251

4 If the line is sufficiently stable, the pins can be removed and the knot transferred.

8 Tighten the knot by working the slack out through the standing parts.

9 A loop can be created by working the slack out through the top corner (or top left, in the original configuration).

Three-strand plait sinnet

Sinnet is basically rope made from two or more strands of cord which can be tied together in various different ways. It's been used for thousands of years by Pacific islanders, and was popular on square-riggers and fishing boats alike due to its excellent hard-wearing character. Nowadays, it features more often in the decorative crafts, including making lanyards, bell ropes, necklaces and key rings.

Here's how to catch a shark, if you ever run out of food while sailing in the Pacific. Get some coconut rope and plait it together to make a two- or three-strand sinnet. Form a noose. Shake a rattle made out of an old coconut shell underwater to attract your shark. When the shark appears, use a bait to guide it into the noose. Tighten the noose and lash it to the side of the boat, until the shark is exhausted. Club it to death, chop it up, and prepare it as a meal.

The above is an accurate description of the traditional method of catching sharks in Samoa (excluding the kava), and demonstrates the impressive strength of plaited rope. Sinnet (or sennit), as this rope is called, is used extensively across the Pacific, not just for catching sharks, but for making houses, canoes and jewellery.

Sinnet line was also used by sailors in the northern hemisphere for signal lines, reefing lanyards, and fishing net lines. Its main advantages are that it has no 'twist', it's less likely to unravel, and it's more resistant to wear.

There are a number of ways of making sinnet line, either by plaiting (as shown here and on page 254), or crowning (page 256) or making a chain (also known as a monkey chain). Like most of the knots in this chapter, the technique is now used extensively in macramé, particularly in its eight-strand formation.

1 Take four lengths of cord, and seize them together at one end. One strand will form the foundation, while the others will make the plaits.

2 Pass the right-hand strand under the strand to its left, then over the next (the foundation strand), and under the last.

6 ... and a right-hand strand goes under and over.

7 Left over...

DECORATIVE KNOTS • 253

KNOT SCORE

Strength
Security
Difficulty Tying
Difficulty Untying
Usefulness

3 Pass what used to be the left-hand strand under the foundation. Pass the right-hand strand under and over, and the left-hand strand over and under.

4 Keep alternating from side to side, passing the right-hand strand under and over, and the left-hand strand over and under.

5 A left-hand strand goes over and under...

8 ... and under. The next right goes under...

9 ... then over. When you reach the end of the line, tighten the knot and either cut off any excess, or plait it in the same way as the rest.

KNOT KNOW-HOW

A typical Samoan shark noose is made from 21mm (7/8in) thick sinnet. It's 6.7m (22ft) long, and is seized for 1.5m (5ft) from the eye. The noose is formed at one end, while the other is split into two to allow it to be lashed around the canoe's rear boom.
Courtesy of Te Rangi Hiroa, aka Mayor Peter H Buck, DSO, MD.

Two-strand plait sinnet

If the three-strand sinnet (page 252) had you scratching your head, try this simpler version. It's more of a wrap than a plait, but will do the job well enough. The outside 'filler' line should be at least six times as long as the two foundation lines. Its job is to guard the foundation lines against chafe, and it adds little in the way of lateral strength to the line.

KNOT SCORE	
Strength	✿✿✿✿✿
Security	✿✿✿✿✿
Difficulty Tying	✿✿
Difficulty Untying	✿✿
Usefulness	✿✿✿✿✿

1 Take three lengths of cord, and seize them together at one end. Two will form the foundation, while the third (longer) strand will act as the filler.

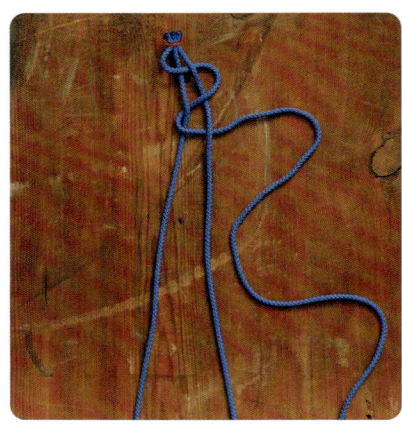

2 Weave the filler strand in and out of the foundation strands, passing between them at every turn.

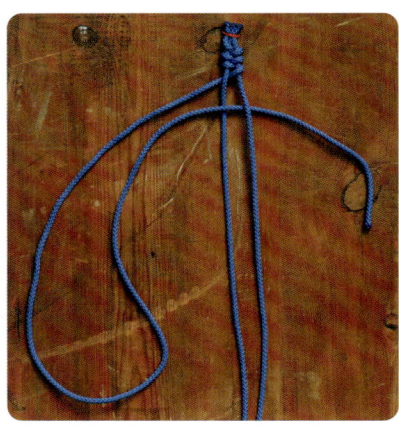

3 Periodically tighten the turns, and bring them up snug against the seizing.

4 Keep weaving the filler strand in and out of the foundation strands...

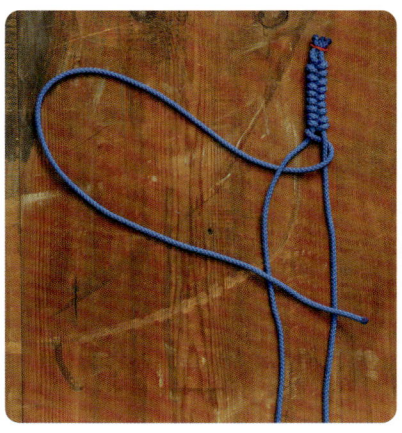

5 ... until they are completely covered.

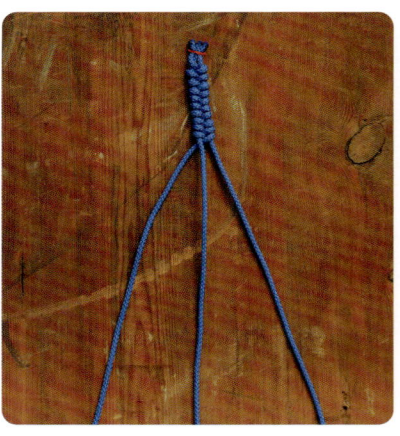

6 Once complete, tie off the end with a whipping (Chapter 9).

DECORATIVE KNOTS • 255

Crown sinnet

You might remember this one from going to scouts or girl guides. Although now more commonly used to make bracelets, it too has its origins aboard ship where it was used for a variety of purposes, including bell ropes. Based on the crown (page 226), its great advantage is that it's unlikely to ever unravel.

KNOT SCORE
Strength
Security
Difficulty Tying
Difficulty Untying
Usefulness

1 Tie a crown (page 226), passing each strand over the standing part of its neighbour.

2 Tighten the knot.

3 Form the next crown, again passing each strand over the standing part of its neighbour.

4 Keep tying a succession of crowns, tightening the knot between each crown.

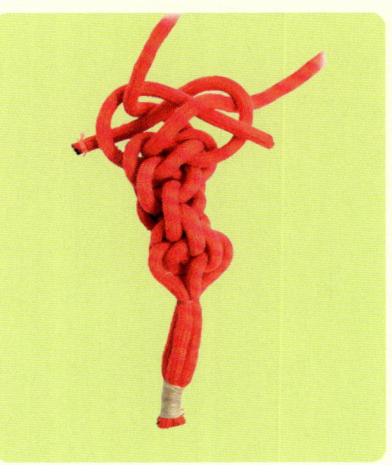

5 Keep straightening the sinnet as you tie it to prevent any 'twist' working its way into the line.

6 Tighten the final crown. The end of the sinnet should be secured with a whipping (Chapter 9).

DECORATIVE KNOTS • 257

BEST FOR making a bellrope key ring

It's all very well learning all these fancy knots, but what can you use them for? One easy project is a bellrope, as featured on the deck of many large sailing ships. Most of us don't own large sailing ships, however, so we've taken the same idea and scaled it down to key ring size, on the principle that most people do own a lot of keys. To make an actual bellrope, simply use thicker rope.

1 Take two 1.3m lengths of 3 or 4mm line, fold them in half and twist the middles together as if laying a rope. Tie the middle into a loop with a piece of string.

2 Use the four strands to tie a Matthew Walker knot, as described on page 238.

3 Next, tie a series of crown knots to create a crown sennit (page 256). You can tie as many as you like, depending on how long you want your key ring to be.

4 For the grand finale, tie a footrope knot (page 234). The picture shows the first pass.

5 Follow the strands around for a second pass – and even a third one – before passing them up through the middle of the knot and out of the centre.

6 Trim the strands and either tuck the ends away in the knot itself or seal them with a butane whipping (page 281).

DECORATIVE KNOTS • 259

Turk's head 3L × 4B – in the round

Once employed to stop sailors' feet slipping while they were stowing sails, the turk's head is now used to decorate everything from wedding rings to fishing rods. Learn to tie this simple version, and you will gain access to a whole world of leads and bights...

KNOT SCORE

Strength ❀❀❀❀❀
Security ❀❀❀❀❀
Difficulty Tying ❀❀❀❀❀
Difficulty Untying ❀❀❀❀❀
Usefulness ❀❀❀❀❀

It seems an injustice to categorise the turk's head as a decorative knot when, historically, it had so many practical applications. On square-riggers, it was used to make footholds and handholds on footropes and lifelines, and to guard against chafe on rails and spars.

If a sailor was feeling creative, he might use one to seize the end of a line, instead of a whipping. Other, more decorative uses were on oars, boathooks, bell ropes, chest handles, whips, lanyards, telescopes, tillers... Well, you get the picture.

Nowadays, however, the turk's head is used almost entirely for decorative purposes, wire having replaced rope for standing rigging, and stainless steel being the material of choice to prevent chafe. One of the few genuinely functional uses of a turk's head is on a ship's wheel, to indicate the position it should be in to be able to centre the rudder.

The obvious decorative appeal of the knot means it has figured in art since at least Celtic times. Even Leonardo da Vinci was a fan, and drew them back in the 15th century.

But the current name for the knot seems to have been coined in 1808 by Darcy Lever who wrote in *The Sheet Anchor* that the knot 'worked with a logline, will form a kind of Crown or Turban.' And back in 1808, anyone who wore a turban – whether Muslim, Hindu or Sikh – was automatically deemed a 'Turk'.

The name is a generic term for the type of knot, which comes in many shapes and sizes. The standard way of describing all turk's heads is by leads and bights. The leads refer to the number of unique circuits the cord makes around the cylinder, while the bights are the arcs formed on the side of the knot each time the cord changes direction.

Thus the knot on this page is a 3L × 4B turk's head, meaning it has three leads and four bights. Curiously, the number of times the strands are doubled doesn't figure in this equation.

1 Take a turn around the pole or spar, and pass the standing end over the standing part. Pass the other end around the pole, over the standing end, and under itself.

2 Pull the line through, and tighten gently so the standing end is locked in place.

3 Turn the knot over, so the turns are visible.

DECORATIVE KNOTS • 261

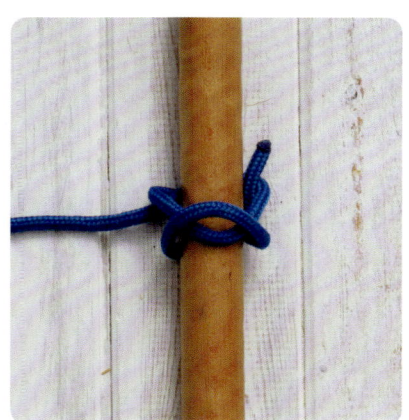

4 Tuck a bight from the upper turn under the lower turn.

5 Pass the working end through the bight.

6 Pass the end over the next bight, and under the next, so it emerges alongside the standing end.

7 The basic shape of the knot (three leads × four bights) has now been established and it's just a matter of doubling the lead.

8 The lead has been doubled once, and the working end is starting its third round.

9 Once three full rounds have been made, work the slack out of the knot (this may take some time!), and trim the ends flush.

Turk's head 4L × 3B – in the round

The shape of a turk's head is determined by the number of leads and bights created at the start: the more leads, the wider the knot, and the more bights, the denser it will be. It's horses for courses…

KNOT SCORE
Strength
Security
Difficulty Tying
Difficulty Untying
Usefulness

1 Tie an overhand knot around the pole or spar, so the working end emerges to the right.

2 Tease the knot open, to create a pair of bights.

3 Pass the working end around the pole, and under and over the bights, working from right to left.

4 Pass the working end around the pole again, and back under itself, working from left to right.

5 Changing direction again, pass the working end over and under the neighbouring strands.

6 Pass the end around the pole and pass it over and under again so it emerges next to the standing end.

DECORATIVE KNOTS • 263

KNOT KNOW-HOW

How to choose the best combination of leads and bights? According to Ashley, any combination can be used, providing the number of leads and the number of bights do not have a common divisor – that is, it should not be possible to divide them by the same number. He recommends using a prime number for the larger dimension, and any smaller number for the other dimension.

7 Follow the lead all the way around, making sure the line stays parallel to the first round. Tighten the knot and cut the ends flush.

Turk's head 3L × 5B in the flat

Slide a turk's head off the pole, rearrange it in the flat, and you've got a turk's head 'clump' mat. Once used to protect decks from clattering blocks, these are now popular as doormats or even coasters.

KNOT SCORE
Strength
Security
Difficulty Tying
Difficulty Untying
Usefulness

1 Put an underhand loop in the standing end, and pass the working end through the loop.

2 Pass the working end over the standing part, and the standing part over the loop.

3 Pull the working end to remove the slack, leaving a bight overlapping the initial loop.

5 Weave the working end over, under and over, so it emerges from the top right-hand bight.

6 Pass the working end under the next strand so it emerges next to the standing end.

7 Once the first lead is complete, follow it around again, making sure the second round sits parallel to the first.

DECORATIVE KNOTS • 265

4 Pass the working end through the top left-hand bight (ie the top of the initial loop).

8 As the second round is fed through, it will automatically remove some of the slack and tighten the knot.

9 Work any remaining slack out through the ends. The ends can be cut flush and hidden under the bights, or kept long and used for tying.

Turk's head 5L × 4B in the flat

Like the turk's head in the round (pages 260–263), the flat version can be made in a variety of shapes and sizes, depending on the number of leads and bights used.

KNOT SCORE

Strength
Security
Difficulty Tying
Difficulty Untying
Usefulness

1 Put an underhand loop in the standing end. Pass the end through the loop and under itself, going under, over and under, right to left.

2 Pass the working end through both the loops formed, going under, over, under and over, left to right.

3 Pass the working end back over itself, then through the initial loops, this time going over, under, over…

4 … then under again, and over itself.

5 Pass the working end around and under, so it emerges next to the standing end.

6 Follow the lead around again, making sure the second round sits parallel next to the first. Trim the ends and hide them under the bights.

DECORATIVE KNOTS • 267

Oval mat

If you've tied the ocean braid mat and you're ready for the next challenge, the oval mat will put your knot-tying skills to the test. If you really get stuck, it's worth pinning the strands down to a polystyrene or plywood board. Tie it in cord for an epaulette or coaster, or use thicker line to make a salty looking door or deck mat.

KNOT SCORE

Strength ❀❀❀❀
Security ❀❀❀❀
Difficulty Tying ❀❀❀❀
Difficulty Untying ❀❀❀❀
Usefulness ❀❀❀❀

1 Put three overhand loops in the end of the line (the standing part is to the right in this picture).

2 Place the right-hand loop over the middle loop, and the left-hand loop under it.

3 Pull a bight from the left-hand loop over the right-hand loop, so they overlap as shown.

4 Pass the working end over and under, over twice, then under and over, working from left to right.

5 Pass the end back through, this time going over and under all the way across, working from right to left.

6 Pass the end through a third time, going over, under, over and under, then crossing over itself, and going under, over, under and over.

Decorative Knots • 269

7 Pull the slack through, leaving a bight on the side.

8 You now have the basic lead, and it's just a matter of doubling it as many times as you wish.

9 Work the slack out through the ends – this may take as long as or longer than tying the knot itself. Trim the ends, and hide them under the bights.

Ocean braid mat

For sailors making long passages during the Age of Sail, the only thing worse than too much wind was too little wind. Stuck aboard ship in the Doldrums, their vessel 'as idle as a painted ship upon a painted ocean', the rigging would creak and groan, wearing away at the vessel's structure. What better than to use the time constructively and make some mats to protect the timber from chafe?

Their starting point was numerous knots that could be turned from hitches into flat objects. The carrick bend, for instance, could be enlarged ad infinitum to make a pleasing rectangular mat. The turk's head, too, normally used to protect spars, could be tied flat to make a circular mat (pages 264–267). Other knots were devised for no other purpose than to make mats, such as the prolong knot and the ocean plait.

The beauty of these knots is they can be produced in any size you like, which means they can be used for anything from epaulettes to ... epaulettes. The size is determined by three basic factors, which will all have an effect on the shape and texture of the final product.

• The first is the number of parts in the knot itself. The more parts you add, the longer or wider the knot becomes, and the more complicated it looks. Because of the way the knot is tied, you usually have to double or triple the whole knot, rather than simply add a bit at a time.
• The second is the number of rounds you make with the rope. The minimum is usually two rounds, and the maximum is six. A two-strand mat will look quite plain and may not sit quite flat, while a six-strand mat may look busy but will sit flat. Three rounds is the usual compromise.
• The third crucial factor is the size and type of rope used. A traditional 9mm (3/8in) hemp rope will produce a roughly textured mat that's ideal as a doormat, while some silken gold braid will

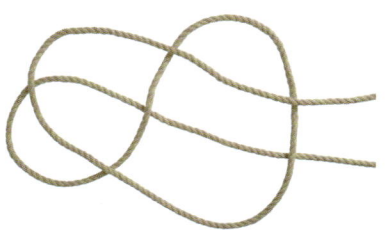

1 Starting with the loop in the bottom left of the picture and working clockwise, lay the line in the pattern shown. The working end is the lower line on the right-hand side.

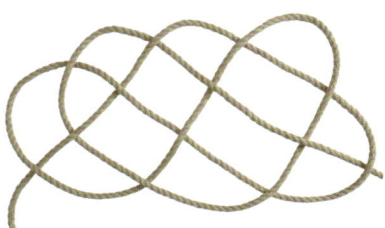

2 Take the working end and go around anticlockwise, tucking it over once, under twice, over once, under once, over once, and under once.

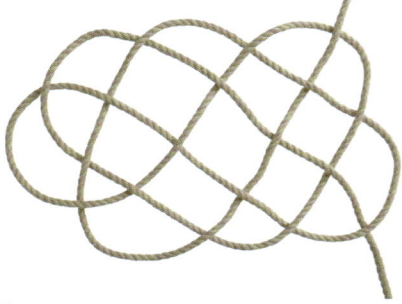

3 Still going anticlockwise, tuck the working end over once, under once, over once, and under once.

DECORATIVE KNOTS • 271

KNOT SCORE

Strength
Security
Difficulty Tying
Difficulty Untying
Usefulness

produce a sumptuous 'frog', which can be stitched onto a uniform as decoration. Modern synthetic ropes also lend themselves well to being tied into mats, and are available in a variety of colours.

As a rough guideline, 10m (35ft) of 10mm (3/8in) rope will produce a 300 × 170mm (12 × 6½in) mat with three 'passes', while 3m (10ft) of 3mm (1/8in) cord will make a 75 × 37mm (3 × 1½in) 'frog'.

KNOT KNOW-HOW

The ocean braid mat is also known as the sailor's true lover mat. To wash it, hose both sides thoroughly, and lay the mat flat while it dries.

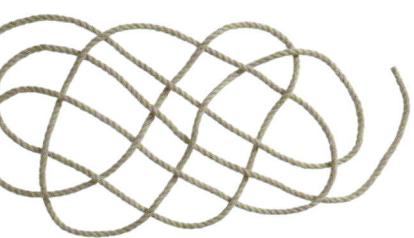

4 Now turn the working end clockwise and feed it in parellel to the standing end.

5 You can use either end of the line for the second pass – just make sure it goes under and over in exactly the same way as the first pass.

6 When the third pass is complete, the mat is tightened by 'chasing' any slack around to either end of the line. Any excess is then cut off, and the ends are stitched or lashed in place.

Doughnut

Served steel rings are used on traditional yachts to slide the foot of the jib out to the end of the bowsprit, thereby saving the crew a possible dunking. But, fear not, if you don't have a steel ring, you can still make a doughnut (or should that be dunking donut?) using cord as a foundation. The serving itself will keep it stiff and shipshape.

KNOT SCORE

Strength ❋❋❋❋
Security ❋❋❋❋
Difficulty Tying ❋❋❋
Difficulty Untying ❋❋❋❋❋
Usefulness ❋❋❋

1 Coil sufficient cord to make a suitably-sized foundation. The number of turns depends on the thickness of the cord.

2 Stop the cord at even intervals using either twine or electrical tape.

3 Tie the end of the serving line using a constrictor knot (page 40) or similar.

4 Wrap the foundation with the serving line, making sure the turns sit snugly side by side.

5 Go all the way round, making sure the foundation is completely covered.

KNOT KNOW-HOW

This variation of the served ring was described by Ashley in his *Book of Knots*. He suggests wrapping the foundation in sheet lead before making the service turns, to make the doughnut more durable. Alternatively, it can be tied in small stuff and used as a hanging switch.

6 Tie the serving line off using a clove hitch (page 32) or similar. The standing part of the foundation can be used to tie the doughnut or to make a loop.

DECORATIVE KNOTS • 273

WHIPPINGS & SEIZINGS 9

Plain whipping

Far from being a dying art, whipping is still the method of choice for many sailors wanting to keep their lines in order. A plain whipping is the simplest and most popular approach, but there are other, more decorative as well as more durable techniques. And if you've just bought some high-modulus line that needs sealing, then you won't do much better than the sailor's whipping (page 278) or the palm and needle whipping (page 279).

KNOT SCORE

Strength ✤ ✤
Security ✤ ✤
Difficulty Tying ✤
Difficulty Untying ✤ ✤
Usefulness ✤ ✤ ✤ ✤ ✤

There's no doubt that yachts have a lot of bits of string to play with. Even the smallest sailing boat has dozens of lines dangling off everything, from reefing points to lifejacket whistles. Trouble is, all those bits of string need to be stopped, or 'whipped', to prevent them becoming frayed.

Not surprisingly, sailors have devised all kinds of ingenious ways to carry out what is one of the most mundane and repetitive jobs aboard ship. Ashley lists at least 20 different methods for whipping rope with twine alone.

The simplest method is to take a couple of turns around the end with some waxed string, and tie a knot. Suitable candidates include a reef knot (page 180), a strangle knot (page 44), or a constrictor knot (page 38). These knots will provide an instant solution until you have time to put in a proper whipping.

The ultimate traditional 'stop' is the back splice (page 294), but this has the drawback of almost doubling the thickness of the line.

Since the invention of synthetic ropes, traditional methods have taken a backseat to the mindless ease of the butane whipping (page 281). A butane whipping will eventually work loose, however, which is why experienced sailors tend to use it as a temporary solution, prior to putting in something more durable.

Other non-traditional solutions include dipping, where the end of the line is dipped into a liquid, which then sets and 'glues' the strands together. There's also adhesive shrink tubing, which is applied with a hot air gun and literally shrinks over the end of the line.

Ironically, none of these methods work very satisfactorily with the latest high-modulus lines, such as Dyneema and Spectra, which just char if attacked with a lighter. The solution? A good old-fashioned whipping, such as those shown on the following pages.

1 Put a bight in the end of a length of twine, and lay it lengthways on the line.

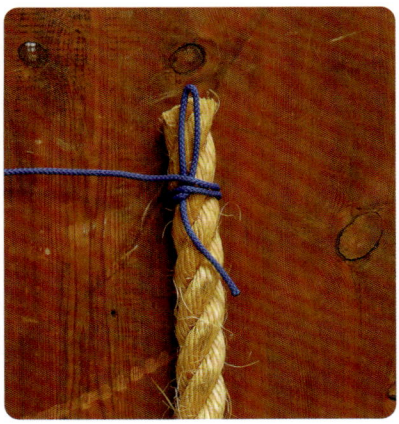

2 Holding the bight in place, wrap a few turns around the line, working towards the bight.

3 Keep going until the width of the whipping is about the same as the diameter of the line.

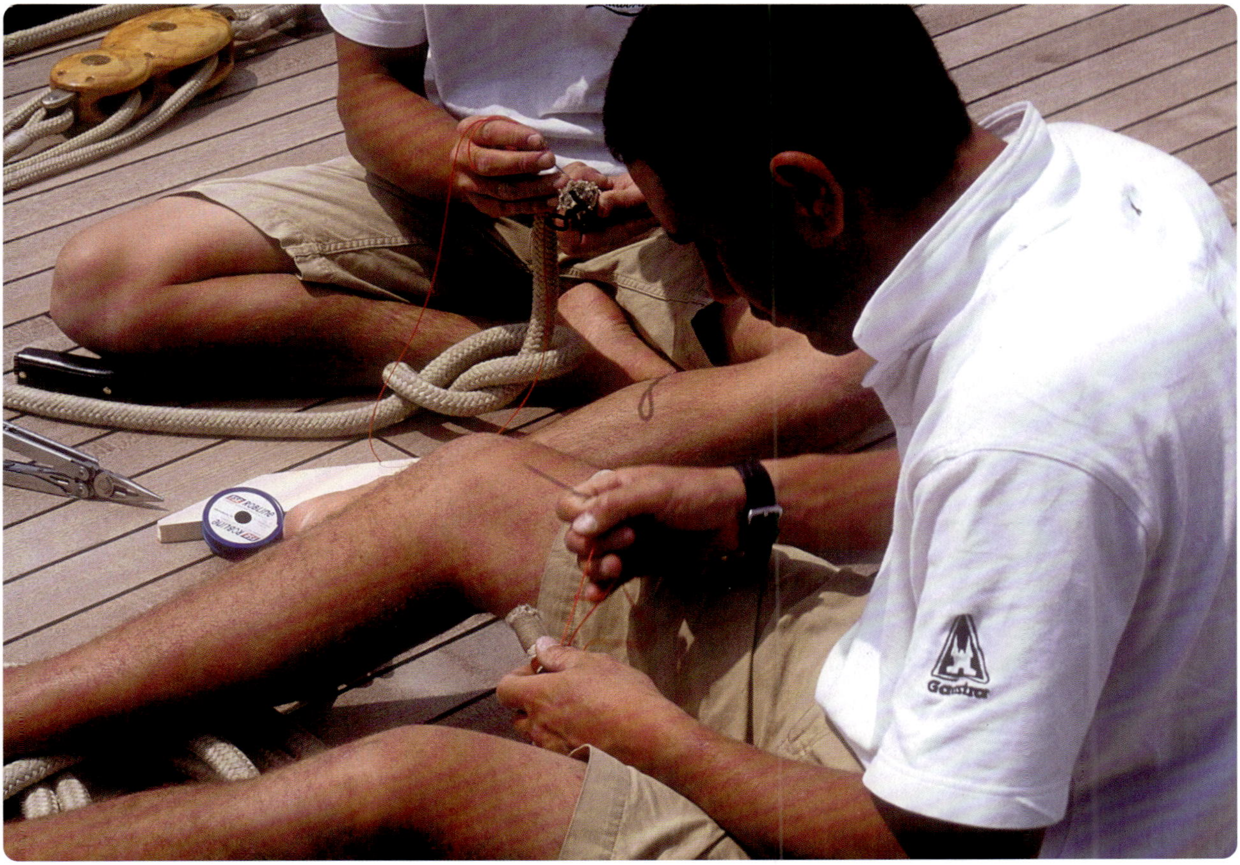

WHIPPINGS & SEIZINGS

4 Tuck the working end through the bight, and pull the standing end until the bight is hidden behind the turns.

5 Once the bight is tucked away, trim both ends flush with the sides of the whipping.

Sailor's whipping

Another whipping made without the use of needles, the sailor's whipping was one of the most popular aboard ship in the Age of Sail. It's an improvement on the plain whipping because the turns don't get disturbed when the ends are locked, and it's less likely to unravel. It's also really quite easy to do, once you get the hang of it.

KNOT SCORE

Strength ✿✿✿
Security ✿✿✿
Difficulty Tying ✿✿✿
Difficulty Untying ✿
Usefulness ✿✿✿✿✿

1 Lay the end of the twine lengthways over the line.

2 Wrap the twine around the line and over its own standing part, until the width of the whipping is about half the diameter of the line.

3 Put a bight in the twine, roughly the same length as used for the first half of the whipping.

4 Use the bight to continue wrapping the twine around the line, until the bight runs out.

5 Pull the standing part of the twine to close the bight, and trim both ends flush with the middle turns.

Palm & needle whipping

If a job's worth doing, it's worth doing well, and this whipping certainly rewards the extra effort put into making it. Not only is it one of the most durable whippings, with the twine actually stitched through the rope, but it also looks just right. And it's suitable for use with braided and high-modulus ropes, where two or three frapping turns are usually applied.

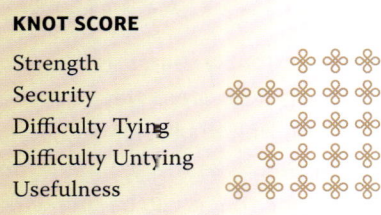

KNOT SCORE
Strength
Security
Difficulty Tying
Difficulty Untying
Usefulness

1 Using a sailmaker's needle, pass the working end of the twine between the strands – or, for an extra strong whipping, through one of the strands.

2 Tuck the standing end between the strands, and wrap the twine around the line until the whipping is as wide as the diameter of the line. Pass the end between the top strands.

3 Follow the groove between the nearest two strands to make the first frapping turn, then insert the needle so it emerges in the neighbouring groove.

4 Run the twine up that groove for the second frapping turn, and insert the needle so it emerges in the next groove.

5 Run the twine down that groove, and insert the needle again so it emerges next to the initial frapping turn.

6 Tuck the working end under a few of the wrapping turns and trim it flush.

French whipping

You've probably seen this whipping at your local nautically-themed pub or bar, as it's a great way to cover railings and poles. You can also use it on a handrail to provide a good grip with an attractive finish. Although not as secure as the palm and needle whipping (page 279), it has the advantage that it can be tied without using a needle.

KNOT SCORE
Strength
Security
Difficulty Tying
Difficulty Untying
Usefulness

1 Tie a running loop in the end of the line, using an overhand loop (page 124) or similar.

2 Pass the working end around the line, going in the same direction as the lay of the line, and tuck it under itself to form the first half hitch.

3 Continue tying hitches with the twine, making sure the row of knots follows the lay of the line.

4 The complete whipping should be at least as wide as the diameter of the line.

5 After tying the last hitch, tuck the end under the last two turns to prevent it coming loose.

Butane whipping

Unlike traditional cordage, modern ropes melt easily so the ends can be sealed to prevent fraying. Unless done properly, however, a butane whipping will eventually crack and come undone. It should therefore be seen as a temporary measure, until such time as a 'proper' whipping is put in. And don't even try it with high-modulus rope, which will just char.

KNOT SCORE

Strength
Security
Difficulty Tying
Difficulty Untying
Usefulness

1 Even plaited rope such as this will soon become frayed with use.

2 If a hot knife isn't available, you can use a traditional lighter or a lighter stick for the job.

3 The end can be melted as it stands, or some masking tape can be applied around it beforehand to prevent the end mushrooming.

KNOT KNOW-HOW

If you're working with small stuff (ie twine and suchlike) it pays to use the correct terminology. A whipping is tied into the end of rope to prevent it fraying. A seizing is used to bind two or more lines (or other objects) together. A stopping is a temporary whipping or seizing, made up of a few turns and a knot. A serving is a protective covering of rope, often used to guard against chafe.

4 All the usual precautions when working with naked flames apply – and make sure the area is well ventilated to get rid of the fumes!

Crown whipping

Another whipping that can double up as a rail wrap (although the initial hitch will need to be adapted), this whipping uses the crown splice as its starting point. The turns are then simply repeated until you end up with three neat ridges, following the lay of the rope. It's a secure and attractive knot, which does have a tendency to bulk up.

KNOT SCORE
Strength
Security
Difficulty Tying
Difficulty Untying
Usefulness

1 Tie a piece of twine to the middle of another piece of twine twice its length. Place the three 'arms' in the centre of the line, as shown.

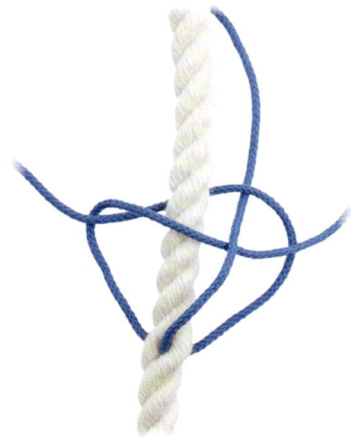

2 Pass each end under the standing part of its neighbour, pulling to the right to follow the lay of the line.

3 Continue weaving the twine under and over, making sure the turns follow the lay of the line.

4 Tighten the crowns as you work your way to the end of the line.

5 To finish off, tuck each end under the previous two crowns, and trim each one flush.

West Country whipping

There's nothing terribly clever about this whipping and it can be tied using the most basic tools (ie a knife), but it's also remarkably hard-wearing. Even if the finishing knot does eventually come undone, the rest of the knots will hold it all together for a good while longer. Use it for slippery lines if you don't have or don't want to use a needle.

KNOT SCORE
Strength
Security
Difficulty Tying
Difficulty Untying
Usefulness

1 Fold a length of twine in half. Centre it, and tie an overhand knot (page 172) around the end of the line.

2 Tighten the knot. A constrictor knot (page 40) also makes a good starting knot, as it binds the strands together.

KNOT KNOW-HOW

There are non-traditional options for those looking for something more contemporary than waxed twine. Electrical tape (yes, that multicoloured stuff they sell at the hardware store) makes an excellent stop-gap whipping. And some people swear by dental floss, which they claim is longer-lasting than twine. Just as long as you don't start using twine in place of dental floss...

3 Take the ends around half a turn, and tie an overhand knot on the other side of the line.

4 Repeat this process until the whipping is the required length. Finish by tying the ends together with a reef knot (page 180).

Flat seizing

Seizings were traditionally used in standing rigging where the thickness of rope or wire made it impractical to splice. Nowadays, they can be used with modern plaited rope which is too complicated or time-consuming to splice. They can also be used to tie metal brackets to wire, or even wire to wire, if suitable fittings are unavailable.

KNOT SCORE
Strength ❁❁❁
Security ❁❁❁❁
Difficulty Tying ❁❁
Difficulty Untying ❁❁
Usefulness ❁❁❁❁❁

1 Tie the two parts together with a running bowline (page 150) or similar, tied in the end of the seizing line.

2 Wrap the seizing line around both parts, sliding the turns snugly side by side. Eight or ten turns are traditionally recommended.

3 Pass the working end up through the turns, using a marlinspike if necessary.

4 Pull the working end to remove any slack.

5 Take a couple of frapping turns around the seizing, so the end emerges inside the loop. Tie a flat knot, as shown.

6 Tighten the knot and trim the end, leaving a short tail.

WHIPPINGS & SEIZINGS • 285

Racking seizing

This method is particularly suited to seizing wire, where the repeated figure-eight turns prevent any slippage. Tied in rope, it can make a trusty loop that is every bit as secure as a splice. Unlike splices, seizings have the advantage that they can be quickly untied or cut loose if the line is needed in its original form.

KNOT SCORE
Strength
Security
Difficulty Tying
Difficulty Untying
Usefulness

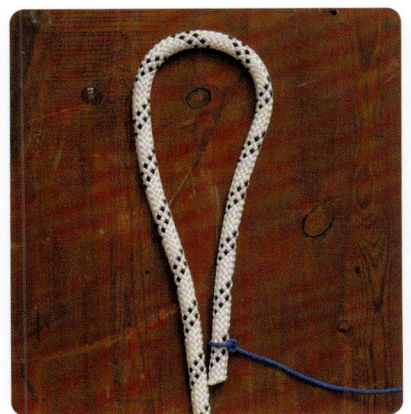

1 Tie the end of the seizing line to one part using a running bowline (page 150) or similar.

2 Weave the line around the two parts, passing between them at every turn.

3 Put in at least five turns. Leave a space the thickness of the seizing line between each turn.

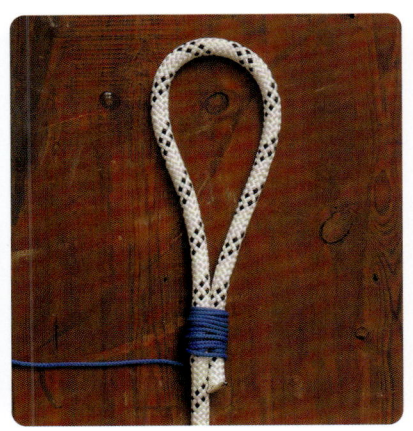

4 Wrap the seizing line around both parts, slipping the line in between each of the existing turns.

5 Take two frapping turns around the seizing and tighten the knot. Tie the end off with a flat knot, as shown opposite, Step 5.

BEST FOR making a chafe guard

Whippings aren't only used as whippings. Tied with thicker rope they can make practical as well as decorative chafe guards to protect various parts of a boat. But probably their most common use nowadays is in nautically themed pubs, where they serve to decorate pillars and posts. Perhaps that's not so surprising, given the long-standing connection between sailors and booze. And cheers to that!

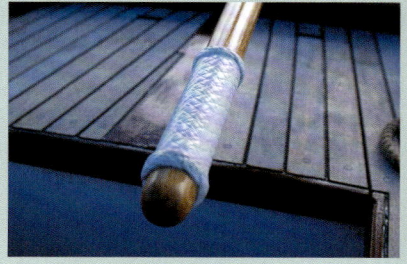

Whipping the end of lines to prevent them unravelling is a dying art, thanks to the ease that modern synthetic rope can be sealed with a so-called butane whipping (page 281). But whippings live on in other forms. Tied using 3mm or 4mm line, instead of twine, they can provide a protective layer on spars and other parts of a boat, whether it's to prevent the boom chaffing against the rigging or to reduce the wear and tear on a pillar in the saloon. They can also provide a useful grip on slippery surfaces, such as a handrail or a tiller handle. Or they can simply be used decoratively to enhance the look of a boat, bar or log cabin.

The simplest option is the aptly named plain whipping (page 276). This creates a plain, even surface with good grip. It's quick to do and can cover quite a large area, though it is limited by the fact that you have to pull the bight through all those turns in order to finish it off. After about 6in, it becomes difficult to pull through – though a pair of pliers can usually sort that out! It's somewhat less secure than the other whippings shown here, as once one end comes loose then the whole thing will quickly unravel.

There's no such problem with the French whipping (page 280), which is basically a series of half hitches. There's something quite magical about the way those half hitches create a perfect spiral with minimal effort from the knot-tyer, winding elegantly around whatever object they're tied to. As a grip, the ridge made by the spiral creates extra friction – or it can just be an annoying lump in your hand, depending how you feel about it. As decoration, it's hard to beat the 'bang for your buck' of this whipping.

It would be nice to say the same about the West Country whipping (page 283) but, while this works perfectly well in its intended purpose as a whipping on the end of a line, it is much less secure tied with slippery modern cordage. Despite being made of a series of overhand knots, it's really no more secure than a plain whipping, while requiring a lot more effort. The overall effect is nice enough, and if that's what you're after then it's worth persevering. It will at least make a change from the ubiquitous French whipping.

Finally, a classic way of creating a chafe guard is by trying a Turk's head – or possibly a series of Turk's heads. Of the various examples shown in this book, the 4L × 3B version on page 262 is the most suitable. You can flesh it out by making three/four passes, or you could tie several side by side. It's more work than any of the whippings shown, but it's also the most secure and, in a happy fusion of form and function, the most decorative.

PLAIN WHIPPING: Simple, easy to tie and effective, the plain whipping (page 276) is the 'full fat milk' candidate of the whipping world.

FRENCH WHIPPING: French whipping (page 280) is a bit more hassle but, if that decorative spiral isn't a problem, it's easily worth it. Every pub landlord's favourite knot.

WEST COUNTRY WHIPPING: It's pretty enough, but the West Country whipping (page 283) is considerably less secure than the French whipping in this context.

TURK'S HEAD: Going further afield, the Turk's head is both secure and extremely decorative – and also a lot more work than any of the others. But it's worth it, right?

SPLICES 10

Short splice

'Splice the mainbrace!' It's one of the best known nautical expressions, which is now only used with reference to alcohol. And splicing a 75mm (3in) line in the middle of an Atlantic storm was something that deserved to be rewarded with alcohol. Nowadays, splicing is a much more genteel affair which can be mastered by anyone who can repeat 'over and under' enough times. If you can plait hair, you can tie a splice.

KNOT SCORE
Strength
Security
Difficulty Tying
Difficulty Untying
Usefulness

It used to be thought that splicing rope was a mysterious art that could only be mastered by the most experienced sailors and craftsmen. Modern how-to books and videos have put paid to that myth, and now splicing is practised by amateur sailors and knot-tyers alike.

Modern materials have contributed to this trend. It's infinitely easier to weave together the silky strands of synthetic three-strand rope than it ever was sisal and manila. The downside is that splices made using modern fibres are more likely to come undone and, where two or three tucks might have sufficed using traditional ropes, nowadays you'd be foolish to put in less than four.

The main arguments for using a splice instead of a knot are clear. Whereas a knot weakens the rope by around 50 per cent, a splice weakens it by just 5–10 per cent. A splice is also generally more secure and creates a more permanent join than a knot. The main disadvantages are that it's more time-consuming to tie, it can't be undone in a hurry, and it increases the diameter of the line by as much as 100 per cent.

The length of a splice is measured in tucks, that is the number of times the strands of one part pass under the strands of the other part.

1 Seize the lines, allowing about three times the diameter of each line per tuck. In this case, five tucks using 10mm (⅜in) line: 3 × 10 × 5 = 150mm (5⅝in).

5 Pick any strand from the top part of the splice, and open the strand directly to its left (or to its right if using left-hand laid rope). Use a marlinspike or fid if necessary.

6 Tuck the first strand under its neighbour, and pull it up firmly. Tuck the other two strands on that side of the splice under the strands immediately to their left too.

7 Repeat the process for a further four tucks, going over and under in a clockwise direction.

2 Tease the strands apart, and reseal or whip the ends if necessary.

3 Marry, or 'crotch', the strands together, so the ends point in alternate directions.

4 Seize the strands on the bottom part of the splice, using either whipping twine or electrical tape.

8 Remove the seizing. Pick any strand from the bottom part of the splice, and tuck in under the strand immediately to its right (or to its left if using left-hand laid rope).

9 Do the same for the rest of the strands. Repeat the process for a further four tucks, going over and under in an anticlockwise direction.

10 Pull the ends tight. The splice can then be rolled underfoot or pounded with a marlinspike or fid to smooth it out. Trim the ends flush, and seal them if necessary.

Long splice

Where it's important that the thickness of the rope remains constant, use the long splice. It's based on the principle of two strands on one line being unlaid and replaced with two strands from the other line. Although it doesn't bulk up the line as much as the short splice, it does weaken the line considerably more – by as much as 50 per cent, according to some.

KNOT SCORE
Strength
Security
Difficulty Tying
Difficulty Untying
Usefulness

1 Mark off each line, allowing about 40 times the diameter for the splice. In this case, 40 × 10mm (⅜in) = 400mm (16in).

2 Tease the strands apart up to the marks, and marry them together so the ends point in alternate directions.

3 Take any strand from the top line and unravel it for about 350mm (14in). Take the matching strand from the lower line and lay it in the groove left by the missing strand.

4 Trim the end of the loose strand, leaving enough length to tie and tuck it later.

5 Take the next strand in the top line and unravel it for about 175mm (7in). Take the matching strand from the lower line and lay it in the groove left by the missing strand.

6 Cross the remaining two strands and tuck the ends under at least two strands, or until they run out.

SPLICES • 293

7 Do the same for the other pairs of strands where they meet further up the line. Trim any excess.

8 Trim the ends flush, and seal if necessary. The splice can then be rolled underfoot or pounded with a marlinspike or fid to smooth it out.

Back splice

A quick and effective way of preventing a line from fraying is to tie a back splice in it. Although this is usually seen as a temporary measure before putting in a whipping (pages 274–287), there's no reason not to leave it in permanently. The only catch is that it does double the line's thickness, which can be a help or a hindrance depending on where it's being used.

KNOT SCORE
Strength
Security
Difficulty Tying
Difficulty Untying
Usefulness

1 Seize the line, allowing about three times the diameter of the line per tuck. In this case, six tucks using 10mm (⅜in) line: 3 × 10mm (⅜in) × 6 = 180mm (6¾in).

2 Tease the strands apart, and reseal or whip the ends if necessary.

3 Pass each strand over the standing part of the strand immediately to its right to form a crown (page 226).

4 Pull the strands down to tighten the crown.

5 Pick any strand, and pass it over the next strand to the right in the standing part, and then under the next one.

6 Do the same for the other two strands.

7 Repeat this process, working down the line in an anticlockwise direction.

8 Once you've made five or six tucks, tighten the splice. The end can then be cut flush and sealed if necessary (not shown here).

Hard eye splice

Wherever a shackle is attached to the end of a line, there will be wear on the rope. It makes sense then to tie a permanent loop, in the form of an eye splice, with a metal or plastic thimble inserted to protect the line. The hard eye splice is widely used aboard ship for halyards, anchor warps, mooring lines and many other purposes.

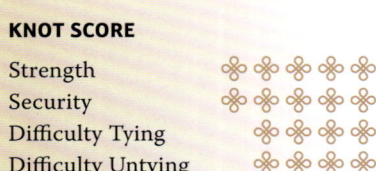

KNOT SCORE
Strength
Security
Difficulty Tying
Difficulty Untying
Usefulness

1 Tease the strands apart, allowing three times the line's diameter per tuck. Four tucks using 10mm (⅜in) line: 3 × 10mm (⅜in) × 4 = 120mm (4½in). Seize the line to the thimble.

2 Bend the line around the thimble, and seize the standing end to it.

3 Marry the working end to the standing part, so the middle and right strand are over it, and the left strand under it. (Note this picture shows a side view.)

4 Pass the right-hand strand over the strand immediately to its right in the standing part, and tuck it under the next one. Do the same for the other two strands.

5 Tuck all the strands again, going over and under in an anticlockwise direction.

6 Repeat the process, pulling the strands tight as you go.

Soft eye splice

If you're not planning to put a shackle or a chain through the end of the line, then a regular 'soft' eye splice will do nicely. This is often used in running rigging on traditional yachts and for mooring lines on vessels of all kinds.

KNOT SCORE

Strength	✥✥✥✥
Security	✥✥✥✥
Difficulty Tying	✥✥✥✥
Difficulty Untying	✥✥✥✥
Usefulness	✥✥✥✥

1 Seize the line and tease the strands apart, allowing three times the diameter per tuck. Splice the end to the standing part, following the same procedure as opposite.

2 At least three tucks are required for traditional ropes (shown) and five or six for modern cordage. Trim the ends flush and sea. if necessary.

7 After at least three tucks (more if using modern cordage), the ends can be teased apart and trimmed by about 50 per cent using a knife.

8 Pass the thinned ends over and under one more time to create a tapered splice. Seal the ends if necessary.

Traditional chain splice

Rather than carry a great weight of chain in the bows of the boat, many sailors extend the scope of their anchor chain with rope. The trouble with this is that a conventional eye splice (with or without a thimble) will usually be too bulky to fit on the anchor winch. The solution is to use a long splice, which hardly bulks out the line at all.

KNOT SCORE
Strength
Security
Difficulty Tying
Difficulty Untying
Usefulness

1 Seize the line and tease the strands apart, allowing about 40 times the diameter of each line for the splice. In this case, 40 × 10mm (⅜in) = 400mm (15in).

2 Pass the middle and right-hand strands through the chain.

3 Pass the right-hand strand back under itself and over the middle strand.

5 Gradually unlay the left-hand strand, putting the middle strand in its place. Make sure you fit the twist already present in the middle strand to the twist of the line.

6 Shortly before the middle strand runs out, cross it over the left-hand strand.

7 Tuck the ends under at least three strands, and pull them tight to hide the join.

4 Bring the right-hand strand up against the chain. Wrap the middle strand around its own and the right-hand strand's standing parts until it meets the left-hand strand.

8 Put a hitch in the right-hand strand, and tuck the end through the top of the knot. Cut the end flush and seal if necessary.

KNOT KNOW-HOW

The traditional method of tapering a splice is to 'thin' each strand with a knife after the last full tuck. You can shave off half the thickness, and put in one more tuck, or you can shave off a third, followed by a tuck, and then another third, followed by a final tuck. Another method is to cut one strand flush and tuck two strands, then cut another strand flush, and tuck the final strand.

9 Tighten the splice, and cut the middle and left-hand strands flush and seal if necessary. Roll the splice underfoot or pound it gently to even it out.

Grommet splice

Rope grommets are 'endless' rings made by splicing rope together. They were used as masthoops, chest handles and for holding blocks together. Spliced to a line, they also made very forgiving rings, with more structural rigidity than a conventional soft eye splice. This method can also be used to splice the end of one line to the bight of another.

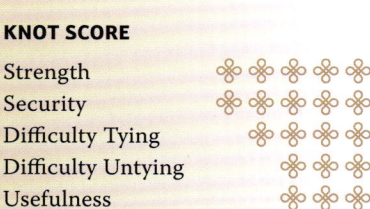

KNOT SCORE
Strength
Security
Difficulty Tying
Difficulty Untying
Usefulness

1 Both the grommet (left) and the line are made of traditional materials, so a short splice will be sufficient. Put in a longer splice if using modern materials.

2 Tease the line apart, allowing at least three times the diameter of the line per tuck. In this case, three tucks using 10mm (⅜in) line: 3 × 10mm (⅜in) × 3 = 90mm (3⅜in).

3 Tuck the left-hand strand of the line under any strand in the grommet.

4 Tuck the centre strand under a strand immediately to the right of the first tuck, and tuck the right-hand strand under a strand immediately to the right of that.

5 Pass the strands through the grommet, and turn it over. Tuck each strand under its own standing part in the line, going in an anticlockwise direction.

6 Put in at least two more tucks if working with traditional ropes; more if working with modern cordage.

7 Tighten the splice. Trim the ends flush, and seal if necessary.

Multiplait eyesplice

With its multiple strands and confusing weave, you might think multiplait is by definition impossible to splice. But keep a cool head, and it can be done. The secret is to be able to identify the right- from the left-twisting strands (there are four of each). Group them together into pairs, and you're already down to four 'double' strands. It's plain sailing from there.

KNOT SCORE
Strength ❋❋❋❋❋
Security ❋❋❋❋❋
Difficulty Tying ❋❋❋
Difficulty Untying ❋❋❋
Usefulness ❋❋❋

1 Seize the line, allowing about 12 times its own diameter. Separate the strands into two right-twisting and two left-twisting pairs, using different coloured electrical tape.

2 Decide on the size of the loop, and tuck the left-hand pair under the nearest pair of strands in the standing part, passing under the strands from left to right.

3 Turn the loop over. Tuck the next pair under the next pair of strands in the standing part, and repeat the process for the remaining two pairs.

5 Pass a pair of strands over the pair immediately to their left, then split them and tuck them under the next pair – one under one strand, the other under the other strand, working from right to left.

6 Turn the loop over, and do the same with an opposite pair (if you started with left-twisting, now choose right-twisting, and vice versa), but this time working from left to right.

7 Keep going, alternating between left- and right-twisting pairs, and changing direction after each round of tucks.

4 Once you've done a complete round, split the pairs but keep them grouped together and make sure they are marked as right- or left-twisting.

8 Once you've made the required number of tucks (a minimum of four is advised), whip the ends ready for cutting.

9 Trim the ends. Alternatively, they can be sealed with a butane whipping (page 281) – but be careful not to scorch the standing part!

Multiplait chain splice

Multiplait is the best modern rope to use for an anchor line, but as with three strand (page 298), you have the problem of joining the rope to the chain without creating an ungainly lump. Once again, the solution is a long splice – but this time going into the chain itself. Once you get your head around all those bits of string, it's not as difficult as it looks. Honest!

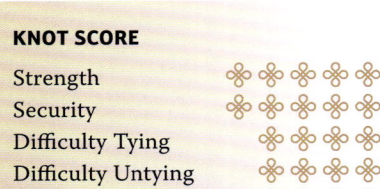

KNOT SCORE
Strength
Security
Difficulty Tying
Difficulty Untying
Usefulness

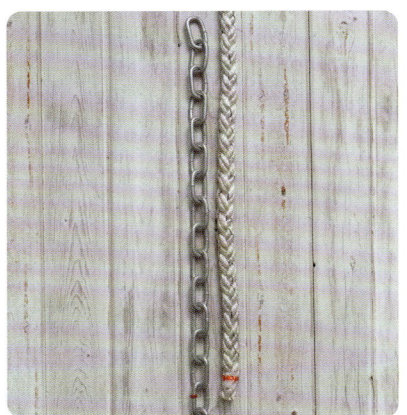

1 Count the number of tucks you're going to make by the links of chain – 15 is sufficient – and mark it off on the line.

2 Seize the line and tease the strands apart. Group the strands together into two left- and two right-twisting pairs. Place a pair of each on either side of the chain.

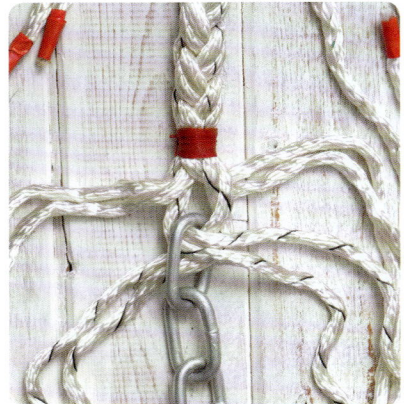

3 Take one pair of strands and pass them through the first link, from left to right. Take the matching pair from the other side, and pass them through the same link from right to left.

4 Continue in this way, threading the first matching pairs through every second link from opposite directions, until 15 links have been spliced.

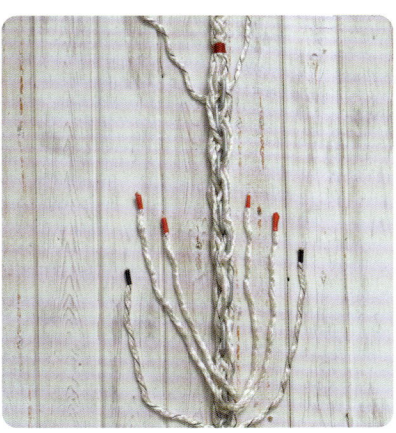

5 Repeat the process, this time with a single matching strand from each side, alternating directions.

6 Repeat the process again with the last two matching strands.

7 Seize the last two pairs of strands around the last link of chain, using whipping twine tied off with a constrictor knot (page 40) or similar.

8 Do the same for the remaining pairs of strands.

Dyneema reduction splice

The astonishing strength of high-modulus ropes such as Dyneema and Spectra is gradually transforming the face of yachting. Suddenly, lashings and 'soft shackles' (page 312) are back in fashion after centuries of neglect. The new materials' reluctance to be tied down also means that other old-fashioned skills are re-emerging in new guises.

KNOT SCORE
Strength
Security
Difficulty Tying
Difficulty Untying
Usefulness

When rope was first created, the main concern was to make it as strong as possible. With the advent of materials such as Spectra and Dyneema, strength is no longer an issue. These ropes are 15 times as strong as wire, weight for weight, and are far more resistant to stretch and chafe than their predecessors. Indeed, a common complaint is that high-modulus lines 'look' too thin for the job, even though they're probably stronger than necessary.

Thin lines can also be hard to handle, so there's a temptation to fit much thicker lines than really needed – a conundrum our ancestors would have been astonished by.

One of the main drawbacks of these lines is that they don't tie well. For one thing, they tend to be very slippery and will pull out of traditional knots such as a sheet bend (page 90). Try a double or triple fisherman's knot (page 114) instead. In terms of loops, the figure-eight loop (page 125) is a better bet than the trusted old bowline (page 126), while the topsail halyard bend (page 58) and cow hitch (page 53) are said to be the most effective hitches.

Slippage aside, tying knots in high-modulus ropes is said to weaken the line far more than traditional cordage. Most manufacturers recommend not tying knots at all, and using splices whenever possible – several of which are shown in the following pages.

As well as having to brush up on their splices, sailors using these ropes are also having to relearn the art of whipping (pages 274–287). Dyneema and her sisters don't melt in the way previous synthetic lines did, so simply burning the ends with a butane whipping (page 281) isn't an option, and the needle and thread are making a comeback.

In order to reduce weight aloft, the casing of high-modulus lines is often removed. The best way to do this is with a reduction splice shown on these pages, which ensures the core doesn't slip when the outside of the rope is gripped by a jamming cleat or similar.

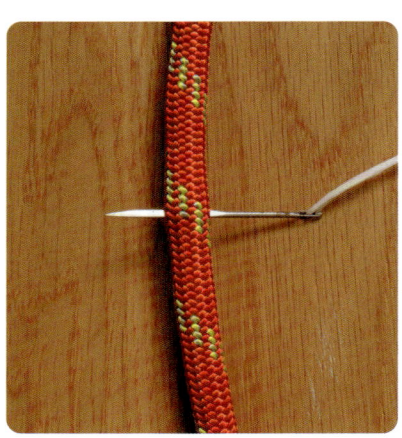

1 Use a sail needle and twine to put a stitch through the case and core of the line. This will prevent any movement while the splice is being made.

2 Prick a hole in the case below the stich, and tease out the Dyneema or Spectra core.

3 Pull the core all the way out, being careful not to damage it in the process.

SPLICES • 307

4 Pass a hollow fid through the centre of the core, and slip the end of the case over one end of the fid.

5 Work the case through the centre of the core using the fid. Reduce, or 'thin', the cover by trimming off some of the braiding with a knife.

6 Slide the core over the case (which effectively becomes the new core). Put three more stitches through the splice and cover it with a whipping (pages 274–287).

Spectra splice

It took centuries of evolution to work out the best way to splice traditional ropes, and no doubt the same will be true of the current generation of high-modulus ropes. Two somewhat different approaches are taken over the following two spreads – and there are other new methods emerging all the time. Try as many as you can and see which works best for you.

KNOT SCORE
Strength ❀❀❀❀❀
Security ❀❀❀❀❀
Difficulty Tying ❀❀❀
Difficulty Untying ❀❀❀❀
Usefulness ❀❀❀❀❀

1 Overlap the two ends and tape them together with electrical tape, so each end is about 250–300mm (10–12in) long.

2 Use a fid to prize apart the strands in the standing part of one line directly next to the tape. Make sure you don't pierce or tear the fibre.

3 Feed the working end of the other line through the gap with the fid, and pull it tight.

5 Pull the working end tight.

6 Skip two strands, and pass the fid through the core of the standing part for about 150mm (6in).

7 Feed the working end through the core using the fid, and pull it tight.

4 Skip over two strands, and pass the fid through the standing part of the first line, without tearing the fibre.

8 Tease apart the strands in the working end.

9 Trim the strands with a knife or scissors to create a tapered end.

10 Work the end back into the core of the other line until it disappears from view. Repeat the process with the opposing end (not shown).

Dyneema loop

Dyneema loops have many uses on modern and traditional yachts alike. Not only are they stronger than their bronze or stainless steel counterparts, but they are also softer and lighter, which means they're less likely to damage the surrounding areas. Use them to attach blocks, secure reefing cringles or simply to hoist an outboard on deck.

KNOT SCORE
Strength ❋❋❋❋❋
Security ❋❋❋❋❋
Difficulty Tying ❋❋❋❋❋
Difficulty Untying ❋❋❋❋❋
Usefulness ❋❋❋

1 Cut enough line for the circumference of the loop, allowing about 200mm (8in) at either end for the splice.

2 Seize the cover to prevent it slipping, and remove it from the working ends using a sharp knife.

3 Use a hollow fid to open the standing part of one side, and pass the other working end through it.

7 Use a splicing needle or wand to feed the tapered end into the core.

8 Slide the end into the core, until it disappears.

9 Taper the other working end in a similar way.

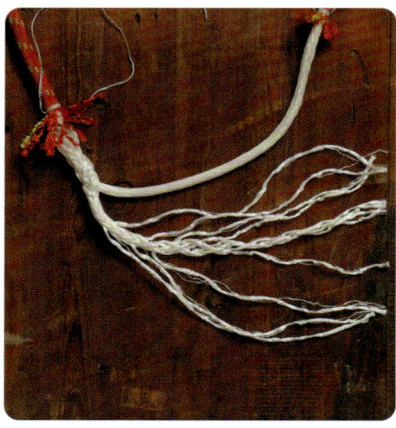

4 Tease apart the strands of the part that has been pierced, and split them into two.

5 Wrap the two sets of strands around the standing part of the other side, and plait them back together.

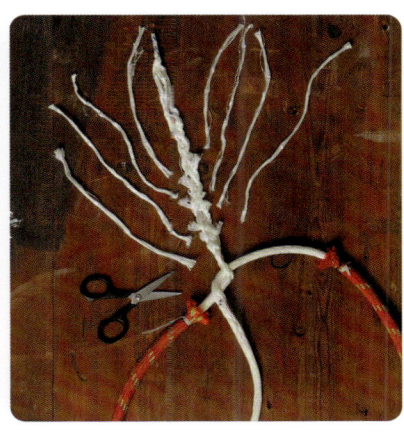

6 Taper the newly-reformed end by trimming the strands out of the plait.

10 Use a splicing needle or wand to feed it into the core. Remove any excess.

11 Slide the cover over as much of the core as possible.

12 Cover the whole splice with a whipping (pages 274–287).

Dyneema soft shackle

The Dyneema soft shackle combines the latest splicing techniques with some very traditional knot-tying to create a functional and yet attractive piece of sailing gear. If only the marriage of old and new was always this successful! Use it for attaching sheets, blocks and halyards. A piece of Velcro taped around the shackle will prevent it opening unexpectedly.

KNOT SCORE

Strength
Security
Difficulty Tying
Difficulty Untying
Usefulness

1 Cut a 0.9m (36in) length of line.

2 Put one mark 300mm (12in) from one end of the line, and another mark 140mm (5½in) from the first.

3 Use a fid to pass the working end through the core, entering at the second mark, and exiting at the first.

7 Put a bight in the standing part and tuck it under the loop, as shown.

8 Pass the standing end around the working end and tuck it under itself, where it is visible through the loop.

9 Tighten the knot, working it down so it forms a cylindrical shape.

4 Slide the working end through the core, using a fid to prevent the loop slipping through.

5 Pass the working end through the standing part, close to where the line emerges from the core.

6 Pull the working end through, and form an underhand loop.

10 Pass the ends around the two strands at the base of the knot, one end around each strand. Pull the ends up through the centre of the knot.

11 Cut the ends flush with the top of the toggle.

12 To use the shackle, ease the loop open, slip the toggle inside, and tighten the loop again.

Glossary

B

barque A sailing ship with three masts, fitted with square sails on the two foremost masts and a fore-and-aft sail on the rearmost mast.

beamshelf The timber that goes around the inside edge of a wooden hull to support the deck beams.

belay To make fast a line by winding it onto a cleat or pin.

belaying pin A wooden or metal bar which is inserted into a rail or bracket and used to make fast a line.

bend A type of knot used to tie two lines together (page 22).

bight a) The part of a line in between the two ends; b) an open loop in which the two legs are not crossed.

block A pulley used to change the direction of a line or as part of a tackle (see below) to gain mechanic advantage.

bolt ropes Rope stitched along the edge of a sail, either to give protection against chafe or to enable the sail to be set in a groove in a spar or in roller reefing.

boom A hinged spar fixed to the bottom of the mast, used to stretch out the foot of the sail.

bosun's chair A chair made either of canvas or wood which is hung from a rope and used to hoist a ship's crew aloft or to lower them over the side.

bowsprit A spar attached to the front of the vessel to which the foremost rigging is attached.

buntline A line which hangs down the leeward side of a square sail and is used to prevent the sail billowing while it is being furled.

C

cable-laid A very thick rope made of at least three hawser-laid ropes twisted together (page 20).

centreboard A retractable keel pivoted near its front edge to enable it to swing upwards either directly under the hull, or within a case inside the hull.

coir A natural fibre made from coconut shells.

cringle A reinforced ring or grommet set into the sail and used to attach it to the spars and rigging.

D

davit A small crane fitted on a ship to hoist dinghies, anchors and other cargo.

deadeye A thick disk of wood with three holes drilled through it. One is attached to the ship's rigging (specifically the shrouds) and the other to the ship's side, and a line is rove between them to tension the rigging.

ditty bag A cloth bag used to hold tools or personal belongings.

Dyneema A high-tech synthetic modern fibre used to make ropes. It is said to be 15 times as strong as steel, weight for weight.

E

elbow A loop with an extra twist (page 22).

F

fairleads A metal fitting through which lines are passed to prevent chafe on the vessel's structure.

fid A tapered pin, usually made of wood or bone, used to separate the strands of rope while splicing (page 18).

fore-and-aft Lining up with the vessel lengthways, ie from front to back rather than from side to side.

frapping turns Lashings wound around at right angles to the wrapping turns (see below) in order to tighten and secure them.

G

genoa A large triangular sail set in front of the mast which overlaps the mainsail.

H

halyard A line used to hoist a sail or flag.

hawser A large rope used to moor or to tow a ship.

hawser-laid When a rope is made of three strands of right-twisting rope, twisted together in a left-hand direction. Also known as plain-laid.

heaving line A thin line which is tied to a much thicker line (usually a mooring warp). The heaving line is thrown ashore and then used to pull the mooring line from the ship to the shore.

high-modulus A material that has a high resistance to being deformed and therefore remains stiff under a load.

hitch A type of knot used to attach a line to an object (page 22).

J

jackyards A short spar used to extend the sail area beyond the scope of the existing spars.

jammer A fitting used to lock a halyard or other part of the running rigging instead of a cleat.

jib A small triangular sail set in front of the mast which does not overlap the mainsail.

junk Old rope no longer fit for purpose which is used for making mats, fenders or caulking.

jury mast A temporary spar, often made out of a boom or spinnaker pole, rigged in place of the normal mast when it has broken.

L

lanyard a) a short length of decorated cord attached to a tool or instrument to prevent it getting lost; b) a length of rope attached between a pair of deadeyes (see above) to tension the rigging.

lighterman A worker employed to transfer cargo on and off ships, especially on the River Thames in London.

M

marlinspike A tapered metal pin, usually with a hole at the thick end, used to separate the strands of rope while splicing (page 18).

masthoop A wooden hoop which slides up and down the mast and holds the front edge (or luff) of a traditional fore-and-aft (gaff) sail.

P

painter A line attached to the front of a small boat, used to secure it to a pontoon or mooring.

palm A reinforced leather strap worn on the hand to protect it while sewing heavy materials.

pin rail A thick wooden plank with holes drilled into it into which the belaying pins (see above) are fitted.

R

ratlines Ropes tied horizontally in the ship's rigging (specifically the shrouds) to act as steps to allow the crew to climb the masts more easily.

reef To reduce the size of the sail by furling a portion of it. This is done when the wind is too strong for the full area of sail.

reefing points A row of cringles, or grommets, set into the sail through which short lengths of line are passed to reef the sail.

rigging The wires and ropes that support the spars or operate the sails.

royal A light square sail set above the topgallant on a square-rigged ship.

rudder A device attached to the back of a ship, used to steer it.

running rigging Ropes used to raise and control sails or spars, such as booms and spinnaker poles.

S

sail ties Short lengths of line or fabric used to secure a sail after it has been furled.

scrimshaw Engravings and small carvings made from the bones and teeth of marine animals such as whales and walruses.

seine fishing A method of fishing using a net hung vertically from floats to encircle and scoop up the fish.

sheet Rope used to control the outer end of a sail once it is hoisted.

shroud Part of the standing rigging that gives lateral support to the mast, running from the top of the mast to the sides of the vessel.

shroud-laid When a rope is made of four strands twisted together (page 20).

small stuff Thin string and twine used for whipping and seizing rope or for decorative purposes.

Spectra A high-tech, synthetic modern fibre used to make ropes.

spinnaker A large, balloon-like sail set at the front of a yacht for downwind sailing.

spinnaker pole A spar temporarily hinged at the base of the mast to hold the spinnaker out.

square-rigger A ship whose principal sails are square and set from yards which run from side to side rather than fore and aft. Most Tall Ships are square-riggers.

standing end The inactive end of a line while tying a knot (page 22).

standing part The part of a line between the standing end and the knot (page 22).

standing rigging The wires that support the mast(s), usually made of stainless or galvanised steel.

stay Part of the standing rigging that gives fore-and-aft support to the mast, running from the top of the mast to the front or back of the vessel.

stevedore Someone employed to load and unload ships.

strake One of the planks that make up the sides of a wooden hull.

studding sails Light sails rigged on the outside of the regular square sails on a square-rigger.

swager A tool used for attaching metal terminals to wire rigging.

T

tackle A combination of ropes and pulleys (or blocks) used to gain mechanical advantage for lifting objects or applying tension.

tiller A length of wood or metal used to lever a ship's rudder in order to steer the vessel.

topgallants The sail set above the topsail on a square-rigger – ie the third sail up!

W

warp A thick line used for mooring or towing a ship.

washboard A removable door in the entrance of a yacht's cabin.

whipping A series of turns wrapped with twine around the end of a line to stop it unravelling or over a splice to protect it from chafe.

working end The active end of the line while tying a knot (page 22).

wrapping turns The turns in rope lashings used to bind two or more objects together – as opposed to the frapping turns (above) which are used to bind the rope itself.

Y

yard The horizontal spars which the sails are set from – usually on square-rigged ships, but also on fore-and-aft rigged vessels.

Index

A

adhesive shrink tubing 276
adjustable bend 62–3, 108
Admiralty, British 232
  The Admiralty Manual of Seamanship 15, 60
Age of Discovery 12
Age of Sail 100, 161, 278
Aldridge, George 192
Alexander the Great 14
Alfa Romeo 175
alpine butterfly bend 88, 92, 144, 162
  variation of 94
alpine coil 218
Alston, Captain Alfred Henry 129
anchor snubber 84, 85
Anderson, RC, *Manuscript on Rigging* 60
angler's loop 133, 172
  double angler's loop 165
artillery loop 138
Asher, Dr Harry
  Alternative Book of Knots 66
  broach bend 99
  clara hitches 66, 67
  Law of Loop, Hitch & Bight 40
  locking loop 155
  simple simon 104
Ashley, Clifford
  The Ashley Book of Knots 15, 70, 92, 176
  Ashley's stopper knot 15, 176, 184, 185
  carrick bend 100
  constrictor knot 42
  doughnuts 272
  end of knot-tying 14–15
  extra turns 56
  good luck knot 248
  hangman's knot 158
  leads and bights in turk's heads 263
  lineman's loop 92
  Matthew Walker knot 238
  overhand bend 88
  reef knot 180
  rigger's bend 95
  round turn and two half hitches 28
  securest bends 106
  timber hitch 60
  types of knots and who tied them 12
  whipping rope 276
  zeppelin bend 25
Ashley's stopper 15, 24, 176–7, 184–5 238
Australian bushmen 146

B

back splice 226, 276
baggage labels, knots for 53
bale sling hitch 53
barques, four-masted 56
barrel knot 95
beeswax 19
belaying pins 75
bell ringer's knot 138, 215
bellrope keyring 258, 259
bends 86–121
  adjustable bend 62–3, 108
  alpine butterfly bend 88, 92, 94
  barrel knot 95
  blood knot 95
  braided splice 120–1, 146
  broach bend 99
  carrick bend 88, 92, 100–101, 110, 137, 230–231, 268
  definition of 22
  double fisherman's knot 115
  double reeving line bend 111
  double sheet bend 88, 91
  double simple simon 105
  figure-eight bend 88, 89
  fisherman's knot 25, 114, 172
  hawser bends 110
  heaving line bend 106, 117
  jamming bend 107
  lapp knot 93
  open carrick bend 101
  overhand bend 88, 89
  racking bend 116
  reeving line bend 110–111
  rigger's bend 94, 98
  sansome bend 119
  sheet bend 25, 88, 90, 104, 119, 127, 306
  simple simon 88, 104
  single stopper 106, 118
  slackline bend 106
  Spanish hawser bend 88, 102
  surgeon's knot 103
  triple fisherman's knot 115
  triple sheet bend 91
  twin bowlines 109, 110
  zeppelin bend 25, 88, 92, 94, 98, 99, 172
bights 22, 260, 262, 263, 266
bill hitch 78
bitts 68, 72
blackwall hitch 78
  double blackwall hitch 15, 78, 79
Blackwall Shipyard, River Thames 78
block and tackles 82
blocks 192
blood knot 95
Boating (magazine) 99
bollards 68
  cleat hitch on a bollard cleat 74
bottle slings 206
  Indian jug handle 195
  Prusik bottle sling 194
bowlines 24, 36, 63, 76–7, 96–7, 112, 126–7, 144–5, 152–3, 168–9
  bowline in the bight 15, 131, 134–5
  breaking bowlines 127, 143
  and effect on line's strength 110
  eskimo bowline 143
  fast bowline 128, 135
  fisherman's bend and bowline 51
  for mooring lines 68

French bowline 15
  interlocked bowline 110
  running bowline 15, 36, 150, 152–3
  seized bowline 129
  Spanish bowline 131, 134–5, 161
  tails on bowlines 130
  triple loop bowline 134–5, 164
  trucker's hitch 82
  tucked bowline 129, 162–3, 168–9
  twin bowlines 109, 110, 112–13
  use in modern ropes 306
  water bowline 130
Bowlings, Tom, *Book of Knots* 42
braided interlocking loops 146, 148–9
braided loop 120, 146–7
braided ropes 21, 279
braided splice 120–1, 146
Bri-Nylon 21
broach bend 99
broach loop 140
Bronze Age 88
bubble knot 81, 145
bucket, tying a 36, 37
Buddhism 250
Budworth, Geoffrey, braided interlocking loop 148
builder's knot *see* clove hitch
buntline hitch 30, 76–7, 162, 169
buntlines 30
butane whipping 258, 276, 281, 286, 306
butterfly bend 92
  variation of 94
butterfly coil 219
butterfly loop 92, 142

C

cable-laid rope 20
camel hitch 38, 84–5
carrick bend 92, 100–1, 110
  knots based on carrick bend 230
  open carrick bend 101
  use for doormats 268
  use in modern rope 88
carrick loop 137, 153
Carrick Roads, Falmouth 100
cat's paw, double 80
Celts 260
chafe 281
chafe guard 286, 287
chain splices
  multiplait 304–5
  traditional 298–299
chain stitch lashing 209
cheesing 216–17, 222–223
Chen, Lydia, *Chinese Knotting* 248
China, knot-tying in 245
Chinese crown loop 247
Chinese lanyard knot 244–245
chrysanthemum knot 248
cinch knot 82
cinquefoil 179, 185
Clayoquot tribes 12
cleat hitch 25, 72–3, 96–7, 152
  cleat hitch on a bollard cleat 74

cleat hitch on a pin 75
slipped cleat hitch 73
cleats 68
climbing 142, 219
clinging clara hitch 66
clove hitch 25, 28, 32–3, 36–7, 40, 48–9, 96–7, 126, 153, 216–17
  exploding clove hitch 23, 33
  reasons for failure 32
  sheepshank with clove hitch 189
  slipped clove hitch 32, 33
  tied in the bight 32, 34
  use on bollards 68
  variations of 25, 38, 39, 45
clove hitch coil 214
coils 16, 210–23
  alpine coil 218
  bell ringer's knot 215
  butterfly coil 219
  clove hitch coil 214
  figure-eight flake 220
  French coil 222
  gasket coil 214, 216–17
  halyard coil 213
  simple coil 212–3
  wrapped coil 218, 221
coir 20
constrictor knot 15, 17, 37, 40–1, 71, 76–7, 276
  alternatives to 44
  double constrictor knot 37, 42, 84–5
  tied in the bight 43
  with loop 41
cotton 20
cow hitch 53, 84–5, 138, 144–5, 306
cowboys 136, 137, 195
crossing knots 52
crossing points 22
crown knot 15, 226–7, 228, 256
crown sinnet 256–8
crown whipping 282
cutting rope 17
Cutty Sark 198

D

Dacron 21
Dana, RH
  A Seaman's Friend 39
  Two Years Before the Mast 78
Dass, Petter 14
deadeyes, knots for 53
decorative knots 224–273
  braided loops 146
  Chinese crown loop 247
  Chinese lanyard knot 244–5
  crown knot 226–7, 228, 256
  crown sinnet 256–7
  diamond knot 230–1, 232, 234
  double diamond knot 232–3
  double Matthew Walker knot 240
  double wall knot 229
  doughnut 272–3
  footrope knot 231, 234–5
  good luck knot 248–9, 250
  Japanese loop 246
  lanyard knot 242–3

INDEX

manrope knot 228
Matthew Walker knot 15, 176, 238–9
Matthew Walker loop 241
mystic knot 250–1
ocean braid mat 268–9
oval mat 270–1
plafond knot 244–5
prolong knot 268
sailor's true lover mat 268–9
star knot 236–7
three-strand plait sinnet 252–3
turk's head 268
turk's head 3L × 4B – in the round 260–1
turk's head 3L × 5B – in the flat 264–5
turk's head 4L × 3B – in the round 262–3
turk's head 5L × 4B – in the flat 266–7
two-strand plait sinnet 254–5
wall knot 15, 226, 228
dental floss 283
Deuteronomy 14
diagonal lashing 15, 201
  alternative to 204
diamond knot 230–1, 232, 234
  double diamond knot 232–233
Diderot, Denis, Encyclopedie 60
dipping rope 276
doormats 264, 266
  ocean braid mat 268–9
  oval mat 270–1
doughnut 272–3
driftnets 46
drying rope 17
Dyneema 21, 88, 306
  bowlines and 126
  knots for 111, 115
  preventing fraying 276
Dyneema loop 310–11
Dyneema reduction splice 306–7
Dyneema soft shackle 312–13
Dyneema splice 308–9

E
East India Company 78
Egyptians, Ancient 12, 180
elbows 22
electrical tape 283
Enkalon 21
ensign, tying a 96, 97
eskimo bowline 143
exploding knots 22–3
  exploding clove hitch 33
eye splices
  hard eye splice 296–7
  multiplait eye splice 302–3
  soft eye splice 297

F
fender, tying a 48, 49
fids 18–19
figure-eight bend 88, 89
figure-eight flake 220

figure-eight knot 24, 96–7, 99, 144–5, 72, 168, 174, 176, 184, 216
  slipped figure-eight knot 174
figure-eight lashing 203
figure-eight loop 82, 124, 125, 169, 306
Filipino lashing 204
fisherman's bend 37, 50, 51, 76–7
fisherman's bend and bowline 37, 51
fisherman's knot 25, 112–13, 114, 162–3, 172
  double fisherman's knot 115, 306
  triple fisherman's knot 113, 115, 306
fishermen, cod 45
flakes
  figure-eight flake 220
  French flake 220
  long flake 220
flax 20
Flemish down 220
Flemish flake 220, 222
Flemish knot 174
Flemish loop 124
footrope knot 231, 234–5, 258
Fortrel 21
frapping turns 200
frayed rope, preventing 276–83, 294–5, 306
French coil 222
French flake 220
French whipping 280, 286–7

G
gaff topsail halyard bend 56, 57
ganging lines 45
gasket coil 214, 216–17
gibbet knot 154, 157, 158
good luck knot 248–9, 250
Gordian knot 14
Gordias, King of Phrygia 14
granny knot 180
great queen clara hitch 66, 67
Greeks, ancient 12, 13, 180, 195
grommet splice 300–1
ground-line hitch 45, 48–9
Grylls, Bear 190
gunner's knot 42
Guthrie, Woody, Hangknot, Slipknot 158

H
hackamore knot 195
half hitch 172
halyards
  halyard coil 212–13, 216–17
  type of rope for 21
  tying, 168, 169
hammocks, stowing 208
handcuff knot 166, 167
hangman's knot 158–9, 182
hangman's noose 138
hard eye splice 296–7
harness loop 138, 142, 162
  double harness loop 139
hawser bends 110
hawser-laid rope 20

heaving line bend 117
  alternatives to 106
heaving line knots 15, 182
  Martha's Vineyard heaving line knot 183
  monkey's fist 186–7
  monkey's paw 187
heaving lines, type of rope for 21
hemp 20
  softening hemp rope 16–17
Heracles knot 13, 180
Heraklas 40, 195
Hercules, knot of 13, 180
high-modulus rope 111, 306
  lashings 198
  splicing 306–309
  whipping 276, 279, 281, 306
hitches 26–83
  bale sling hitch 53
  bill hitch 78
  blackwall hitch 78
  bubble knot 81, 145
  camel hitch 38, 84–5
  cinch knot 82
  cleat hitch 25, 72–3, 96–7, 152
  cleat hitch on a bollard cleat 74
  cleat hitch on a pin 75
  clinging clara hitch 66
  clove hitch 25, 28, 32–3, 36–7, 40, 48–9, 96–7, 126, 153, 216–17
  clove hitch tied in the bight 32, 34
  constrictor knot 17, 40–1, 71, 276
  constrictor knot tied in the bight 43
  constrictor knot with loop 41
  cow hitch 53, 138, 306
  crossing knot 71
  definition of 22
  double blackwall hitch 78, 79
  double cat's paw 80
  double constrictor knot 42
  double trucker's hitch 83
  exploding clove hitch 23, 33
  fisherman's bend 50, 51
  fisherman's bend and bowline 51
  gaff topsail halyard bend 56, 57
  great queen clara hitch 66, 67
  ground-line hitch 45, 48–9
  half hitch 172
  hook hitch 78
  horse dealer's hitch 59
  innomiknot 31
  killick hitch 64, 226
  knute hitch 55
  lifting hitch 65
  lighterman's hitch 68–9, 70
  Magner's hitch 39
  Magnus hitch 39
  marling hitch 15
  marlinspike hitch 15, 52, 78
  midshipman's hitch 15
  ossel hitch 46
  ossel knot 47
  pile hitch 70
  queen clara hitch 66

ring hitch 53
rolling hitch 25, 39, 48–9, 84–5, 96, 132
round turn and buntline hitch 30
round turn and two half hitches 24, 28–9, 50, 68, 172
seized round turn and two half hitches 29
slipped cleat hitch 73
slipped clove hitch 32, 33
spar hitch 45
stopped half hitch 61
strangle hitch 40
strangle knot 44
studding sail bend 56–7
stunner hitch 78
timber hitch 15, 60, 64
topsail halyard bend 56, 58, 306
transom hitch 54
trucker's hitch 62–3, 82–3
tugboat hitch 68
wagoner's hitch 82–3
honda knot 136–8
hook hitches 78
horns 18
horse dealer's hitch 59
hot knives 17, 19
Hunter, Dr Edward 95

I
ichabod knot 150, 154, 157, 158
IGKT (International Guild of Knot Tyers) 59
Incas 12
Indian jug handle 195
innomiknot 31
International Guild of Knot Tyers (IGKT) 15, 59
Izzo, Foldo 191

J
jamming bend 107
Japan, knot-tying in 246
Japanese lashing 205
Japanese loop 246
Jewish Bible 14
jib sheet, tying a 144, 145
jury mast knot 206–7

K
Kevlar 21
killick hitch 64, 226
killicks 64
kinbaku 246
king of knots 126
knives 18
  hot knives 17, 19
Knotting Matters 15
knot-tying, history of 12–15
knots
  Ashley's stopper knot 15, 24, 176–7, 238
  bell-rope keyring 258, 259
  bell-ringer's knot 138
  cincquefoil 179
  definition of 22, 114

double blackwall knot 15
double fisherman's knot 306
double overhand knot 173
figure-eight knot 15, 24, 99, 172, 174, 176
Flemish knot 174
granny knot 180
hackamore 195
heaving line knot 15, 182
Heracles knot 13, 180
Indian jug handle 195
knot of Hercules 13, 180
knots named after people 15, 176–7, 238
love knot 180
manrope knot 183
Martha's Vineyard heaving line knot 183
monkey's fist 15, 182, 186–7, 226
monkey's paw 187
moonshiner's 195
new knots 59, 66, 70, 81, 104
number in existence 15, 70
overhand knot 172
oysterman's stopper 15, 176
Poldo tackle 191, 238
Prusik bottle sling 194
quatrefoil 178
reef knot 13, 25, 40, 103, 180, 276
sheepshank 172
sheepshank in the bight 188
sheepshank tied with ends 189
sheepshank with clove hitch 189
slipped figure-eight knot 174
slipped overhand knot 173
square knot 180
stevedore knot 175
stopper knot 184, 185, 89, 226
strangle knot 172, 195, 276
symbolism of knots 13, 180, 245
thief knot 180
top ten knots 24–5
triple fisherman's knot 306
versatackle 192–3
yardarm knot 190
knots, decorative 224–273
braided loops 146
Chinese crown loop 247
Chinese lanyard knot 244–5
crown knot 226–7, 228, 256
crown sinnet 256–7
diamond knot 230–1, 232, 234
double diamond knot 232–3
double Matthew Walker knot 240
double wall knot 229
doughnut 272–3
footrope knot 231, 234–5
good luck knot 248–9, 250
Japanese loop 246
lanyard knot 242–3
manrope knot 228
Matthew Walker knot 15, 176, 238–9, 258
Matthew Walker loop 241
mystic knot 250–1
ocean braid mat 268–9

ocean plait knot 17
oval mat 270–1
plafond knot 244–5
prolong knot 268
rope to use 20
sailor's true lover mat 268–9
star knot 236–7
three-strand plait sinnet 252–3
turk's head 15, 268
turk's head 3L × 4B – in the round 260–1
turk's head 3L × 5B – flat 264–5
turk's head 4L × 3B – in the round 262–3
turk's head 5L × 4B – in the flat 266–7
two-strand plait sinnet 254–5
wall knot 15, 226, 228
knute hitch 55
Kon-Tiki 198
Koran 14

L
lanyard knot 242–3
lanyards 226, 236, 242
 braided loop 146–7
 carrick bend 100
 knots for 53, 55
Lapland 93
lapp knot 93
lashings 62, 63, 196–209, 306
 chain stitch lashing 209
 diagonal lashing 15, 201, 204
 figure-eight lashing 203
 Filipino lashing 204
 Japanese lashing 205
 jury mast knot 206–7
 marline hitches 208
 masthead knot 206–7
 pole hitch 198–9
 shear lashing 202
 square lashing 15, 200, 205
 tightening 200
lassos 136, 137, 150
leads 260, 262, 263, 266
Leonardo da Vinci 260
Lever, Darcy, *The Sheet Anchor* 229, 260
lifting hitch 65
lighterman's hitch 68–9, 70
lineman's loop 92
lineman's rider 142
lines 23
locking loop 155
London Boat Show (1986) 67
long-nosed pliers 19
longships 198
loops 22, 122–67
 adjustable loop 157
 angler's loop 133, 172
 artillery loop 138
 bowline 24, 68, 82, 126–7, 306
 bowline in the bight 131
 braided interlocking loops 146, 148–9
 braided loop 120, 146–7

broach loop 140
butterfly loop 142
carrick loop 137, 153
Chinese crown loop 247
Chinese lanyard knot 244–5
double angler's loop 165
double harness loop 139
Dyneema loop 310–11
eskimo bowline 143
fast bowline 128, 135
figure-eight loop 82, 124, 125, 169, 306
Flemish loop 124
gibbet knot 154, 157, 158
handcuff knot 166, 167
hangman's knot 158–9, 182
hangman's noose 138
harness loop 138, 142, 162
honda knot 136, 137, 138
ichabod knot 150, 154, 157, 158
interlocked bowlines 110
Japanese loop 246
lineman's rider 142
locking loop 155
Matthew Walker loop 241
midshipman's loop 132, 152–3
overhand loop 62–3, 124
peace knots 141
plafond knot 244–5
running bowline 150
scaffold knot 158, 160
seized bowline 129
slip and nip loop 156
Spanish bowline 131, 161
tom fool's knot 166
tucked bowlines 129
water bowline 130
love knot 13, 180
Luce, Admiral Stephen 28

M
macrame 226, 252
magical properties of knots 14
Magner's hitch 39
Magnus hitch 39
manila 20
manrope knot 15, 228
marline hitches 208
marling hitch 15
marlinspike hitch 15, 52, 78
marlinspikes 18, 19, 52
Martha's Vineyard heaving line knot 183
masthead knot 206–7
mats
 doormats 264, 266
 ocean braid mat 268–9
 oval mat 270–1
 rope mats 226
 sailor's true lover mat 268–9
Matthew Walker knot 15, 176, 238–9, 258
 double Matthew Walker knot 240
Matthew Walker loop 241
merchant navy 12
metaphors, knots and 13–14

midshipman's hitch 15
midshipman's loop 132, 152–3
modern rope 111
 and bowlines 130
 coiling 212
 decorative mats 271
 knots for 140
 lashings 198
 seized round turn and two half hitches 29
 whipping 276, 279, 281, 306
monkey chain 252
monkey's fist 15, 182, 186–7, 226
monkey's paw 187
moonshiner's knot 195
mooring lines, joining 100, 112, 113
mooring lines, tying to a bollard 152, 153
mooring lines, tying to a ring 76, 77
multiplait chain splice 304–5
multiplait eyesplice 302–3
mystic knot 250–1
myths and legends 14

N
natural rope 20
nippers 203
Nootka tribes 12
'number records' (Inca) 12
nylon 21

O
ocean braid mat 270–1
ocean plait mat 17
Oribasius 12
ossel hitch 46
ossel knot 47
ossels 46
Ötzi the Iceman 88
oval mat 268–9
overhand bend 88, 89
overhand knots 172, 184
 double overhand knot 173, 184–5
 slipped overhand knot 173
overhand loop 62–3, 124
oysterman's stopper 15, 176

P
Pacific 198, 252
palm 19
palm and needle whipping 276, 279, 280
peace knot 141
pile hitch 70
plafond knot 244–5
plaited ropes 21
pliers, long-nosed 19
Poldo tackle 191, 238
pole hitch 198–9
Polyamide 21
polyester 21
polyethylene 21
polypropylene 21
Practical Boat Owner 81
prolong knot 268
Prusik, Dr Karl 194

INDEX

Prusik bottle sling 194
Prusik knot 84–5, 162–3, 194
purchase 192

Q
Qing Dynasty 245
quatrefoil 178
queen clara hitch 66
quipus 12

R
racking bend 116
racking seizing 285
reef knot 13, 25, 40, 103, 180, 276
reeving line bend 110–11
  double reeving line bend 111
religion and knots 14
Repolusthöhle 12
rescue lines, type of rope for 21
rigger's bend 94, 98
rigger's knives 18
ring hitch 53
rings, served 272–3
rolling hitch 25, 39, 48–9, 84–5, 96, 132
Romans 12, 13, 180
rope
  adhesive shrink tubing 276
  braided 21, 279
  cable-laid 20
  cheesing 222–3
  coiling 16, 210–23
  cutting 17
  dipping 276
  drying 17
  fraying 276
  grommets 300–1
  hawser-laid 20
  hemp 16–17
  joining 86–121
  natural 20
  rope care 16
  shroud-laid 20
  softening 16–17
  types of 20–1
  washing 17
  weave 21
  see also high-modulus rope; modern rope; seizing; whipping
rope harness, tying a 134, 135
rope ladder, making a 162, 163
Rosendahl, Charles 99
round turn 23
round turn and buntline hitch 30
round turn and two half hitches 24, 28–9, 36–7, 48–9, 50, 68, 76–7, 96, 152–3, 162, 172
Royal Aircraft Establishment 95
Royal Navy 12, 78
running hitches, alternatives to 56
running rigging, type of rope for 21

S
sailors, and knot-tying 12
sailor's true lover mat 268–9
sailor's whipping 277, 278
samson posts 68, 72
sansome bend 119
Savoy, House of 175
scaffold knot 158, 160
sealing rope ends 17
seine netters 46, 47
seized round turn and two half hitches 29
seizings 281, 284–5
  flat seizing 284
  racking seizing 285
  temporary seizing 40
serving 281
  served rings 272–3
shackles
  Dyneema soft shackles 312–13
  eye splices 296–7
  lashings as substitutes for 203
shamisen, Japanese three-stringed 117
shear lashing 202
sheepshanks 82, 172
  in the bight 188
  sheepshank with clove hitch 189
  tied with ends 189
  variations of 190
sheet bends 25, 78, 90, 96–7, 119, 127, 306
  alternatives to 104
  double sheet bend 88, 91, 112
  triple sheet bend 91
shroud-laid rope 20
simple simon 66, 88, 104
  double simple simon 105
sinnet
  crown sinnet 256–7
  three-strand plait sinnet 252–3
  two-strand plait sinnet 254–5
sisal 20
slackline bend 106
slings 80
slip and nip loop 156
slipped knots 22
slungshots 186
Smith, Captain Charles W 234
Smith, Captain John, *A Seaman's Grammar & Dictionary* 126
Smyth, Admiral 28
soft eye splice 36, 297
soft shackles 198, 306
  Dyneema soft shackles 312–13
Spanish hawser bend 88, 102
spar hitch 45
Spectra 21, 88, 306
  bowlines and 126
  knots for 111, 115
  preventing fraying 276
Spectra splice 308–9
splices and splicing 15, 110, 288–313
  back splice 226, 276, 294–5
  definition of 22
  Dyneema loop 310–11
  Dyneema reduction splice 306–7
  Dyneema splice 308–9
  grommets 300–1

hard eye splice 296–7
long splice 292–3
multiplait chain splice 304–5
multiplait eyesplice 302–3
short splice 290
soft eye splice 297
Spectra splice 308–9
spliced loop 36
tapering 299
tools 18
traditional chain splice 298–9
square knot 13, 180
square lashing 15, 200
  alternative to 205
square-riggers 30, 56, 75, 206, 252, 260
standing end 22
standing part 22
star knot 236–7
Steel, David, *The Elements and Practice of Rigging and Seamanship* 60
stevedore knot 175, 184
stopped half hitch 61
stopper, single 106, 118
stopper knots 84, 85, 89, 226, 231
  Ashley's stopper 176–7, 184–5
  cinquefoil 179
  double wall knot 229
  figure-eight knot 174, 176
  oysterman's stopper 176
  quatrefoil 178
  stevedore knot 175
stoppings 17, 40, 281
strands 20
strangle knot 40, 44, 76–7 172, 195, 276
studding sail bend 56–7
studding sails 56
stunner hitch 78
superstition and knots 14
surgeon's knot 103
Swedish fid 19
symbolism of knots 13–14
synthetic rope 21
  cutting 19
  washing 17
  see also high-modulus rope; modern rope

T
tackles, rope 192
taking a turn 23
tapering splices 299
Tergal 21
terminology 22–3
Terylene 21
thief knot 180
tightening knots 17
timber hitch 15, 60
  variations of 64
tom fool's knot 166, 206
tools 18–19
topsail halyard bend 56, 58, 306
Toss, Brian 55
transom hitch 54

trucker's hitch 62–3, 82–3
  double trucker's hitch 83
tugboat hitch 68
turk's head 15, 226, 268, 286–7
turk's head 3L × 4B – in the round 260–1
turk's head 3L × 5B – in the flat 264–5
turk's head 4L × 3B – in the round 262–3
turk's head 5L × 4B – in the flat 266–7
turk's head 'clump' mat 264
Tutankhamun 12
twine, whipping 19
tzitzit 14

U
US Cavalry 45
US Navy 98, 99

V
versatackle 192–3
vice versa 66
Vikings 98

W
wagoner's hitch 82–3
Walker, Matthew 176, 238
wall knot 15, 226, 228
  double wall knot 229
washing rope 17
weave 21
West country whipping 283
whaling ships 12–13
Wharram, James 198
whipping twine 19
whippings 15, 17, 19, 40, 274–283
  butane whipping 258, 276, 281, 286–7, 306
  chafe guard 286, 287
  crown whipping 282
  French whipping 280
  high-modulus rope 279
  non-traditional whipping 283
  palm and needle whipping 276, 279, 280
  plain whipping 276–7, 286–7
  sailor's whipping 276, 278
  West country whipping 283, 286–7
wind-knots 14
working end 22
wrapped coil 218, 221
wrapping turns 200

Y
yardarm knot 190
yarns 20

Z
zeppelin bend 25, 98, 99, 172
  variations of 94

Acknowledgements

The publisher would like to thank the following for their kind permission to reproduce photographs in this book.

(Abbreviations key: t = top, b = bottom, c = centre, r = right, l = left, bkg = background)

Nic Compton: 2 (c), 9 (t), 12 (tr), 13 (bc), 16 (bc), 19 (t), 23 (tr), 32 (bl), 36, 37, 48, 49, 56 (bl), 62, 63, 69 (t), 74 (br), 76, 77, 79 (b), 84, 85, 93 (b), 96, 97, 107 (bc), 112, 113, 134, 135, 136 (br), 144, 145, 149 (t), 152, 153, 159 (t), 162, 163, 168, 169, 184, 185, 193 (t), 194 (br), 199 (b), 216, 217, 221 (b), 223 (t), 245 (t), 247 (b), 255, 257, 258, 259, 263, 267, 273 (t), 277 (t), 286, 287, 293 (t), 295 (t), 309 (t), 314 (tr), 315 (br)

Corbis: 6 (c) © Onne van der Wal/CORBIS, 13 (tr), 14 (tr), 14 (bc) © Bettmann/Corbis

Fotolia: 28 (b), 51 (bkg), 69 (bkg), 82 (bkg), 120 (bkg), 256 (bkg)

Getty Images: front cover, 15 (bl), 94 (bkg), 108 (bkg), 130 (bkg), 178 (bkg), 219 (bkg)

Rupert Holmes: 21 (bl)

istockphoto: 46 (bkg), 200 (bkg), 229 (bkg)

Andrew Perris: 8 (tr, bl), 10 (c), 17 (br), 18, 20, 22, 24, 25, 28, 29, 30, 31, 32 (br), 33, 34, 35, 38, 39, 40, 41, 42, 43, 44, 45, 46, 47, 50, 51, 52, 53, 54, 55 (except b), 56, 57, 58, 59, 60, 61, 64, 65, 66, 67, 68, 69 (except t), 70, 71, 72, 73 (except b), 74 (except br), 101, 78, 79 (except b), 80, 81, 82, 83, 86, 88, 89, 90, 91, 92, 93 (except b), 94, 95, 98, 99, 100, 101, 102, 103, 104, 105, 106, 107, 108, 109, 110, 111, 114, 115, 116, 117, 118 (except br), 119, 120, 121, 122, 123, 126, 127, 128 (except b), 129, 130, 131, 132, 133, 136 (except br), 137, 138 (except bl), 139, 140, 141, 142, 143, 146, 147, 148, 149 (except t), 150, 151, 154, 155, 156, 157, 158, 159 (except t), 160, 161, 164, 165, 166, 167, 171, 172, 173, 174, 175, 176, 177, 178, 180, 181, 182, 183, 186, 187, 188, 189, 190, 191, 192, 193 (except t), 194, 195, 197, 198, 199 (except b), 200, 201, 202 (except br), 203, 204, 205, 206, 207, 208, 209, 210, 212, 213, 214, 215, 218, 219, 220, 221 (except b), 222, 223 (except t), 224, 226, 227, 228, 229, 230, 231, 232, 233, 234, 235, 236, 237, 238, 239, 240, 241, 242, 243, 244, 245 (except t), 246, 247 (except b), 248, 249, 250, 251, 252, 253, 254, 256, 260, 261, 262, 263, 264, 265, 266, 268, 269, 270, 271, 272, 273, 274, 276, 278, 279, 280, 281, 282, 283, 284, 285, 288, 290, 291, 292, 293 (except t), 294, 295 (except t), 296, 297, 298, 299, 300, 301, 302, 303, 304, 305, 306, 307, 308, 309 (except t), 310, 311, 312, 314.

Shutterstock: 50 (bkg), 73 (b), 103 (b), 128 (b), 138 (bl)

The author would like to thank Vanessa Bird and Anna Kisby for their invaluable editorial input. Thanks also to Tom and to the good ship *Wanda* for their help with the final photoshoot.